Off the Page

Activities to bring lessons alive and enhance learning

Cambridge Handbooks for Language Teachers

This series, now with over 50 titles, offers practical ideas, techniques and activities for the teaching of English and other languages, providing inspiration for both teachers and trainers.

Recent titles in this series:

Teach Business English
SYLVIE DONNA

Teaching English Spelling
A practical guide
RUTH SHEMESH AND SHEILA WALLER

Using Folktales
ERIC K. TAYLOR

Learner English (Second edition)
A teacher's guide to interference and other problems
EDITED BY MICHAEL SWAN AND BERNARD SMITH

Planning Lessons and Courses
Designing sequences of work for the language classroom
TESSA WOODWARD

Teaching Large Multilevel Classes
NATALIE HESS

Using the Board in the Language Classroom
JEANNINE DOBBS

Writing Simple Poems
Pattern poetry for language acquisition
VICKI L. HOLMES AND MARGARET R. MOULTON

Laughing Matters
Humour in the language classroom
PÉTER MEDGYES

Stories
Narrative activities in the language classroom
RUTH WAJNRYB

Using Authentic Video in the Language Classroom
JANE SHERMAN

Extensive Reading Activities for Teaching Language
EDITED BY JULIAN BAMFORD AND RICHARD R. DAY

Language Activities for Teenagers
EDITED BY SETH LINDSTROMBERG

Pronunciation Practice Activities
A resource book for teaching English pronunciation
MARTIN HEWINGS

Drama Techniques (Third edition)
A resource book of communication activities for language teachers
ALAN MALEY AND ALAN DUFF

Five-Minute Activities for Business English
PAUL EMMERSON AND NICK HAMILTON

Games for Language Learning (Third edition)
ANDREW WRIGHT, DAVID BETTERIDGE AND MICHAEL BUCKBY

Dictionary Activities
CINDY LEANEY

Dialogue Activities
Exploring spoken interaction in the language class
NICK BILBROUGH

Five-Minute Activities for Young Learners
PENNY MCKAY AND JENNI GUSE

The Internet and the Language Classroom (Second edition)
A practical guide for teachers
GAVIN DUDENEY

Working with Images
A resource book for the language classroom
BEN GOLDSTEIN

Grammar Practice Activities (Second edition)
A practical guide for teachers
PENNY UR

Intercultural Language Activities
JOHN CORBETT

Learning One-to-One
INGRID WISNIEWSKA

Communicative Activities for EAP
JENNI GUSE

Memory Activities for Language Learning
NICK BILBROUGH

Vocabulary Activities
PENNY UR

Classroom Management Techniques
JIM SCRIVENER

CLIL Activities
A resource for subject and language teachers
LIZ DALE AND ROSIE TANNER

Language Learning with Technology
Ideas for integrating technology in the classroom
GRAHAM STANLEY

Translation and Own-language Activities
PHILIP KERR

Language Learning with Digital Video
BEN GOLDSTEIN AND PAUL DRIVER

Discussions and More
Oral fluency practice in the classroom
PENNY UR

Interaction Online
Creative activities for blended learning
LINDSAY CLANDFIELD AND JILL HADFIELD

Activities for Very Young Learners
HERBERT PUCHTA AND KAREN ELLIOTT

Teaching and Developing Reading Skills
PETER WATKINS

Lexical Grammar
Activities for teaching chunks and exploring patterns
LEO SELIVAN

Off the Page

Activities to bring lessons alive and enhance learning

Craig Thaine

Consultant and editor: Scott Thornbury

CAMBRIDGE
UNIVERSITY PRESS

CAMBRIDGE
UNIVERSITY PRESS

University Printing House, Cambridge CB2 8BS, United Kingdom
One Liberty Plaza, 20th Floor, New York, NY 10006, USA
477 Williamstown Road, Port Melbourne, VIC 3207, Australia
4843/24, 2nd Floor, Ansari Road, Daryaganj, Delhi – 110002, India
79 Anson Road, #06–04/06, Singapore 079906

Cambridge University Press is part of the University of Cambridge.

It furthers the University's mission by disseminating knowledge in the pursuit of education, learning and research at the highest international levels of excellence.

www.cambridge.org
Information on this title: www.cambridge.org/9781108814386

First published 2020

20 19 18 17 16 15 14 13 12 11 10 9 8 7 6 5 4 3 2 1

Printed in Italy by L.E.G.O S.p.A.

A catalogue record for this publication is available from the British Library

Library of Congress Cataloging in Publication data

ISBN 978-1-108-81438-6 Paperback
ISBN 978-1-108-81440-9 Apple iBook
ISBN 978-1-108-81441-6 Google eBook
ISBN 978-1-108-81443-0 Kindle eBook
ISBN 978-1-108-81442-3 ebooks.com eBook

Contents

Thanks

I would like to thank the following people who have helped me in the writing of *Off the Page*.

Gillian Lowe for indirectly suggesting the idea to me and letting me run with it;
Karen Momber for initial and on-going insight, encouragement and support;
Scott Thornbury for his constructive, creative and always stimulating guidance (*Kia ora e hoa.*);
Greg Sibley for his expert, detailed and dedicated attention to improving the text;
Jo Timerick for managing everything so well and keeping it all on track;
Hemalatha Bakthavatchalam for getting the book smoothly through production;
Marcus Fletcher for his care and thoroughness in checking the text;
Rosie Wood for enhancing readers' access to the book by creating the index;
Purnima Singh, Aradhna Mishra and Sushmita Sharma for their diligent and efficient pursuit of extract permissions;
Rajan Karthikeyan for his creative and responsive development of original artwork.

It has been a real pleasure to work with such a great team.

Finally, a thanks from long ago – to Susie Abell and Philip Dale, my pre-service teacher trainers, who first taught me to get the lesson off the page.

Acknowledgements

The authors and publishers acknowledge the following sources of copyright material and are grateful for the permissions granted. While every effort has been made, it has not always been possible to identify the sources of all the material used, or to trace all copyright holders. If any omissions are brought to our notice, we will be happy to include the appropriate acknowledgements on reprinting and in the next update to the digital edition, as applicable.

Text

Chapter 1: Extracts from *Evolve Level 2 Student's Book* by Lindsay Clandfield, Ben Goldstein et al. Copyright © 2019 Cambridge University Press; Extract from *Evolve Level 2 Teacher's Book* by Genevieve Kocienda, Gareth Jones et al. Copyright © 2019 Cambridge University Press; Extract from *Listening in the Language Classroom* by John Field. Copyright © 2008 Cambridge University Press; Extracts from *Cambridge English Empower B1* by Adrian Doff, Craig Thaine et al. Copyright © 2015 Cambridge University Press; Extract from *Eyes Open Level 3 Student's Book* by Ben Goldstein, Gareth Jones et al. Copyright © 2015 Cambridge University Press; Extract from *Think Level 2 Student's Book* by Herbert Puchta, Jeff Stranks and Peter Lewis-Jones. Copyright © 2015 Cambridge University Press; Extract from *Think Level 2 Teacher's Book* by Herbert Puchta, Jeff Stranks and Peter Lewis-Jones. Copyright © 2015 Cambridge University Press; Extracts from *English Unlimited B1+ Intermediate Coursebook* by David Rea, Theresa Clementson et al. Copyright © 2011 Cambridge University Press; Extracts from *Cambridge English Empower Student's Book B1* by Adrian Doff, Craig Thaine et al. Copyright © 2015 Cambridge University Press; Extracts from *face2face Elementary* by Chris Redston and Gillie Cunningham. Copyright © 2012 Cambridge University Press; Extract from *Interchange Level 1 Student's Book* by Jack C. Richards et al. Copyright © 2017 Cambridge University Press; Extracts from *English Unlimited Elementary A2* by Alex Tilbury, Theresa Clementson et al. Copyright © 2010 Cambridge University Press; Extracts from *face2face Pre Intermediate* by Chris Redston and Gillie Cunningham. Copyright © 2012 Cambridge University Press; Extract from *Evolve Level 1 Student's Book* by Leslie Anne Hendra, Mark Ibbotson, Kathryn O'Dell. Copyright © 2019 Cambridge University Press; Extract from *Interchange Level 2 Student's Book* by Jack C. Richards et al. Copyright © 2017 Cambridge University Press; Extracts from *Eyes Open Level 3 Student's Book* by Ben Goldstein and Ceri Jones. Copyright © 2015 Cambridge University Press; Extracts from *Cambridge English Empower A2* by Adrian Doff, Craig Thaine et al. Copyright © 2015 Cambridge University Press; Extracts from *Think Level 1 Student's Book* by Herbert Puchta, Jeff Stranks and Peter Lewis-Jones. Copyright © 2015 Cambridge University Press; **Chapter 2:** Extracts from *Cambridge English Empower A2* by Adrian Doff, Craig Thaine et al. Copyright © 2015 Cambridge University Press; Extract from *How much time should we give to speaking practice?* by Philip Kerr. Copyright © 2017 Cambridge University Press; Extracts from *face2face Intermediate* by Chris Redston and Gillie Cunningham. Copyright © 2012 Cambridge University Press; Extracts from *face2face Elementary* by Chris Redston and Gillie Cunningham. Copyright © 2012 Cambridge University Press; Extracts from *Interchange Level 1 Student's Book* by Jack C. Richards Copyright © 2017 Cambridge University Press; Extracts from *Eyes Open Level 2*

Student's Book by Ben Goldstein and Ceri Jones. Copyright © 2015 Cambridge University Press; Extracts from *Think Level 1 A2 Student's Book* by Herbert Puchta, Jeff Stranks and Peter Lewis-Jones. Copyright © 2015 Cambridge University Press; Extracts from *Unlock Level 3 Listening, Speaking and Critical Thinking* by Sabina Ostrowska, Nancy Jordan et al. Copyright © 2019 Cambridge University Press; Extracts from *Interchange Level 2 Student's Book* by Jack C. Richards. Copyright © 2017 Cambridge University Press; Extracts from *Unlock Level 2 Reading and Writing Skills* by Richard O'Neill. Copyright © 2019 Cambridge University Press; Extract from *Think Level 2 Student's Book* by Herbert Puchta, Jeff Stranks and Peter Lewis-Jones. Copyright © 2015 Cambridge University Press; Extract from *Interchange Level 1 Student's Book* by Jack C. Richards et al. Copyright © 2017 Cambridge University Press; Extract from *Eyes Open Level 3 Student's Book* by Ben Goldstein and Ceri Jones. Copyright © 2015 Cambridge University Press; Extract from *Evolve Level 3 Student's Book* by Leslie Anne Hendra, Mark Ibbotson, Kathryn O'Dell. Copyright © 2019 Cambridge University Press; Extracts from *Interchange Level 3 Student's Book* by Jack C. Richards et al. Copyright © 2017 Cambridge University Press; Extracts from *Cambridge English Empower B1* by Adrian Doff, Craig Thaine et al. Copyright © 2015 Cambridge University Press; Extract from *English Unlimited B1* by Alex Tilbury et al. Copyright © 2010 Cambridge University Press; Extract from *English Unlimited B1+ Intermediate Coursebook* by David Rea, Theresa Clementson et al. Copyright © 2011 Cambridge University Press; Extract from *Think Level 3 Student's Book* by Herbert Puchta, Jeff Stranks and Peter Lewis-Jones. Copyright © 2015 Cambridge University Press; Extracts from *Cambridge English Empower B1+* by Adrian Doff, Craig Thaine et al. Copyright © 2015 Cambridge University Press; **Chapter 3:** Extracts from *Cambridge English Empower B1* by Adrian Doff, Craig Thaine et al. Copyright © 2015 Cambridge University Press; Extract from *Cambridge English Empower B1* by Adrian Doff, Craig Thaine et al. Copyright © 2015 Cambridge University Press; Extract from http://www.englishprofile.org/wordlist. Copyright © 2015 Cambridge University Press. Extract from *Evolve Level 2 Student's Book* by Lindsay Clandfield, Ben Goldstein et al. Copyright © 2019 Cambridge University Press; Extract from *face2face Pre Intermediate* by Chris Redston and Gillie Cunningham. Copyright © 2012 Cambridge University Press; Extract from *Empower A2* by Adrian Doff, Craig Thaine et al. Copyright © 2015 Cambridge University Press; Extracts from *Think Level 1 Student's Book* by Herbert Puchta, Jeff Stranks and Peter Lewis-Jones. Copyright © 2015 Cambridge University Press; Extracts from *Interchange Level 3 Student's Book* by Jack C. Richards et al. Copyright © 2017 Cambridge University Press; Extract from *Empower B1+* by Adrian Doff, Craig Thaine et al. Copyright © 2015 Cambridge University Press; Extract from *Think Student's Book Starter* by Herbert Puchta, Jeff Stranks and Peter Lewis-Jones. Copyright © 2015 Cambridge University Press; Extract from *Evolve Level 1 Student's Book* by Leslie Anne Hendra, Mark Ibbotson, Kathryn O'Dell. Copyright © 2019 Cambridge University Press; Extract from *Teaching and Developing Reading Skills* by Peter Watkins. Copyright © 2017 Cambridge University Press; Extract from *English Unlimited A2* by Alex Tilbury, Theresa Clementson et al. Copyright © 2010 Cambridge University Press; Extract from *Eyes Open Level 3* by Ben Goldstein and Ceri Jones. Copyright © 2015 Cambridge University Press; Extract from *Empower B1+* by Adrian Doff, Craig Thaine et al. Copyright © 2015 Cambridge University Press; Extract from *Unlock Level 2 Reading, Writing and Critical Thinking* by Carolyn Westbrook, Lida Baker, with Chris Sowton. Copyright © 2019 Cambridge University Press; Extract from *face2face Elementary* by Chris Redston and Gillie Cunningham. Copyright © 2012 Cambridge University Press; Extract from *Eyes Open Level 3* by

Ben Goldstein and Ceri Jones. Copyright © 2015 Cambridge University Press; Extract from *Evolve Level 2* by Lindsay Clandfield et al. Copyright © 2019 Cambridge University Press; **Chapter 4:** Extracts from *Think Level 1 Student's Book* by Herbert Puchta, Jeff Stranks and Peter Lewis-Jones. Copyright © 2015 Cambridge University Press; Extracts from *Interchange Level 1 Student's Book* by Jack C. Richards et al. Copyright © 2017 Cambridge University Press; Extracts from *Cambridge English Empower A2* by Adrian Doff, Craig Thaine et al. Copyright © 2015 Cambridge University Press; Extracts from *Think 2 Student's Book* by Herbert Puchta, Jeff Stranks and Peter Lewis-Jones. Copyright © 2015 Cambridge University Press; Extract from *Eyes Open Level 3 Student's Book* by Ben Goldstein and Ceri Jones. Copyright © 2015 Cambridge University Press; Extracts from *Evolve Level 3 Student's Book* by Leslie Anne Hendra, Mark Ibbotson, Kathryn O'Dell. Copyright © 2019 Cambridge University Press; Extract from *Unlock Level 3 Reading, Writing and Critical Thinking* by Carolyn Westbrook, Lida Baker, with Chris Sowton. Copyright © 2019 Cambridge University Press; Extracts from *Cambridge English Empower A1* by Adrian Doff, Craig Thaine et al. Copyright © 2015 Cambridge University Press; Extract from *Eyes Open Level 2 Student's Book* by Ben Goldstein, and Ceri Jones. Copyright © 2015 Cambridge University Press; Extract from *English Unlimited A2* by Tilbury, Clementson et al. Copyright © 2010 Cambridge University Press; Extract from *Unlock Level 2 Reading, Writing and Critical Thinking* by Richard O'Neill, Michele Lewis et al. Copyright © 2019 Cambridge University Press; Extract from *Evolve Level 2 Student's Book* by Lindsay Clandfield et al. Copyright © 2019 Cambridge University Press; Extract from *Unlock Level 4 Reading, Writing and Critical Thinking* by Chris Sowton, Alan S. Kennedy et al. Copyright © 2019 Cambridge University Press; **Chapter 5:** Extracts from *Cambridge English Empower A2 Student's Book* by Adrian Doff, Craig Thaine et al. Copyright © 2015 Cambridge University Press; Extracts from *face2face Elementary* by Chris Redston and Gillie Cunningham. Copyright © 2012 Cambridge University Press; Extract from *Empower B2 Student's Book* by Adrian Doff, Craig Thaine et al. Copyright © 2015 Cambridge University Press; Extracts from *Evolve Level 2 Student's Book* by Lindsay Clandfield, Ben Goldstein et al. Copyright © 2019 Cambridge University Press; Extracts from *Eyes Open 3* by Ben Goldstein and Ceri Jones. Copyright © 2015 Cambridge University Press; Extract from *English Unlimited B1+ Intermediate Coursebook* by David Rea, Theresa Clementson et al. Copyright © 2011 Cambridge University Press; Extract from *face2face Upper Intermediate* by Chris Redston and Gillie Cunningham. Copyright © 2013 Cambridge University Press; Extract from *face2face Pre-intermediate* Chris Redston and Gillie Cunningham. Copyright © 2012 Cambridge University Press; Extract from *Think Student's Book Level 1* by Herbert Puchta, Jeff Stranks and Peter Lewis-Jones. Copyright © 2015 Cambridge University Press; Extract from *Interchange Level 1 Student's Book* by Jack C. Richards et al. Copyright © 2017 Cambridge University Press; Extract from *face2face Elementary* by Chris Redston and Gillie Cunningham. Copyright © 2012 Cambridge University Press; Extract from *Eyes Open Level 2* by Ben Goldstein and Ceri Jones. Copyright © 2015 Cambridge University Press; Extract from *Cambridge English Empower A1* by Adrian Doff, Craig Thaine et al. Copyright © 2015 Cambridge University Press; Extract from *Think Level 1 Student's Book* by Herbert Puchta, Jeff Stranks and Peter Lewis-Jones. Copyright © 2015 Cambridge University Press; Extract from *Interchange Level 2 Student's Book* by Jack C. Richards et al. Copyright © 2017 Cambridge University Press; Extract from *Cambridge English Empower B1+* by Adrian Doff, Craig Thaine et al. Copyright © 2015 Cambridge University Press; Extract from *Think Level 3 Student's Book* by Herbert Puchta, Jeff Stranks and Peter Lewis-Jones. Copyright © 2015

Cambridge University Press; **Chapter 6:** Extracts from *Cambridge English Empower A1* by Adrian Doff, Craig Thaine et al. Copyright © 2015 Cambridge University Press; Extracts from *Interchange Level 1 Student's Book* by Jack C. Richards et al. Copyright © 2017 Cambridge University Press; Extract from *Unlock Level 3 Reading, Writing and Critical Thinking* by Carolyn Westbrook, Lida Baker et al. Copyright © 2019 Cambridge University Press; Extracts from *Think Level 2 Student's Book* by Herbert Puchta, Jeff Stranks and Peter Lewis-Jones. Copyright © 2015 Cambridge University Press; Extract from *face2face Pre Intermediate* by Chris Redston and Gillie Cunningham. Copyright © 2012 Cambridge University Press; Extracts from *Cambridge English Empower A2* by Adrian Doff, Craig Thaine et al. Copyright © 2015 Cambridge University Press; Extract from *Learning Vocabulary in Another Language* by I. S. P. Nation. Copyright © 2013 Cambridge University Press; Extracts from *face2face Elementary* by Chris Redston and Gillie Cunningham. Copyright © 2012 Cambridge University Press; Extract from *Interchange Level 3 Student's Book* by Jack C. Richards et al. Copyright © 2017 Cambridge University Press; Extract from *Think Level 2 Student's Book* by Herbert Puchta, Jeff Stranks and Peter Lewis-Jones. Copyright © 2015 Cambridge University Press; Extracts from *Cambridge English Empower B1* by Adrian Doff, Craig Thaine et al. Copyright © 2015 Cambridge University Press; Extract from *Eyes Open Level 2 Student's Book* by Ben Goldstein and Ceri Jones. Copyright © 2015 Cambridge University Press; Extract from *Think Level 3 Student's Book* by Herbert Puchta, Jeff Stranks and Peter Lewis-Jones. Copyright © 2015 Cambridge University Press; Extract from *Unlock Level 3 Reading, Writing and Critical Thinking* by Carolyn Westbrook, Lida Baker et al. Copyright © 2015 Cambridge University Press; Extract from *face2face Upper intermediate* by Chris Redston and Gillie Cunningham. Copyright © 2012 Cambridge University Press; Extract from *Evolve 2 Student's Book* by Lindsay Clandfield et al. Copyright © 2019 Cambridge University Press; Extract from *Eyes Open Level 2 Student's Book* by Ben Goldstein and Ceri Jones. Copyright © 2015 Cambridge University Press; Extract from *Interchange Level 1 Student's Book* by Jack C. Richards et al. Copyright © 2015 Cambridge University Press; Extract from *Evolve Level 3 Student's Book* by Leslie Anne Hendra, Mark Ibbotson, Kathryn O'Dell. Copyright © 2019 Cambridge University Press; **Chapter 7:** Extract from *Interchange Level 1 Student's Book* by Jack C. Richards. et al. Copyright © 2017 Cambridge University Press; Extracts from *Cambridge English Empower A2* by Adrian Doff, Craig Thaine et al. Copyright © 2015 Cambridge University Press; Extracts from *Cambridge English Empower B1* by Adrian Doff, Craig Thaine et al. Copyright © 2015 Cambridge University Press; Extract from *face2face Elementary* by Chris Redston and Gillie Cunningham. Copyright © 2012 Cambridge University Press; Extract from *Evolve 2 Level Student's Book* by Lindsay Clandfield et al. Copyright © 2019 Cambridge University Press; Extracts from *Cambridge English Empower A2* by Adrian Doff, Craig Thaine et al. Copyright © 2015 Cambridge University Press; Extract from *Think Level 2 Student's Book* by Herbert Puchta, Jeff Stranks and Peter Lewis-Jones. Copyright © 2015 Cambridge University Press; Extract from *Interchange Level 1 Student's Book* by Jack C. Richards et al. Copyright © 2017 Cambridge University Press; Extract from *Eyes Open 2 Student's Book* by Ben Goldstein, and Ceri Jones. Copyright © 2015 Cambridge University Press; Extract from *Unlock 2 Listening, Speaking and Critical Thinking* by Stephanie Dimond-Bayir and Kimberley Russell. Copyright © 2019 Cambridge University Press; Extract from *Interchange Level 3 Student's Book* by Jack C. Richards et al. Copyright © 2017 Cambridge University Press; Extract from *English Unlimited Elementary* by Leslie Anne Hendra, Mark Ibbotson, Kathryn O'Dell. Copyright © 2019

Cambridge University Press; Extract from *English Unlimited Elementary* by Alex Tilbury et al. Copyright © 2010 Cambridge University Press; Extract from *Eyes Open Level 2 Student's Book* by Ben Goldstein and Ceri Jones. Copyright © 2015 Cambridge University Press; Extract from *Unlock 2 Listening, Speaking and Critical Thinking* by Stephanie Dimond-Bayir and Kimberley Russell. Copyright © 2019 Cambridge University Press; Extract from *Cambridge English Empower A2* by Adrian Doff, Craig Thaine et al. Copyright © 2015 Cambridge University Press; Extract from *Evolve 3 Student's Book* by Leslie Anne Hendra, Mark Ibbotson, Kathryn O'Dell. Copyright © 2019 Cambridge University Press; Extract from *Unlock 3 Listening, Speaking and Critical Thinking* by Sabina Ostrowska, Nancy Jordan et al. Copyright © 2019 Cambridge University Press; **Chapter 8:** Extract from *Discourse Analysis for Language Teachers* by Michael McCarthy et al. Copyright © 1991 Cambridge University Press; Extract from *Cambridge Grammar of English* by Ronald Carter and Michael McCarthy et al. Copyright © 2006 Cambridge University Press; Extract from *Cambridge English Empower A2* by Adrian Doff, Craig Thaine et al. Copyright © 2015 Cambridge University Press; Extract *from Eyes Open Level 2 Student's Book* by Ben Goldstein, and Ceri Jones. Copyright © 2015 Cambridge University Press; Extract from *face2face Pre Intermediate* by Chris Redston and Gillie Cunningham. Copyright © 2012 Cambridge University Press; Extract from *Interchange Level 1 Student's Book* by Jack C. Richards et al. Copyright © 2017 Cambridge University Press; Extracts from *Think Level 1 Student's Book* by Herbert Puchta, Jeff Stranks and Peter Lewis-Jones. Copyright © 2015 Cambridge University Press; Extract from *face2face Elementary* by Chris Redston and Gillie Cunningham. Copyright © 2012 Cambridge University Press; Extract from *Cambridge English Empower B1* by Adrian Doff, Craig Thaine et al. Copyright © 2015 Cambridge University Press; Extract from *Cambridge English Empower A1* by Adrian Doff, Craig Thaine et al. Copyright © 2015 Cambridge University Press; Extract from *face2face Pre intermediate* by Chris Redston and Gillie Cunningham. Copyright © 2012 Cambridge University Press; Extract from *Interchange Level 2 Student's Book* by Jack C. Richards et al. Copyright © 2017 Cambridge University Press; Extract from *Cambridge English Empower A1* by Adrian Doff, Craig Thaine et al. Copyright © 2015 Cambridge University Press; Extracts from *face2face Elementary* by Chris Redston and Gillie Cunningham. Copyright © 2012 Cambridge University Press; Extract from *Think Level 2 Student's Book* by Herbert Puchta, Jeff Stranks, Peter Lewis-Jones. Copyright © 2015 Cambridge University Press; Extract from *Interchange Level 1 Student's Book* by Jack C. Richards et al. Copyright © 2017 Cambridge University Press; Extracts from *Eyes Open Level 3 Student's Book* by Ben Goldstein and Ceri Jones. Copyright © 2015 Cambridge University Press; Extracts from *Cambridge English Empower A2* by Adrian Doff, Craig Thaine et al. Copyright © 2015 Cambridge University Press; Extract from *Think Level 2 Student's Book* by Herbert Puchta, Jeff Stranks and Peter Lewis-Jones. Copyright © 2015 Cambridge University Press; Extract from *Eyes Open Level 2 Student's Book* by Ben Goldstein and Ceri Jones. Copyright © 2015 Cambridge University Press; Extract from *Unlock 3 Reading, Writing and Critical Thinking* by Carolyn Westbrook, Lida Baker et al. Copyright © 2019 Cambridge University Press; Extract from *Unlock Level 2 Reading, Writing and Critical Thinking* by Richard O'Neill, Michele Lewis et al. Copyright © 2019 Cambridge University Press; Extract from *Unlock Listening, Speaking and Critical Thinking* by Sabina Ostrowska and Nancy Jordan, with Chris Sowton. Copyright © 2019 Cambridge University Press; Extract from *Cambridge English Empower B1+* by Adrian Doff, Craig Thaine et al. Copyright © 2015 Cambridge University Press; **Chapter 9:** Extract from *Listening in the Language Classroom* by

John Field. Copyright © 2008 Cambridge University Press; Extract from *Teaching Speaking – A Holistic View* by Goh, C. C. M. and A. Burns. Copyright © 2012 Cambridge University Press; Extract from *Teaching and Developing Reading Skills* by Peter Watkins. Copyright © 2017 Cambridge University Press; Extract from *https://www.coe.int/en/web/common-european-framework-reference-languages/table-2-cefr-3.3-common-reference-levels-self-assessment-grid* by Common European Framework of Reference for Languages (CEFR) Self-assessment grid; Extract from *Second Language Writing* by Ken Hyland. Copyright © 1996 Cambridge University Press; Extract from *Learning Grammar* by Scott Thornbury and *The Cambridge Guide to Learning English as a Second Language* by Anne Burns and Jack C. Richards et al. Copyright © 2018 Cambridge University Press; Extract from *Learning Vocabulary in Another Language* by I. S. P. Nation. Copyright © 2013 Cambridge University Press; Extract from *Reading in a Second Language* by William Grabe et al. Copyright © 2009 Cambridge University Press; Extract from *Key Issues in Language Teaching* by Jack C. Richards. Copyright © 2015 Cambridge University Press; Extract from *Conversation: From Description to Pedagogy* by Scott Thornbury and Diana Slade. Copyright © 2006 Cambridge University Press.

Images

Cover photography by PM Images/Stone/Getty Images.

URL

The publisher has used its best endeavours to ensure that the URLs for external websites referred to in this book are correct and active at the time of going to press. However, the publisher has no responsibility for the websites and can make no guarantee that a site will remain live or that the content is or will remain appropriate.

Introduction

What does 'off the page' mean?

In English language teaching schools and institutions around the world, a great many teachers use material from a published course book as the basis of the lessons they teach. A course book may be the core element of a language teaching programme, or it could be a teaching and learning resource that is dipped into from time to time. In the past, course books reflected a range of methodological approaches that, in turn, reflected the belief systems of writers. However, these days most course books tend to subscribe to a 'soft version' of the communicative approach, and are arguably more standardised as a result.

Course books have also become more user friendly than they were 30 years ago, and those produced by publishers in the UK and the US for an international market mostly provide logically sequenced learning activities with a student-centred focus. It is now possible for a teacher to work through the activities in the course book when delivering a lesson, and the result will generally be well-balanced and varied. But, no matter how well designed, a lesson that is mechanically delivered runs the risk of failing to fully engage learners and, therefore, it may not be such a motivating experience for a student.

In some contexts, teachers are observed by senior peers or teacher educators as part of a teacher development programme. These observers often praise teachers for the clarity of the lesson as a whole and for a proficient display of teaching skills. However, they often note that the lesson did not fully engage students and it needed more animation. Observers sometimes make the comment that the lesson 'didn't get off the page'. This is what is meant by the title of this book. It investigates ways of bringing course book-based lessons to life so they are more dynamic and engaging for students.

The role of course books in English language programmes

The importance of course books for English language teachers is not lost on Richards (1993) or Tomlinson (2003). Richards states that:

> ... coursebooks are the main teaching resource used by many of the world's English teachers. The extent of English teaching worldwide could probably not be sustained without the support of many different kinds of textbooks and their ancillaries (2014:19)

This suggests a central and dominant role of course books in the teaching and learning of English. Richards goes on to note that, in many institutions, the course book is in effect the syllabus that teachers follow. In schools where there might be an independent syllabus, it is often cross-referenced to a specific course book.

The quote above also highlights the supportive role course books can play. Apart from providing logically sequenced activities, they often include a range of activities that encourages students to speak – information gap activities, role plays, discussions and personalisation activities all feature prominently in contemporary course books. These activities are usually designed in such a way that they are easy to set up and manage. This is the area in which course books have perhaps improved most in the past 30 years, and it is here we can see the influence of a more communicative approach to language teaching. Previously, there were fewer speaking activities, and language practice was often limited to oral pattern practice drills or controlled written practice of target vocabulary and grammar.

Course books are usually published with accompanying notes for teachers typically provided in a Teacher's Book. These notes often include methodological ideas and language notes from which novice teachers can learn. The support that they offer might also include a teacher development dimension. With the advent of information technology (IT), much of this extra support material has been placed online. Publishers now provide a wide range of extra resources that includes extra language practice, additional reading and listening material, short videos and assessment material that all aim to make a teacher's job easier in terms of availability of resources. The course book is sometimes like the tip of a resource iceberg. Nevertheless, it is the tip from which everything else pivots.

While playing a central role in the teaching and learning process, course books are not always seen in a positive light. The most common criticism levelled at course books is their inability to meet the needs of specific learner groups or to reflect the local context in which learning is taking place. Tomlinson (2016) questions the ability of course books to aid 'durable language acquisition' while also conceding there is no evidence to indicate they do not.

Meddings and Thornbury (2009) proposed an alternative approach to English language teaching they termed Dogme that involved very limited use of course book material. They noted that, among other things, the predominantly grammar-focused syllabus of most course books acted as an impediment to the students' own emergent language. They aimed to move English language learning away from the topics and themes introduced in course books and to situate it more firmly in the experience of students' lives. This meant teachers provided their students with opportunities to talk about what was relevant to them. In turn, teachers could respond to the language that students produced. A Dogme classroom involves the construction of knowledge shared by the teacher and learners and by way of input from a course book.

The underlying principle of teachers responding to emergent language remains a powerful one, and it means teachers cannot mechanically work through a series of course book tasks. It also mitigates against what Akbari (2008) calls 'textbook-defined practice', methodology that is determined by the course book. He notes that this can become default methodology for teachers because of institutional constraints or time pressure.

These criticisms of the way course books can affect classroom delivery lead to a salient point made by McGrath (2016) about needing to make a distinction between a course book and the way it is used. He has a constructive view of this relationship and notes that course books can provide teachers with a structure for teaching. He also notes that course books provide a map for teachers to follow; they can offer variety in terms of topics; and they can save teachers a lot of time. On balance, he concludes that they are a 'convenient aid'.

It is also worth noting that many teachers enjoy using course books. Course book writers typically have substantial teaching experience and good awareness of what does and does not work in the classroom. Furthermore, publishers conduct extensive market research with teachers and students when they create a course and sample materials are trialled. The results of this research and trialling feed directly into the writing process. This means the end product is likely to meet the broader needs of at least some teachers and students. Any adaptations that need to be made are often related to the local context in which the course book is used.

The discussion above is a very limited summary of different points of view that teachers, researchers and materials writers have of course books. Attitudes can vary enormously, and this is often informed by the amount of teaching experience a teacher has. Hadley summarises this clearly in the following diagram:

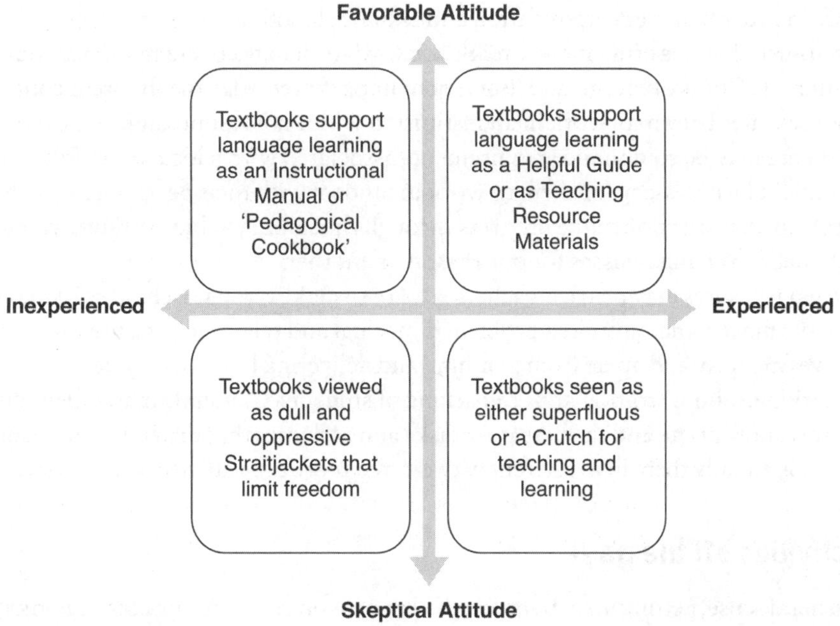

Figure 0.1: Interaction Between Teachers, Teacher Experience and Attitudes Towards Textbooks (Hadley 2018: 301).

Course book adaptation

If, as noted above, course books are unable to respond to specific student needs and represent localised learning contexts, then some kind of adaptation to the material is desirable. McGrath (2016) provides a useful framework for course book adaptation:

- the teacher completely *changes* what is in the course book – the contexts, the language and the methodology (*adaptation as change*);
- the teacher *adds* to the course book material in some way either when planning the lesson or during its delivery (*adaptation as addition*).

Adaptation as addition can be further broken down:

- *Extemporisation*: the teacher responds spontaneously to a learning event that arises during the course of a lesson, for example, the teacher may note that a reading text includes examples of a previously taught grammar item and points this out to learners;

- *Extension*: the teacher provides extra material to supplement what is already in the course book, for example, another reading text on the same topic as the one in the course book or more vocabulary practice activities of lexis presented in the course book;
- *Exploitation*: the teacher uses what is in the course book but exploits it in a slightly different way, for example, rather than getting students to read an example dialogue aloud, the teacher may provide key-word prompts and get students to perform a role play of the dialogue.

The activities in *Off the Page* adhere to the exploitation strategy of course book adaptation. In effect, they take what is in the course book and exploit it in a different way so the activity is animated to some degree in order to increase motivation and enhance learning.

It could be argued that it is often more straightforward to change course book material for something different. This is often the case, but it does not acknowledge the different contexts in which many teachers operate. They may work in an institution where it is not possible to deviate from the course book. There may be compliance requirements associated with a local or national curriculum. Conversely, it might be necessary for them to work in tandem with their peers to ensure that students at a certain level in an institution make progress through the same syllabus at a similar rate because students might need to change classes for one reason or another.

While external pressures may restrict teachers' ability to make dramatic changes to the course book they are using, the most commonly cited problem is internal and relates to time pressure. Teachers' professional lives are busy and apart from planning and delivering lessons, they need to attend to assessment, marking, administration and counselling of students. Changing material involves finding something that is appropriate and then creating tasks and activities that turn it into a learning resource. Exploiting what is already there in a different way is often more time efficient and less stressful.

Getting activities off the page

In the most general sense, getting an activity off the page involves mediating course book material. The aim is to avoid a lesson where students seem stuck in a continuous cycle of:

students do a task → check in pairs → check answers with the teacher → do the next task

There may be some opportunities for speaking practice in amongst this, but the lesson mostly proceeds in this predictable way. The tasks may be of good quality, and there are likely to be opportunities for students to learn and practise language. However, the lesson may not fully engage students in the learning process.

In order to interrupt this cycle, teachers need to evaluate activities with a critical eye when they are planning their lessons. They need to ask themselves if they could do a task in a slightly different way and call on their experience and their creativity in order to make a change. In doing so, they should bear in mind some core principles associated with getting material off the page and they should also question themselves:

- *Providing a communicative focus*: Is there some way I can create an information gap with this activity that gives students a reason to communicate?
- *Giving more opportunities for student speaking*: Is there something that students can talk about with this activity? Can I suggest they have a personal response to a topic? Is there potential for a role play or discussion associated with this topic/context?

- *Being alert to student-centredness*: Do I, the teacher, need to maintain control of this activity? Could I hand things over to students and get them to think / talk about this in pairs or groups?
- *Offering a variety of interaction*: Would it be more interesting for students to do this in pairs or small groups? Can I move some students from one group to the next? Does it help to get them up and moving around the classroom and talking to each other?
- *Allowing more student-generated content*: Is there an opportunity for students to make their own examples? What if students wrote the questions and not the answers?
- *Introducing a fun element*: Can I turn it into some kind of language game? Can this activity become some kind of competition that means they all become involved?

In making these adaptations, the aim is to bring a task or activity to life in such a way that students will be more motivated to do it and become more engaged as they carry out the task or activity. Ideally, at the same time, it should provide students with more by way of learning opportunities. These opportunities will sometimes be explicit and students will learn something new about language, or they may be implicit and students learn to do something with language as they are using it.

This book provides examples of how teachers can get course book material off the page. In doing so, it aims to act as an initial guide and jumping off point that stimulates teachers' own creativity. Ultimately, the exploitation adaptations that you, the teacher, make in relation to your student group and the context you are working in are likely to be the most successful.

Organisation of the book

The organisation of *Off the Page* is based on the way that course book material is typically organised within a unit, where different sections focus on different language skills and language systems. As a result, there are four chapters in *Off the Page* that relate to the four language skills of listening, speaking, reading and writing; and four chapters that relate to the four language systems of pronunciation, vocabulary, grammar and discourse. (Chapter 8 combines discourse with language used in social contexts, often called functional or situational language in course books.) The aim of organising the book in this way is for ease of reference in relation to whatever course book you are using.

It is, however, worth remembering that the aims of course book activities are never entirely singular. For example, an activity that aims to get students speaking may also be providing practice of a grammar point while a reading activity may involve a text that includes previously taught vocabulary and, apart from practising reading skills, may also be aiming to revise that vocabulary.

Each chapter begins with an introduction that outlines how that language system or skill is typically represented in course books and then describes a generic methodological procedure implicit in the material. Alternatives to typical approaches and possible exceptions are also discussed in the chapter introductions.

Each example activity refers to a specific example of course book material and outlines a procedure of how this material can be animated. A rationale is provided for the approach and, after the procedure, there is a comment that shows how the idea can be generalised and applied to other course book activities. In doing so, there are often suggestions for how the idea can be varied according to the language level you are teaching.

Following each activity, there are reflection questions for students and for you, the teacher. In providing these questions for students, the aim is to develop language skills and not just practise them. They also encourage students to become more aware of their own learning, and therefore a little more independent in determining their learning goals. The teachers' reflection questions aim to get you thinking critically about methodology and, at times, they ask you to consider the activity in light of your student group and to consider what the activity revealed about learners in your class.

At the end of each chapter, you are directed to Chapter 9 to find suggestions for further teacher development. Each teacher development activity begins with an extract from a publication that focuses on a point of interest associated with the language system/skill. This is followed by questions that encourage you to reflect on the content of the reading. Next there is a suggestion for some kind of teacher development activity, for example, an action research project or a methodological experiment. Finally, there are general reflection questions.

The teacher development activities can be done alone, but there is obvious benefit in carrying them out together with a colleague or group of colleagues as you will doubtless gain insights from each other's point of view. In effect, the teacher development activities could form the basis of a systematic programme in an institution.

How to use *Off the Page*

Off the Page is the kind of book that you can dip into according to your interests and needs, and the activities do not follow any prescriptive order. A first step is to decide for yourself what kind of activity you wish to experiment with. Find the relevant chapter and then scan the chapter headings to find the kind of activity you wish to try out. If the example course book material for the activity is something that you can use with your students, then it is merely a question of following the preparation instructions and the procedure. However, if the material is not suitable, for example, it is not the correct level, then you will need to identify a similar activity in a course book – either the one you are using or an alternative.

Once you have carried out the activity, it is useful to find out students' comments in answer to their reflection questions. Beyond this, consider the teacher reflection questions and perhaps discuss them with a colleague. Actively engaging in this process will help inform how you might adapt or alter the teaching idea in future lessons. This is what is meant above when it is suggested that *Off the Page* is a jumping off point for your own ideas.

A final word on classroom management and interaction patterns. Throughout the book the following interaction patterns are referred to.

pair work – two students working together

small group work – three or four students working together

large group work – more than four students working together

mingle – when students stand up and move around the room in order to speak to different peers

onion ring – students form two circles, one inside the other; the outer group face in towards the inner circle who face out; one circle moves in a clockwise direction and the other anti-clockwise to create new pairs

If you are working in a teaching space where it is difficult to carry out mingle and onion ring interactions, feel free to adapt the suggestions to suit your teaching space.

References

Akbari, R. (2008) 'Postmethod discourse and practice', *TESOL Quarterly*, 42/4, p. 647.

Hadley, G. (2018) Learning Through Textbooks. In A. Burns and J. C. Richards (eds.), *The Cambridge Guide to Learning English as a Second Language* (pp. 298–306). Cambridge: Cambridge University Press.

McGrath, I. (2016) *Materials Evaluation and Design for Language Teaching* (2nd ed.). Edinburgh: Edinburgh University Press.

Meddings, L. O. and Thornbury, S. (2009) *Teaching Unplugged*. Peaslake: Delta Publishing.

Richards, J. C. (1993) 'Beyond the textbook: the role of commercial materials in language teaching', *RELC Journal*, 24(1): 1–14.

Richards, J. C. (2014) The ELT Coursebook. In S. Garton and K. Graves (eds.), *International Perspectives on Materials in ELT* (pp. 19–36). Basingstoke: Palgrave Macmillan.

Tomlinson, B. (2016) Achieving a match between SLA theory and materials development. In B. Tomlinson (ed.), *SLA Research and Materials Development for Language Learning* (pp. 3–22). New York: Routledge.

Tomlinson, B. (2003) Introduction: Are Materials Developing? In B. Tomlinson (ed.), *Developing Materials for Language Teaching* (pp. 1–14). London: Continuum.

1 Listening

Introduction

Listening activities in course books

All course books provide some kind of listening material. This can be either audio or video, but, on balance, there is likely to be more audio material. Listening material has two key roles to play in English language programmes:

- it gives students an opportunity to practise and develop their listening skills;
- it provides a context for specific language items: grammar, expressions, vocabulary and pronunciation features.

Figure 1.0a (page 10) is an example of a course book listening lesson that includes typical steps (or stages) in a listening lesson. *Figure 1.0b* (page 11) is the audio script of the listening.

Broadly speaking, the material follows the steps of a listening lesson that combine the two key roles of listening material noted above (listening practice and language feature contextualisation):

lead in → initial listening → second, more detailed listening → follow up speaking activity→ focus on a language feature

While this broad overview applies to a wide range of listening lessons, the nature of the listening text will result in variations – these are examined below.

In *Figure 1.0a*, exercise 1A is the lead in activity. As is usually the case, this involves some kind of speaking, and course books will often provide visual prompts to stimulate spoken language. Apart from providing spoken fluency practice, lead in activities also aim to generate student interest in the topic or theme of the listening text, and perhaps activate any related background knowledge they might have. Activating background knowledge can often compensate for gaps in students' linguistic knowledge and any possible deficit in their language competence. Exercise 1A above encourages students to speculate on how these different images might be linked and predict the content of the listening text. To some degree, it creates a kind of mystery that students might be curious to solve. This gives them motivation to listen.

Exercise 1B is the initial listening activity. Students listen without reading the audio script and find out whether their predictions about the photographs are correct or not. In order to complete this task, students will not need to understand a lot of detailed information in the listening text, so they 'listen for the gist'. The principle here is that it would be too difficult and unfair to expect students to understand a lot of detail the first time they listen to a text or a conversation, particularly when they are at a lower level. It is likely to have a negative impact on their motivation if we expect them to understand a lot of detailed information during an initial listening. However, providing them with a task that requires a gist understanding of the listening text is likely to be more manageable.

1 LISTENING

A PREDICT **Look at the pictures from an unusual event. Can you guess what it is?**

B 1.44 **Listen to a news report about the event. Was your prediction correct?**

C 1.44 LISTEN FOR DETAIL **Listen to the report again and answer the questions.**

1 Where does the festival take place?
2 Where do the bats come from?
3 What moment are the people waiting for?
4 How many bats are there?

D 1.45 PAIR WORK **What other things do you think happen at the festival? Think of four to six possibilities. Listen and check your ideas.**

E THINK CRITICALLY **Not everyone in Austin likes the festival. Think of who these people are. Why don't they enjoy it? Would you like to go to the festival? Why or why not?**

2 PRONUNCIATION: Listening for single sounds

A 1.46 **Listen. Focus on the letters in bold. Can you hear one or two sounds?**

1 We know them from ba**d** **d**reams.
2 Bats a**r**e **r**eally scary.
3 There'**s** **s**o much happening.

B 1.47 **Find two letters in the sentences that can connect to make one sound. There are two pairs of letters in sentence 1. Listen and check.**

1 They can eat ten thousand kilograms of insects in one night.
2 It's home to music festivals and car racing.
3 I can't wait to try the barbecue.

C **Complete the sentence.**

Two sounds often become *one / three* if they are *similar / different* at the end of a word and the start of the next word.

Figure 1.0a: Clandfield, L., B. Goldstein et al. (2019) *Evolve 2*, p. 40.

In most cases, the more students listen to a text or conversation, the more they understand. As a result, course books usually provide a second listening task that aims to help students understand more information in the listening text. Again, students listen, but they do not follow the audio script. Exercise 1C encourages students to do this. Given that students have already listened to the text once, this should be an achievable task. Also, the questions in exercise 1C focus the attention of the listener, and the

Lesson 4.4, page 40, Exercises 1B and 1C

Reporter We know them from bad dreams and scary movies. Creatures of the night that drink our blood and become vampires! I'm talking, of course, about bats! But not everyone thinks bats are really scary. There is a place where these little animals are very popular. So popular, in fact, that once a year there is a festival to celebrate them. That place is Austin, Texas, and the festival is Bat Fest.

Every year, bats from Mexico fly north and spend the summer under the Congress Avenue Bridge in downtown Austin, right under my feet. At the moment it's daytime, so they're sleeping. In a few hours, when the sun starts to go down, it's dinnertime. And these bats are hungry. Together, they eat about 10,000 kilograms of insects in one night. That's what everyone at Bat Fest is waiting for now – the moment when 1.5 million bats wake up, leave the bridge, and fill the evening sky. And I'll be right here to see it.

Bats or no bats, Austin is a cool city. It's a college town, so there are a lot of young people. It's also home to music festivals and car racing. People in Austin like to celebrate everything, so why not the bats? But Bat Fest is about more than bats. There's so much happening.

Figure 1.0b: Kocienda, G., G. Jones et al. (2019) *Evolve 2 Teacher's Book*, p. 174.

information in the questions themselves provide students with clues about the information in the text. In other words, providing some kind of focused task makes detailed listening easier than it would be if the teacher gave a very general instruction such as 'listen again for more details'.

Exercise 1D provides students with a third opportunity to listen in more detail. As is the case with exercises 1A and 1B, students are asked to predict and then listen to check their ideas. However, this time, they do so on the basis that they are already familiar with some of the information in the listening text. Exercise 1D is a less typical detailed listening task, but it is an interesting one because it gives students some degree of choice in terms of what information they are listening for.

The follow up speaking activity is found in exercise 1E. This asks students to respond to the content of the listening text in a critical light and is likely to take the form of a discussion in pairs or small groups. Follow up speaking activities do not always involve critical thinking skills and will often get students to personalise information in the text, voice their own opinion of it or perhaps do a role play that is similar to the conversation they have just heard.

The next stage of a typical course book listening lesson is to focus on a particular language feature. In the example in *Figure 1.0a* above, exercises 2A–C focus on pronunciation. Students listen to examples from the news report that illustrate a feature of connected speech – the way adjacent consonant sounds can combine to become one sound (known as 'assimilation'). At this stage in a listening lesson, students can be asked to listen for any language feature: grammar structures, useful expressions and individual words. This kind of very intensive listening requires bottom-up processing of language. Not all course books include this step in a listening lesson.

Listening subskills and texts

In outlining typical stages of a listening lesson, some listening subskills have been referred to. Students might practise some of the following core listening subskills:

- listening for gist
- listening for detail
- listening for language items
- scan listening
- listening to infer information (e.g. speaker's point of view)
- listening for text or discourse patterns

The kind of subskill they practise will depend on the nature of the listening text and the task that the course book or the teacher provides. In the example material above, listening for the gist of a news report is a reasonably natural way to listen. However, if the listening text were a series of flight announcements at an airport, then it would be less natural to practise gist listening and it would make more sense to provide a scan listening task where students have to pick out individual flight and gate numbers – as travellers do at an airport.

Conversely, if the listening text is a university lecture (or an excerpt from one), then a first listening task that asks students to scan listen for key vocabulary items in the lecture would not be a natural response to that listening text. It would make more sense to get students to understand the main ideas in the lecture (the gist) and perhaps get them to listen and understand if the structure of the lecture follows some kind of specific text pattern, for example, the lecture might introduce a problem and then provide a solution. As you consider listening lessons in course books, it pays to evaluate the tasks critically to see that they practise the listening subskill they say they aim to practise, and whether that subskill is natural in relation to the nature of the listening text.

Methodological considerations

Teachers also need to think about the way they deliver listening lessons from course books. Some very simple ideas can ensure that students feel supported and get benefit from listening. Here are four key steps that can be good practice to follow:

1. Set listening tasks before playing the audio, so students know what they are listening for and have a reason to listen;
2. Get students to check their answers together in pairs before you check their answers – this gives them more confidence and students can often learn from each other when checking their understanding in pairs;
3. Monitor students carefully during pair checking stages and try to determine how well they have understood the listening text;
4. Play the audio more than once if necessary, particularly for detailed listening activities – students will usually understand more with each subsequent listening.

Many course books provide an audio script of listening material at the back of the book. After following the four steps above, it would be an appropriate time for students to listen again and follow the audio script. It is a good way to round off a listening activity, particularly at lower levels. This can be an opportunity for students to resolve any uncertainties they might have had, and for you to answer any questions they might have about language. It is also a way of helping learners tune into differences between the way English is written and the way it is spoken.

Issues with listening lessons

The description of course book based listening lessons above is often described as the 'comprehension approach' to listening (Field 2008). Criticism of this approach includes the following:

- students have little control over the listening text;
- when students use English outside the classroom, they not only have to listen but they also have to speak;
- there is not sufficient attention paid to bottom-up processing of spoken language.

Some of the activities in this chapter suggest ways of helping with these challenges, but these are key points for teachers to consider whenever they are planning listening lessons. They also suggest that teachers need to encourage their learners to listen outside the classroom as much as possible. Digital technology and the amount of material that is freely available online has made this a far more achievable goal.

Reference

Field, J. (2008) *Listening in the Language Classroom*. Cambridge: Cambridge University Press.

A Before listening

1.1 Role play first

Level	B1 and above
Time	10 to 15 minutes
Outline	In this activity students do a role play of a conversation in the same situation as the listening they are going to listen to.
Aim	To get students interested in the topic; to prepare them for listening; to provide speaking fluency practice.
Preparation	Copy the role cards below to use with the *Figure 1.1a* below or create your own role cards for another listening text.
Rationale	A typical way of leading into a listening activity is by getting students to discuss questions about the topic of a listening. This activity is a variation on this typical lead in. Getting students to do a role play more actively puts them in the speaker's role and it may help generate ideas that they don't consciously think of in a normal lead in. You can also focus students on some of the content of the listening in the role cards you give them. In addition, a role play provides extra speaking practice, of course.

Procedure

1 Establish the topic or the situation of the role play and pre-teach any useful vocabulary students can use.
2 Hand out role cards and give students time to prepare.
3 Put students in A–B pairs to do the role play.
4 Do whole class feedback and make notes on the board.
5 Students listen to the audio and see if it's similar to the conversation they had.
6 In their pairs, students discuss similarities. Then do whole class feedback.

Notes

Possible next steps in the lesson are for students to do a detailed listening task and then listen and follow the audio script in order to notice useful language items. You could then ask students to repeat their role play trying to include new ideas and language they have noticed from the listening. This follows a task-teach(noticing)-task approach to the skills work.

Learner reflection questions

1 What ideas from your conversation were similar to the ideas in the listening?
2 How did this help you to understand the listening?
3 When you practise listening on your own, is it a good idea to think about the topic of the listening before you listen? Why / Why not?

Teacher reflection

How motivated were students to listen to the conversation the first time? Why do you think this was the case?

1 LISTENING AND SPEAKING

a Look at the different ways of learning and answer the questions.

- reading about a topic
- listening to someone explain
- group work
- online or with an app
- in a classroom with a teacher
- one-to-one with a teacher
- studying on your own

1 What different ways have you experienced?
2 Are there any other ways you can think of?
3 Which ways do you prefer?

b 3.19 Listen to Janina and Roberta talking about online learning. Who is worried about online learning? Why?

c 3.19 Listen again. Are the sentences true (*T*) or false (*F*)? Correct the false sentences.

1 ☐ Janina's going to do an online course next year.
2 ☐ Roberta prefers learning in a classroom.
3 ☐ Roberta likes to choose when she studies.
4 ☐ Roberta couldn't meet her teachers during her online course.
5 ☐ Roberta liked reading the students' online profiles.
6 ☐ Janina needs to have excellent IT skills for the course.
7 ☐ Janina must do the introduction course very soon.

d Make a list of good and bad points for studying in class with a teacher and studying online.

in class with a teacher
good points | bad points

online
good points | bad points

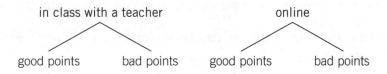

3.19

ROBERTA Hi, Janina. What are you reading?
JANINA I'm just looking at the course information for next year.
R Oh, OK.
J It says that one of the psychology courses I have to do is going to be online.
R That's good.
J You think so? I've never done an online course.
R I did one this year – it was great. I wouldn't mind doing my whole degree online.
J Really, Roberta? What's so good about it?
R Well, we only had about two classes on the whole course. And they recorded them and put them online anyway. I was free to study whenever I wanted. Good for people like me who are always late for classes!
J Yeah, I don't have a problem with that but it sounds good.
R I mean, you still have to write essays and hand things in on time and all that kind of thing.
J Of course.
R And I got good grades on that course.
J But did you … I mean, didn't you miss asking your teachers questions? And what about meeting other students?
R Well, we could go and meet the teachers if we wanted to … you know, make an appointment and ask about something one-to-one. And at the beginning of the course, we had to write an online profile. We had students from all round the world in our class, so the profiles were really interesting.
J How many international students were there?
R About 15, I think. And from all kinds of different places – Colombia, China, Morocco, Turkey, Oman – all over the place.
J And did they talk about their countries a lot?
R Yeah, that's what I really enjoyed.
J The only thing I'm not sure of … well, you know that my IT skills aren't very good. Like, I'm OK making documents and using the Internet. But this could be a bit more … I don't know ... difficult?
R Not really. You don't need any special skills. It's quite easy. And there's an introduction course you can do.
J Yeah, I was just reading about that. At least it's free.
R Yeah, you should do it, Janina. It's only two weeks long and you can do it any time. It really helped me.
J OK – sounds like a good idea.

Figure 1.1a: Doff, A., C. Thaine et al. (2015) *Cambridge English Empower B1*, pp. 94 and 173.

Role cards

Student A

Read the instructions and write answers to the questions. Speak to Student B who has already done an online course.

You are planning to study university courses next year. One of the courses you really want to do is online.

- *What is the topic of the course?*

You're not sure you want to do a course online. There are some things you're not sure about.

- *What do you want to know about online studying?*

You're not sure if your IT skills are good enough.

- *Why not?*

Student B

Read the instructions and write answers to the questions. Speak to Student A.

Student A is your friend. She/He is thinking about doing a university course online next year, but she/he isn't sure about it. You did an online course last year and really enjoyed it. You liked being free to study when you wanted.

- *What other things did you enjoy about the course?*
- *In what ways are online courses similar to face-to-face courses?*

For the listening exercise in *Figure 1.1b*, you could also provide students with some of the useful language on the role play cards.

3 1.50 **Listen to Gemma talking to an activity guide. What is she going to do?**

4 **Complete the conversation with the useful language.**

Useful language

Where can I sign up?
Can I ask you a few things about (…)?
What about … ?
What do I need to bring?
How long is … ?
Does the price include (…)?

Gemma: Can I [1] ....*ask you*..... a few things about the **canyoning trip**?
Guide: The **Blue Canyon** one? Sure. What would you like to know?
Gemma: Well, is it only for people who've already done it?
Guide: No, you don't need any experience. We give training with qualified guides, and the **Blue Canyon** is fine for **beginners**.
Gemma: Great! [2]… need to bring? I haven't got **a wetsuit or anything**.
Guide: That's OK. We provide a **wetsuit, helmet, shoes and life jacket**. Just bring **your swimsuit** and **towel** and **some warm clothes for after**.
Gemma: OK, good! How [3]… is the trip to **Blue Canyon**?
Guide: It's **all day**, from **nine until six**.
Gemma: I see. [4]… **food**, then? Does the price [5] … ?
Guide: **Food is included** in the price. We look after everything, so you just enjoy the adventure!
Gemma: Wow! It sounds fantastic. Where [6]… sign up?
Guide: Right here!

Figure 1.1b: Goldstein, B. and C. Jones (2015) *Eyes Open 3*, p. 48.

1.2 Find someone who first

Level	A2 and above
Time	15 minutes
Outline	Students do a *Find someone who* activity related to the topic of the listening before they listen in order to personalise the topic and create interest in the listening text.
Aim	To activate background knowledge and interest in the topic by relating it to students' previous experience; to revise question forms; to provide spoken fluency practice.
Preparation	Copy the *Find someone who* worksheet below to use with the example listening activity *Figure 1.2a* or create your own question prompts for another listening text.
Rationale	Another way to bring lead in questions to life is by turning them into a *Find someone who* activity. These activities are often done as a post-listening speaking task, but they can work just as well as a pre-listening activity. It means that students relate the topic to their own experience before they listen, and it gets them up and moving before having to sit still and listen.

Procedure

1. Check that students know something about the topic of the listening – Black Friday sales in *Figure 1.2a*.
2. Give students prompts for *Find someone who* questions and tell each student which question they should ask other students. Allow time for students to think of the question they should ask and monitor and help if needed.
3. Students stand up and move around and ask and answer questions. Each student asks their question to as many other students as possible. If they get a 'yes' answer, they should ask a follow-up question using the suggested question word.
4. Put students in pairs and get them to tell each other what they found out about their classmates, and then do whole class feedback.
5. Set the first listening task and ask students to listen and see if anyone in the conversation says something similar to what their classmates said.

Notes

The *Find someone who* worksheet below is only a suggestion. You could, for example, easily create a *Find someone who* worksheet for the material in activity 1.1 above, about students' experiences of learning online and in class. The more you can relate the questions to what you know about your students' interests the better. With a weaker class, you may need to elicit examples of the direct questions students will need to ask from the *Find someone who* prompts.

Learner reflection questions

1. Who in your class had a similar experience to one of the speakers in the listening?
2. What language from the *Find someone who* activity helped you with the listening?

Teacher reflection

What is likely to be the difference in energy levels with the *Find someone who* activity compared to students discussing the lead in questions in pairs?

6.1 BLACK FRIDAY FUN

LESSON OBJECTIVE
- plan a shopping trip

1 LANGUAGE IN CONTEXT

FIND IT

A 1.58 PAIR WORK **What do you know about Black Friday? You can go online to find out more. Then listen to four people talking about Black Friday. Who likes the day?**

B 1.58 **Listen to the program again. Who … ?**

1 ______ wants a new television.
2 ______ works at the store.
3 ______ is with someone.
4 ______ made a mistake.

1.58 Audio script

Black Friday is back! We asked some people what they think of it. Here's what they said.

Katie I didn't know today was Black Friday. I only came here to **return** a shirt but forget it! I'm going to come back next week – when it's not so crazy!

Seb I love Black Friday. I **save** for months and months and even **borrow** money from friends. I go crazy! I usually **spend** my money on clothes and shoes, but this year I'm going to buy a TV.

Marcia I hate Black Friday! I have to work all day and, excuse me… . Are you going to buy that?

Adam I'm here with my wife, but I can't find her now! I really want to go home. We're not going to come back next year. We're going to **shop online** in the future.

Figure 1.2a: Clandfield, L., B. Goldstein et al. (2019) *Evolve 2*, p. 54.

Find someone who …

1 always goes to sales. Why?
2 got a good bargain at a sale recently. What?
3 bought some clothes at a sale. What?
4 bought an IT product at a sale. What?
5 saves money to spend at a sale. How much?
6 only buys from online sales. Why?
7 bought something that didn't work at a sale. What?
8 works / worked in a shop during sale time. When?
9 gets up very early to go to a sale. What time?
10 is happy to spend all day shopping at sales. Why?
11 only buys one thing from a sale. What?
12 loves the crowds at a sale. Why?

For the listening exercise in *Figure 1.2b*, the *Find someone who* task could include the activities in the pictures as well as extra ones you know your students will be familiar with.

LISTENING

1 **Work in pairs. Match the activities with the photos.**

1 make a fire | 2 spend a night outdoors | 3 climb a tree | 4 drive a car | 5 spend an hour blindfolded

2 SPEAKING **Which of these things have you done? Tell your partner.**

3 1.16 **Listen to David talking about a book his father has just read. Which of the activities in Exercise 1 do they talk about?**

4 1.16 **Listen again. Mark the sentences T (true) or F (false).**

1 David is babysitting his little brother. ___
2 David thinks the book his father read is nonsense. ___
3 The book says children should spend an hour blindfolded alone. ___
4 David is not sure his dad will let Nick drive a car. ___
5 Nick drove the car straight into a tree. ___
6 David thinks Nick will enjoy showing that he can make a fire. ___

Audio Script Track 1.16

John	Hi, David.
David	Oh, hi, John.
John	I'm going to the pool. Want to come along?
David	I can't. My dad has asked me to do some things with Nick.
John	Your little brother? Oh, you're babysitting. Too bad.
David	No, I'm not actually babysitting. My dad's going to be with us, too.
John	So what are you doing?
David	Well, it's a long story. It all started with a book my dad read recently. It's called *50 Dangerous Things You Should Let Your Children Do*.
John	What? Seriously?
David	Yeah.
John	And?
David	And …, the book's cool, really. Parents are normally 'don't do this' and 'don't do that', right?
John	Yeah, tell me about it.
David	Well, this book says that parents should let children do things that most parents don't let them do.
John	Wow! OK. Let children do things like what?
David	So, for example, parents should let children make a fire.
John	Really? Isn't that dangerous?
David	Well, of course, kids shouldn't be alone when they make a fire. Parents should be with them, so they learn that fire can be dangerous. And of course they must not make a fire in a place where it is forbidden.
John	Uh-huh. What else?
David	Kids should spend an hour blindfolded.
John	Really, young children? That's dangerous.
David	That's right. That's why they couldn't do that on their own. Their parents need to make sure that nothing happens to them.
John	OK, but why?
David	The child learns something new. It's a new experience. And it's interesting for the child, too. They learn to be cautious.
John	Hmm. Cool.
David	Oh, something else.
John	What's that?
David	Parents should let their children drive a car.
John	Really? In the street?
David	No, no. In an empty space where there are no other cars, obviously.
John	Wow!
David	Yeah, but I'm not sure Dad will try this one with Nick.
John	He thinks he'll probably drive straight into a tree, right?
David	Look, I need to go now. I need to get some sausages.
John	Sausages?
David	Yes, Dad and I are going to show Nick how to make a fire. And then we want to grill some sausages.
John	Really, wow! I'd love to come along.
David	Why don't you?
John	Would that be OK with your dad?
David	Of course. He'd be happy if you could join us. And Nick …
John	What about him?
David	Well, he'll be proud to show you he can make a fire!
John	Of course!

Figure 1.2b: Puchta, H., J. Stranks and P. Lewis-Jones (2015) *Think Level 2*, pp. 23 and 35.

1.3 Ranking pictures

Level	B1 and above
Time	10 minutes
Outline	Turn a simple brainstorming activity into a ranking activity that gets students moving around the room.
Aim	To find out what students know about the topic; to get them to share information and evaluate their own knowledge; to provide spoken fluency practice.
Preparation	Find a series of interesting images associated with the topic of the listening. You can paste these into an electronic file that you project on the board or you can print them and put them up around the classroom. For example, for the listening activity in *Figure 1.3* you could find images of the following: email, text messaging, Skype, Facetime, postcards, a mobile phone, social media websites etc.
Rationale	Many pre-listening activities ask students to think about the topic and tell each other what they know. While course books include photographs and illustrations to support this, they may not be the best images to motivate your students. Getting students to rank the ideas they think about adds a task element to the activity.

Procedure

1 If using printed pictures, put them up in the classroom before the lesson begins.
2 Students make decisions about the pictures you have put up according to criteria. For example, if using pictures of different types of communication ask them to put them in order from *most* to *least useful* for staying in touch with friends and family when they are away from home.
3 Students move around the room and look at each image and think about how they will rank them.
4 In pairs, students compare their lists and give reasons for their order. They also think about other ways of communicating not included in the visuals.
5 Do whole class feedback and find the most popular way of communicating in the class.
6 Students then do the gist listening activity in exercise 2 in *Figure 1.3*.

Notes

A key to the success of this activity is finding images that are interesting for your students. Putting the images up around the room or projecting them on to the board means that students have their heads up and are more likely to talk to each other. Students will often automatically move into pairs for this activity and start talking about the images and commenting on them before they begin to rank them. When doing this activity with another listening text, you need to think of your own ranking criteria related to the topic of the listening and the images you choose.

Learner reflection questions

1 When you listened, did you think about any of the images you saw before you listened?
2 Do images sometimes help you to understand and remember information you listen to? Why / Why not?

Teacher reflection

To what extent did your images motivate students? Would you use the same ones again or would you change them? Why / Why not?

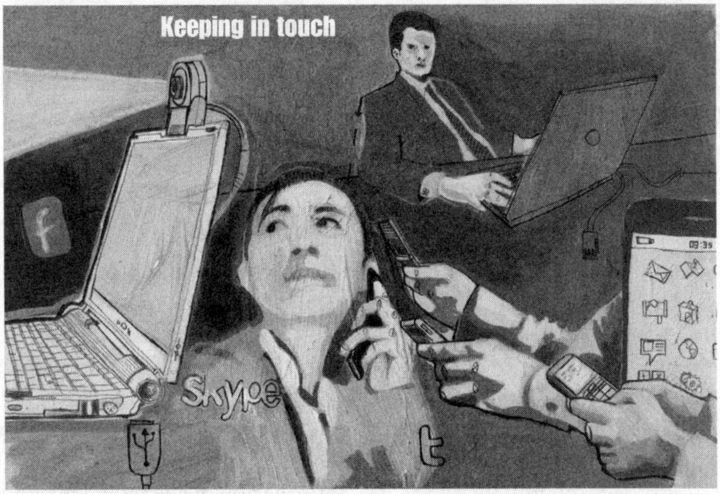

LISTENING **1** **Look at the pictures. How do you keep in touch with your family and friends?**

2 **1.10 Listen to two conversations. What method of communication is each about? What do the people think about it?**

Unit 2

1.10

PAULA I think Facebook is a waste of time. I'm totally addicted, I have to say. But, er, there really isn't much going on. You just spend hours just, sort of, making friends, checking other people's profiles, looking at the, erm, pictures they've, er, posted and it's just, I don't know, I mean, nothing happens. It's just that, I don't know, it's very voyeuristic and it, erm, really is a waste of time, I think.

MEGAN I find myself wasting a lot of time on Facebook. I'm now back in touch with people I knew in primary school but we don't actually say anything to each other. You just go onto their page, look at their pictures and then that's it, but for some reason I still find myself checking it constantly.

P Yeah, it's incredibly addictive. Erm, it's happened to me as well. Like, er, I was contacted by people I hadn't seen, er, in a very long time, and then you realise that you've changed a lot and you actually have nothing to talk about so there's no point in being friends, really. You know, all this, like, sort of, virtual friendship, it just leads nowhere, I think. It's not like a real friendship.

M It's such a huge waste of time that I've heard that some workplaces are banning its use because so many of us are wasting so much time looking at it.

GRAHAM How are you doing? Busy?

DENIZ I'm so busy! It's great to get out and have some fun.

G But you're always messing around with your phone when we're talking.

D Oh, am I? That's terrible. I ... I'm just trying to keep up with my emails.

G Yeah, but they say you need to take breaks from work, in the evening and weekends and stuff. Apparently, if you don't it really affects your performance. I read it somewhere.

D No, I don't think that's true.

G Do you really have to answer everything straight away?

D Yeah, it saves such a lot of time.

G And do you ever turn it off? I mean, what do you do at night?

D I screen my calls and if it's someone I need to talk to it pings, which wakes me up. Then I can call them back.

G Couldn't they wait till the morning?

D Well, the thing is, I have to talk to people in New York and Tokyo. So I have to be in contact during their work hours.

G That must be hard. I reckon you must get tired.

D Yeah, it's tiring being on call all the time. But you know, it's so interesting – I love the job.

G And what about holidays?

D Yeah, I know some people say you shouldn't take your work on holiday, but I take my phone.

G Really?

D Yeah. There's no harm in checking your emails from time to time, you know.

G You couldn't leave it at home?

D Er, no, no, I couldn't.

G I'd say it must be impossible to relax, though.

D Yeah, it's difficult to relax sometimes, but I love what I do ... it's amazing how much I miss the buzz of work when I'm away, even for a few days.

G Really? I don't have that problem.

Figure 1.3: Rea, D., T. Clementson et al. (2011) *English Unlimited B1+*, pp. 14 and 147.

B While listening

1.4 Order the text

Level	A2 and above
Time	10 to 15 minutes
Outline	After listening once to a simple situational dialogue, students are given a piece of a cut up audio script and have to put themselves in the correct order according to the original text.
Aim	To provide a student-centred focus to understanding the text; to focus on coherence and cohesion in a dialogue; to encourage students to listen to each other.
Preparation	If using *Figure 1.4*, cut up the dialogue from the audio script (see below) so each line is on an individual piece of paper. If using a different listening, and the audio script lines are close together, you may prefer to word process the dialogue so it's easier to cut up.
Rationale	Often second, detailed listening tasks such as comprehension questions or *True/False* questions focus on individual pieces of information in a listening text. This activity aims to focus students on all the information in a listening text and the way in which it fits together. It highlights the overall coherence of the listening text.

Procedure

1 Do a first listening task with students, e.g. as suggested in the course book exercise 4 in *Figure 1.4*, and check the answers.
2 Give students the individual lines of dialogue of the audio script that you prepared – one line for each student.
3 Ask students not to show their lines to each other.
4 Tell students to stand in the same order as the dialogue they listened to. They should say which speaker they are and read out their line.
5 Make sure students listen to each other by saying their lines aloud and not silently reading each other's strips of paper.
6 When students think they have the order correct, play the audio for them to check.

Notes and variation

In this activity, students get extra listening practice by having to listen carefully to each other. In *Figure 1.4*, the information is divided up into sentences. Also note how this activity gets students to focus on useful language items in an indirect way. It's an alternative to the course book exercise 5. With higher level or stronger groups, you could also do this activity with a monologue, for example, a narrative.

Learner reflection questions

1 The first time you listened, did you have to understand all the details of the conversation or just the main things that happened?
2 How did this help you order the dialogue?
3 What do you think helped you most to order the dialogue – the information you understood from the listening or the expressions used by the speakers?

Teacher reflection

To what degree do you think students were using their gist understanding from the first listening to help them? To what degree do you think they were using their language knowledge to help them order the dialogue? What does this tell you about top-down and bottom-up processing of information?

Can I help you?

4 VIDEO 7 CD2 40 Look at the photos. Paul and Clare are at the shops. Watch or listen to their conversations. Answer these questions.

	Paul	Clare
1 Which shop is he/she in?		
2 What does he/she buy?		
3 How much does he/she spend?		

HELP WITH LISTENING What sales assistants say

5 **a** Read these things that sales assistants say. Check new words with your teacher.

CONVERSATION 1

a Here's your change and your receipt.
b Anything else?
c Can I help you?
d Yes, they're over there.
e Would you like a bag?

CONVERSATION 2

f Would you like anything else?
g Your pin number, please.
h That's £17.50, please.
i Do you need any help?
j They're on the second floor.

b VIDEO 7 CD2 40 Watch or listen again. Put sentences a–j in **5a** in the order you hear them (1–10).

VIDEO 7 CD2 40

1 SALES ASSISTANT 1 Hi. Can I help you?
PAUL Yes, please. Have you got any guide books for London?
SA1 Yes, they're over there.
P Oh yes, I see. Thanks. ... I'll have this one, please. How much is this map?
SA1 This one is ... £5.95.
P OK, I'll have the map too.
SA1 Sure. ...
P And can I have four stamps for Europe, please?
SA1 I'm sorry, we don't sell stamps for Europe.
P No problem.
SA1 Anything else?
P No, that's all, thanks.
SA1 Right, that's £19.45, please.
P Here you are.
SA1 Would you like a bag?
P No, thanks. I've got one.
SA1 OK. Here's your change and your receipt.
P Thank you.
SA1 Have a nice day.
P You too. Bye.
SA1 Bye.

Figure 1.4: Redston, C. and G. Cunningham (2012) *face2face Elementary* (2nd ed.), pp. 60 and 160.

1.5 Interactive narrative

Level	B1 and above
Time	15 to 20 minutes
Outline	You, the teacher, re-tell a narrative listening from the course book as if it were your own story, as a stop-start activity and students predict what will happen next.
Aims	To encourage interactive listening; to practise the skill of prediction before listening.
Preparation	Find a narrative listening and select key words that students can predict from. If you re-tell the story in your own words, make notes from the audio script to refer to when you speak (see the example below).
Rationale	The key reason for providing audio recordings is to practise listening and give students an opportunity to listen to different voices and accents in English. However, sometimes we need to balance this against the fact that a lot of real-life listening is interactive and the person listening can interrupt and ask questions. It's sometimes useful if the teacher provides a listening text that allows students to interact. If students ask about information that is not included in the listening text, you can invent answers.

Procedure

1 Put three or four words/phrases or picture clues that relate to the first part of the story on the board. For *Figure 1.5* below use: *ride a cow, sister, horse noises, cowboy.*
2 In pairs, students predict what will happen. Put their predictions on the board.
3 Use the notes to tell the first part of the story, then ask the class if their predictions were correct.
4 Students can ask you questions about the part of the story you've just told them.
5 Write up clues for the next part of the story: *jumped off the fence, surprised, dirty, guilty.*
6 Follow the same procedure: students predict in pairs, you write up key predictions, tell the next part of the story, check predictions, invite questions.
7 For *Figure 1.5*, two steps are enough. For a longer story, repeat the process as necessary.

Notes

You can just read the story aloud, but it will sound more natural if you use key word prompts and tell your own version of the story. Try to look for good 'cliff hanger' (what-will-happen-next?) moments in the story to maintain students' interest. Students could repeat this activity in pairs and listen to each other's stories. When they prepare stories, encourage them just to make notes in preparation to speak (set a time limit) and not write out the story – the aim should be speaking and listening and not writing and listening.

Learner reflection questions

1 What extra information did you find out when you and your classmates asked questions?
2 When we understand the first part of a story, why does it help us understand what happens next?

Teacher reflection

How accurate were the students' predictions? How much were you able to give them hints about the content in your answers to their questions? Although it wasn't your story, did the interactive nature of this listening feel natural?

1 LISTENING

a When you were a child, did you get on well with other children? How about with your brothers and sisters?

b Look at the pictures below. What do you think is happening in each picture?

c 3.54 Listen and match stories 1–3 to the pictures. Were you right about what was happening?

d 3.54 Listen again. Are the sentences true (*T*) or false (*F*)? Correct the false sentences.

Claire

1 ☐ Claire told her sister that the cows were horses.
2 ☐ Claire found it funny when her sister jumped on the cow.
3 ☐ Claire's sister went back home on her own.
4 ☐ Claire told her mum the truth about what had happened.

3.54

CLAIRE My little sister and I have always had our fights. I think the funniest time was when I made her ride a cow. We lived in a house with a field of cows on one side and I told my sister that they were horses. I went into the field and stood behind the cows making horse noises. When the cows were right next to our garden fence, I said she could ride one of the horses … just like a cowboy! I still can't believe she listened to me! She just jumped off the fence onto a cow's back! The cow was very surprised. It ran away with my sister holding onto its back. I couldn't stop laughing. In the end, my sister fell off. Her clothes were really dirty and she was crying. Then, I felt bad and helped her back home. When we got back, I told my mum my sister had tried to ride a cow and I had saved her. She believed me … I still feel guilty.

Figure 1.5: Doff, A., C. Thaine et al. (2015) *Cambridge English Empower B1*, pp. 120 and 175.

Example notes (all verbs in base form)

little sister – fights – funniest time – ride a cow – house – field of cows on side – tell sister horses
field – behind cow – horse noises – cow near fence – ride horse – cowboy
can't believe! – jump off fence – cow's back – surprised – run away – sister holding on – laugh
fall off – dirty clothes – crying – feel bad – help
tell mother – sister ride cow – save – mother believe – guilty!

1.6 Half the script

Level A2 and above
Time 10 to 15 minutes
Outline After hearing the recording once, students form pairs with each student given a different part of the audio script to support their partner's listening comprehension.
Aim To lower the level of challenge for intensive listening; to encourage communicative interaction as students negotiate the listening task.
Preparation Copy the audio script of the listening and cut into two halves (or you could just direct students to the audio script if it is in the course book).
Rationale Some longer listening texts can present a challenge for certain groups, and this activity is a way for making that challenge more manageable. Allowing some students to read the audio script as they listen makes it easier for them to understand, and places them in the situation of being the 'knower' who can help their partner. This activity works best with listening texts that either have two conversations or monologues or where there are two clear parts to the listening. This means both students have the chance to take the 'knower' role. It also means that the listener has the opportunity of checking their understanding. This negotiation can provide good communicative interaction.

Procedure

1. All students do the first, gist listening task – exercise 1 in *Figure 1.6* below.
2. Students work in A and B pairs. Give the first part of the audio script to Student A. Play the audio for this part of the script only, once again. Student A listens and reads, but Student B only listens.
3. After the audio finishes, ask Student A to turn over their audio script so they can no longer read it.
4. A and B pairs complete as much of the detailed listening task – exercise 2 in *Figure 1.6* – as they can. Make sure A students don't turn over the audio script.
5. If necessary, play the first part again and allow Student A to read the audio script at the same time while Student B again just listens.
6. When most students seem confident of their answers to the first part of the listening, move on to the second part. Roles are reversed so Student B has the audio script and Student A just listens. Repeat the same steps above.
7. When most students have completed the intensive listening, check the answers.

Notes and variation

When a student has the audio script, the listening is easy, but it becomes more challenging when they don't. Also, getting the student to turn over the audio script after each listening maintains a level of challenge – the student can't just refer back to the script, and they have to recall information as they would in a conversation. The interaction for this activity can be varied according to the structure of the audio. For example, students can work in groups of three when the listening is in three parts. Getting students to read and listen at the same time can be a useful way of helping them to notice the relationship between spelling and pronunciation in English. If you have more than one audio device and a large classroom (or access to an empty classroom), students can do a split listening whereby one group of students listens to one text and the other group to a different text. They then tell each other what they heard. This is more challenging than listening with the audio script.

Learner reflection questions

1 How much did your partner understand when they didn't have the audio script?
2 When you turned over the audio script after each listening, how easy was it to remember information? Was this similar to having a conversation?

Teacher reflection

What kind of listening practice did students get when they were discussing the task in pairs? What kind of speaking practice did the student who was the 'knower' get?

Across cultures Transport culture

1 a Which cities do you think the pictures show?

b 2.52 Listen to Marike and Hasan talking about their cities and check your ideas.

2 a What do Marike and Hasan say about these things?

1 the government
2 traffic lights
3 the price of petrol
4 taxis
5 roads
6 bike lanes

b 2.52 Listen again to check.

2.52

MARIKE One of the best things about Amsterdam is we don't have a big car culture. In fact, the government here thinks about public transport and bicycles first, and cars second. I think that's different from many other countries. People say Amsterdam's a centre of bicycle culture and, erm, that's true. I mean, we have about 400 kilometres of bike lanes. And also, we have bike traffic lights. They look the same as traffic lights but they, erm, they have the shape of a bicycle. Do other countries have those? I don't know. Anyway, some streets don't have bike lanes but you can cycle on them and cars will go around you or follow you. As I said, we're really bicycle-friendly.

HASAN In Dubai, everyone I know uses a car. They're cheap because they're tax free and petrol's not too expensive ... well, actually, prices are going up. We also use taxis a lot but it's harder to find a taxi than before. There aren't enough these days. There are some buses, too, but it's easier and people really love their cars. They're air-conditioned, quiet and private ... Of course the roads in Dubai are very crowded, but we have a new metro now so maybe that will change things. But if you want to go to the desert or mountains or to, say, Abu Dhabi, the car's the best way. We have great roads.

Figure 1.6: Tilbury, A., T. Clementson et al. (2010) *English Unlimited A2*, pp. 79 and 155.

C After listening

1.7 Half dictation

Level	A1 and above
Time	15 to 20 minutes
Outline	Before students read and listen to a dialogue, you dictate one speaker's half of the dialogue and ask students to guess and write in the responses. They then listen and read to check their answers.
Aims	To provide students practice in bottom-up, very intensive listening; to give students practice in predicting language content.
Preparation	Decide how many exchanges in the dialogue you will use and decide if you will read a complete utterance when you dictate or only part. If the latter, decide how you will break up the utterances.
Rationale	Most course books provide suitable gist and detailed listening tasks for listening comprehension. However, they do not always provide activities that focus on very intensive bottom-up listening. Once students have completed gist and detailed listening tasks, dictation is one way to practise very intensive listening. This means students have to accurately decode the language they hear. The dictation is made more meaningful as students write down only one speaker's part in a dialogue, and then have to predict and write in the replies of the other speaker. Having done this activity, students are more motivated to listen and read because they want to check what they've written against the original.

Procedure

1. Students do a gist listening comprehension task to understand the dialogue as a whole – exercise 1.B in *Figure 1.7* below. Don't let students listen and read, they should cover the audio script.
2. For *Figure 1.7* dictate what Antonio says with students leaving a gap after each line so they can write in a reply by Jonathan. Use the first eight exchanges (down to where Jonathan says 'Good idea').
3. Get students to check what they have written in pairs or small groups. Don't check their dictation or show them the correct answers at this stage.
4. Students then work in pairs and complete Jonathan's part of the conversation. They can then check their finished version with another pair.
5. Once most students have finished, play the audio of the conversation to check against their own version.
6. Finally, students open their course books, and listen once more and read the audio script, checking their dictated lines and responses.

Notes

This activity is best suited to parts of a dialogue of between four to eight lines – more than that could make the activity long-winded. Having done the dictation and predicted some of the language, students are more motivated to listen and read because they want to check what they've written against the original. They are also more likely to notice any target language more actively.

Learner reflection questions

1. What was the difference between listening to the complete dialogue for the first time and the last time?
2. What did you have to listen for during the dictation?

Teacher reflection

Which lines from the dictation were most difficult for students during the dictation? Why was that the case? How motivated were they to listen and read at the end of the activity?

1 FUNCTIONAL LANGUAGE

A **Jonathan is in Mexico City for a meeting with his coworker, Antonio. They're making plans to go out in the evening. What do you think they are saying?**

B 2.34 **Read and listen. Where are Antonio and Jonathan going to have dinner? Where are they going to meet? What time are they going to meet?**

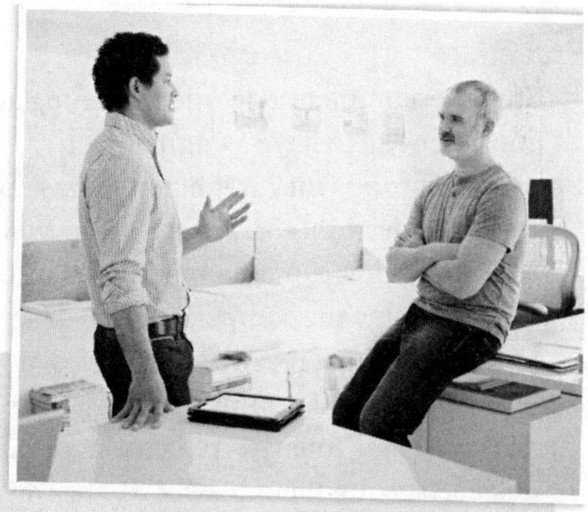

2.34 Audio script

Antonio So, Jonathan, **why don't we go out tonight?**
Jonathan **OK, sounds good.**
Antonio Do you like Mexican food?
Jonathan I love it! Are there any good Mexican restaurants in town?
Antonio Um, in Mexico City? Yeah, I know one or two places!
Jonathan I'm sure you do!
Antonio There's a very good restaurant near your hotel. Why don't we go there?
Jonathan **Good idea.**
Antonio So **let's meet at the hotel.**
Jonathan OK. What time? Eight o'clock?
Antonio Um ... **I'm sorry, but I can't.** How about eight-thirty?
Jonathan **Yes, sure.**

Figure 1.7: Hendra, L. A., M. Ibbotson and K. O'Dell (2019) *Evolve 1*, p. 102.

1.8 What can you remember?

Level	A2 and above
Time	5 minutes
Outline	In small groups, students have a competition to recall as much as they can from a listening and evaluate it.
Aim	To highlight the value of content in listening material; to practise critical evaluation of a text; to provide spoken fluency practice.
Preparation	If the course book doesn't include an evaluation question for the listening text, you will need to think of one.
Rationale	Many course books include a post-listening speaking activity where students respond to the information in a listening text. For example, they might talk about what ideas they agreed with, what they liked or disliked about the topic of the listening. Sometimes these activities don't generate as much spoken language as they could. By asking students to recall information as well as evaluate it, they are likely to speak more, and it's likely to be a better check of understanding. Turning this into a competition helps with motivation.

Procedure

1 Students complete a detailed listening activity – exercise 2 in *Figure 1.8a* below – and close their course books to have a competition.
2 In small groups they: 1) remember as much information as they can from the listening; 2) answer a suitable question, e.g. *What do you think was the biggest change for Onyinye? Why?*
3 The group that can remember most information and give the most interesting answer to the question wins the competition.
4 Students discuss, recall and note down what they remember.
5 Do feedback and get the group with the largest number of points to read them out. Other groups can challenge, for example, two notes are the same point.
6 Ask each group their answer to the evaluation question. If a group with fewer notes gives a really interesting answer, they can win.
7 Optional follow on: students listen and read the audio script to see if there is any information they didn't recall.

Notes

This activity suits listening texts which prompt a response, such as an opinion or evaluation. It probably wouldn't work for a text which is simply designed to display a grammatical structure. The evaluation can be viewed as practice of 'soft' critical thinking skills. The suggested optional follow on activity can help learners make connections between the way language sounds and the way it is written. It may also help with incidental acquisition of language.

Learner reflection questions

1 In your group, did you all remember exactly the same things? Why / Why not?
2 Was it easier to answer the teacher's question about the listening after you remembered most of the information? Why / Why not?

Teacher reflection

How much do you feel making the recall a competition helped motivate students? As you monitored, did you hear students refer to any new language they heard from the listening or perhaps picked up from each other in the discussion?

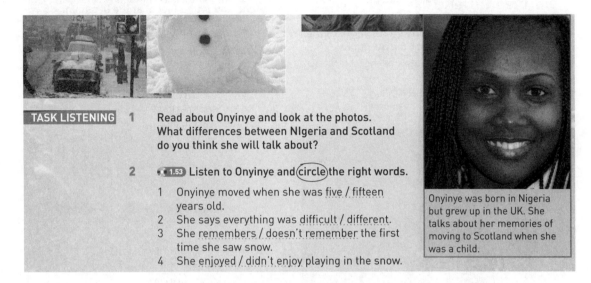

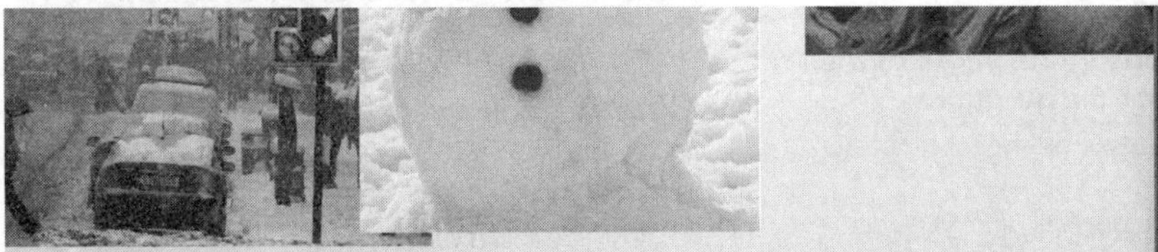

Onyinye was born in Nigeria but grew up in the UK. She talks about her memories of moving to Scotland when she was a child.

TASK LISTENING

1 Read about Onyinye and look at the photos. What differences between NIgeria and Scotland do you think she will talk about?

2 1.53 Listen to Onyinye and circle the right words.

1. Onyinye moved when she was five / fifteen years old.
2. She says everything was difficult / different.
3. She remembers / doesn't remember the first time she saw snow.
4. She enjoyed / didn't enjoy playing in the snow.

1.53

ONYINYE I remember when my family moved from Nigeria to Scotland. That was an important event. I was, erm, five years old so I was very young and it's a very different country because Nigeria is very hot and sunny – in Africa – and, uh, Scotland is very cold and, uh ...

CHIE Wet?

O ... wet, yes. And in, in Europe. And the country itself is very different. My memories of Nigeria – I was only five so I don't have too many – but a lot of red sand, and the trees were different, erm, the houses were different. Everything was different. But, erm, when I moved to Scotland, at first it was like a big holiday because we were moving and it was very exciting, until the first winter, and I saw snow for the first time which was a shock. And, uh, it was a big thing. We all went outside and we built a snowman and we had lots of fun, but it made us all realise that it wasn't a holiday any more.

Figure 1.8a: Tilbury, A., T. Clementson et al. (2010) *English Unlimited A2*, pp. 38 and 151.

For the listening exercise in *Figure 1.8b* the evaluation question could be: *Why do you think some people are afraid of some machines but not others?*

Listening Conversations between friends

1 Work with a partner. Look at the photo of the roller coaster and answer the questions.

1 How do you think the people on the roller coaster are feeling?
2 The ride is called *The Scream Machine.* Why do you think so?
3 Do you like roller coasters? Why/Why not?

2 2.16 Listen to two conversations betwe[en] a group of friends in a theme park. How do Anita and Bruno feel a) at the beginning of [the] day and b) at the end of the day?

3 2.16 Listen again. Choose the correct answers.

Conversation 1

1 Which ride is Anita scared of?
  a The Scream Machine b The Colossus
  c The Tidal Wave
2 How does Bruno feel about The Tidal Wave?
  a He's terrified. b He's worried.
  c He's relaxed.
3 Why does Claudia suggest starting with The Scream Machine?
  a The queue is short. b It's very scary.
  c It's lots of fun.

Conversation 2

4 What was Claudia's favourite ride?
  a The Colossus b The Tidal Wave
  c The Scream Machine
5 What is the problem at the end of the day?
  a They miss the bus home.
  b They've spent a lot of money.
  c They can't get anything to eat.

Audioscript

Conversation 1

Anita: OK, so where are we going first?
Bruno: I want to go on The Scream Machine.
Claudia: Me too.
Anita: Yeah, but there are too many people! Look at the queue, Bruno …
Bruno: It's not that bad. Anita, are you scared?
Anita: Scared? Well, yeah! I'm terrified of roller coasters – and it's called *the Scream Machine*! Why don't we go on The Tidal Wave? Look, there are only a few people in the queue …
Bruno: I'm a bit worried about the water on that one.
Anita: Don't be silly Bruno! You don't have to swim!
Bruno: Yeah, but you know, I don't really like water …
Claudia: Listen, there's enough time to do everything. Don't worry about the queues. Let's start with The Scream Machine – really, Anita it looks worse than it is – it's great when you're on it … honest.
Anita: Mmm … I'm still not sure … How many loops has it got?
Bruno: Not many. Just ten. You'll love it!
Anita: Ten? I don't know …!
Claudia: Come on! You can scream as much as you want!
Anita: OK. But then we're going on the Tidal Wave! Bruno?
Bruno: OK! That's fair. Come on, before the queue gets bigger…

Conversation 2

Anita: That was brilliant … what a fantastic day! The Scream Machine was great! I loved it!
Claudia: I told you! And what about the Tidal Wave Bruno? Scary?
Bruno: Nah, not at all! I loved the water. It was so nice and fresh!
Claudia: But The Colossus was the best … it was so exciting!
Bruno: Yeah, that was my favourite too. It was amazing! I've been on a lot of rides and that was the best ride ever.
Anita: Everything was great fun, except we spent too much money, right?
Claudia: And I'm exhausted now!
Bruno: And I'm hungry. How much money have we got? Can we get something to eat?
Anita: Yeah, I think so, we've got a little time before the bus comes … There are some food stalls over there, let's get something.
Claudia: OK, I want a burger!

Figure 1.8b: Goldstein, B. and C. Jones (2015) *Eyes Open 3*, pp. 66 and 96.

1.9 A kind of bingo

Level A2 and above
Time 5 minutes
Outline Students listen to a text containing numbers and tick off what they hear on a worksheet that is similar to a bingo card.
Aim To provide practice of listening accurately for information details.
Preparation If you use *Figure 1.9a*, you will need to copy the bingo worksheet below. If you are using another listening text, you will need to create your own bingo worksheet. Include numbers that are in the dialogue as well as other numbers.
Rationale Some listening texts include a variety of numbers. These might be prices, times, years or statistical information. Giving students a detailed listening task that focuses on these numbers in the form of a game can be a fun follow on from more typical intensive listening tasks such as *True/False* or comprehension questions. It also means that students get practice in listening for specific pieces of information accurately. This is often important with numbers, for example, when someone gives their telephone number.

Procedure

1 Students listen to the text to understand it to a good level of detail. In *Figure 1.9a*, students complete exercises 1 to 3.
2 Hand out the bingo worksheets (see below). Tell students they will listen to the complete dialogue again – in the example material this means all three parts.
3 Tell students to tick or cross the numbers on the worksheet that they hear in the dialogue.
4 Play the audio and let students check their answers in pairs. Offer to play the audio again if you think students would like or need this.
5 Do whole class feedback – perhaps stop and start the audio and isolate the numbers.

Notes and variation

You can make this activity more or less difficult depending on the difference in sound between correct and incorrect numbers. For example, if one of the correct numbers is 30, putting the number 13 on the bingo worksheet as an incorrect alternative is more challenging than putting the number 50. A variation to this activity would be to include words on the bingo worksheet. For example, at a lower level the bingo card could include different kinds of clothes or food; at a higher level you could focus on multi-word verbs and students have to listen for the correct particle – *come in* vs. *come on*.

Learner reflection questions

1 What was harder to do: understand the number or find the correct number on the card?
2 In a real situation (for example, in a shop), if you don't understand a number, what can you do?

Teacher reflection

Which of the numbers did students find most difficult – the times, sizes or prices? What kinds of numbers do they need more practice listening to? What kind of listening practice of numbers could you give students yourself?

1 LISTENING

a Ask and answer the questions.

1 How often do you buy clothes?
2 Which sentence a–c describes you best?
  a I love buying clothes. I buy something new every week.
  b I only buy clothes if I really need them.
  c I don't often buy clothes, but I like looking round clothes shops.

b 3.31 Watch or listen to Part 1. Who wants to buy clothes: Dan, Annie or both?

c 3.31 Change three incorrect things in the text below. Watch or listen to Part 1 again to check your answers.

Dan's meeting Martina to go to a concert. He wants to wear new clothes as a surprise. Annie says she'll meet Dan at 5 pm. She isn't very happy about it.

d 3.32 Watch or listen to Part 2 and answer the questions.

1 What clothes does Dan want to buy?
2 What size does Dan wear?
3 Do you think Dan enjoys shopping?

e Do you ever ask friends or family to help you buy clothes? Who do you ask and why?

2 USEFUL LANGUAGE Choosing clothes

a Match 1–4 with a–d.

1 What are you looking for?
2 What size are you?
3 What colour would you like?
4 Why don't you try them on?

a In trousers? 32.
b Oh, I don't know. Something dark?
c A shirt and trousers.
d OK. Excuse me, where are the fitting rooms?

b 3.32 Watch or listen to Part 2 again and check your answers in 2a.

c In pairs, practise saying the questions and answers in 2a.

d Take turns helping your partner choose clothes.

A You want a jacket. B You want a pair of jeans.

3 LISTENING

a 3.33 Watch or listen to Part 3 and answer the questions.

1 Does Annie like the clothes Dan tries on?
2 What does Annie think about the last set of clothes Dan comes out in?

b 3.33 Watch or listen to Part 3 again and complete Dan's receipt.

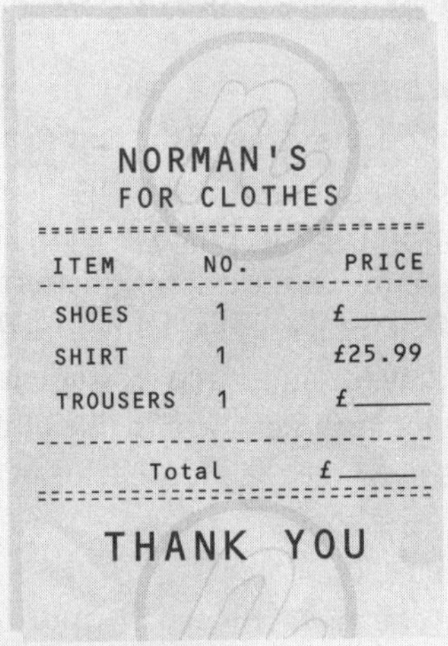
NORMAN'S
FOR CLOTHES

ITEM	NO.	PRICE
SHOES	1	£____
SHIRT	1	£25.99
TROUSERS	1	£____
Total		£____

THANK YOU

3.31 PART 1

ANNIE Dan! Hi!
DAN Hi, Annie, how are things?
A Fine.
D Um, look. Are you free at lunchtime?
A Yes.
D Great. Could we meet? I need help to buy some clothes for this evening.
A Yeah, sure. But what about Martina? Can't she help?
D Well I'm meeting her this evening for dinner. She always says I wear the same old clothes, so I want to get something new. I want to surprise her.
A OK, sure. I'm free at 12:30.

3.32 PART 2

ANNIE So what are you looking for?
DAN I don't know really. A shirt and trousers. Just something casual.
A OK. What size are you?
D In trousers. 32. ... OK, 34.
A Or 36? And probably a large for the shirt?
D Yeah, I think so.
A What colour would you like?
D Oh, I don't know. Something dark?
A What about this? ... Why don't you try them on?
D OK, excuse me, where are the fitting rooms?
SHOP ASSISTANT The fitting rooms are just over there, sir.
D Thanks.
SA Thank you.

3.33 PART 3

DAN What do you think?
ANNIE No …
D This one?
A Ugh …
D And this?
A No. Try the next one.
D How about this one?
A No, Dan … That's it! That looks great.
D These are mine! This is what I came in!
A Well, it looks really good on you …
SHOP ASSISTANT Can I help you, sir?
D Hi. There's no price on these shoes. How much are they?
SA They're £49.99.
D Great. I'll take them.
A And these trousers and this shirt, please.
SA All together that's £115.97 please.
D Can I pay by card?
SA Yes, of course. Just enter your PIN, please. ... Shall I put the receipt in the bag?
D Yes – thanks.
SA There you go, sir.
D Thank you.
SA Thank you. Take care now.
A Bye.

Figure 1.9a: Doff, A., C. Thaine et al. (2015) *Cambridge English Empower A2*, pp. 94 and 173.

Bingo worksheet

1 12.30	2 59.99	3 2.30	4 115.97
5 39.99	6 150.97	7 35	8 113.97
9 34	10 10.30	11 36	12 49.99

Answer key: squares: 1, 4, 9, 11, 12

Off the Page

For the listening exercise in *Figure 1.9b*, you could create bingo cards with vocabulary of rooms and furniture.

LISTENING

1 **SPEAKING** **Work in pairs. Describe the pictures.**

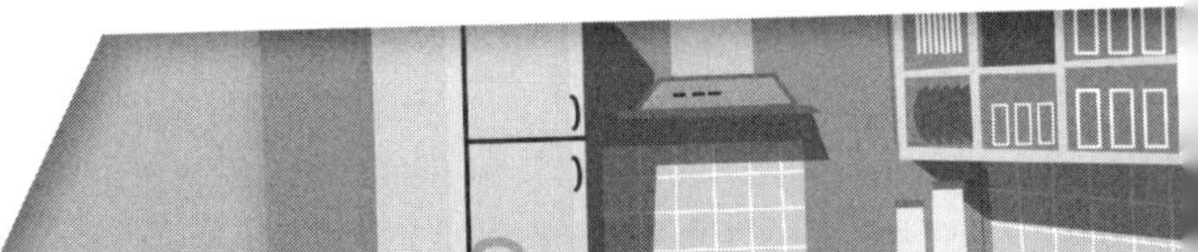

2 1.51 **Listen to four people talking about 'home'. Write the names under the correct pictures.**

Sophie | James | Mia | Daniel

3 1.51 **Listen again. Complete the table with the missing information.**

	What is home?	**What I like doing there.**
Sophie	Home is where I feel [1] ____________ .	2 ____________
James	Somewhere [3] ____________ .	4 ____________
Mia	The [5] ____________ in our flat.	6 ____________
Daniel	With [7] ____________ in the garden.	8 ____________

Audio Script Track 1.55

1 Sophie

Interviewer	Where's home for you, Sophie?
Sophie	For me, home is the place where I can be happy. I'm thinking of my bedroom. I feel really happy there.
Interviewer	What do you like best there?
Sophie	My desk. It's got the docking station for my MP3-player, of course, with two very good speakers, so I can listen to my favourite music. That's cool.

2 James

Interviewer	Where's home for you?
James	That's a difficult question. I feel at home where it isn't noisy. Hmm. I think for me home is the living room at my grandparents' house.
Interviewer	What things do you like best there?
James	The big soft armchair. It's very comfortable. I love sitting in it and watching TV.

3 Mia

Interviewer	Where's home for you?
Mia	The kitchen in the flat where I live with my mum and my sister.
Interviewer	What do you like best there, Mia?
Mia	It's quite small but it's always busy and full of people talking and having fun. My mum's always cooking something and I love helping her. She asks me all about school and my friends. I love telling her about my life and then at the end there's a delicious cake to eat!

4 Daniel

Interviewer	Where's home for you?
Daniel	My garden.
Interviewer	Your garden?
Daniel	Yes, we've got a really big garden.
Interviewer	And what do you like best there?
Daniel	I like playing football there with my friends. It's great. I can forget about everything and just enjoy myself. I think when I'm with my friends I always feel like I'm at home.

Figure 1.9b: Puchta, H., J. Stranks and P. Lewis-Jones (2015) *Think Level 1*, pp. 51 and 57.

You can find teacher development activities about listening on pages 253 to 256.

2 Speaking

Introduction

Why do we get students to speak in the classroom?

Most students who attend English language classes have an ultimate aim of wanting to be able to *speak* English well or well enough in situations or contexts that are relevant to their needs. If students voice a learning objective, they often say they want to speak more or speak more confidently. One of the broader aims of this book is to provide students with more speaking opportunities. Getting a lesson 'off the page' means bringing language to life in oral communication.

In a general sense, we can say there are two main reasons for getting students to speak:

- to give students practice of language items;
- to develop students' ability to speak fluently and interactively.

Once language items (vocabulary, grammar, functional/situational language) have been presented, it is usual to provide varying degrees of spoken practice from controlled to semi-controlled to freer practice. When teachers do this, their emphasis is usually to help students use new language when they speak. It fits with what is known as the PPP (Presentation → Practice → Production) paradigm and it suggests that teachers have a specific linguistic agenda in mind. They want students to speak, but they also want them to use specific language items when they do so (see also the introduction to Chapter 5 for further mention of PPP).

Conversely, the broad aim of developing students' ability to speak well is connected to the idea of getting students to speak for the sake of speaking. Teachers might be less concerned about them using specific language items (and using them correctly) and be happy for them just to experience the sensation of using English to communicate orally with each other. The teacher might want students to become more fluent speakers of English, and she may want them to improve their ability to interact with and respond to other speakers.

While it is possible to delineate these two broad aims on paper, the reality of classroom practice is not quite as black and white. Experienced teachers are more often than not aiming to do two or three things at once. For example, they may set up a speaking activity with a primary aim of developing students' spoken fluency, but, at the same time, they know that there are certain grammatical and lexical items that should ideally be used during the activity in order to communicate effectively. As a result, the teacher may be listening in to see whether their students are using those language items. On the other hand, a teacher may set up an activity in which the students get freer practice of a grammar item (the 'production' stage in a PPP style lesson), but they may not be overly concerned if the students are not using the target grammar so long as they feel they are getting a useful opportunity to speak freely.

An information gap

Regardless of the broader aim of a speaking activity, a key consideration for any speaking task is the idea of an 'information gap'. This is related to a real-world idea of communication and means that one speaker knows something that another speaker does not, and they, therefore, have a reason to say something to each other and, just as importantly, listen to each other. A typical classroom information gap activity is where Student A has a picture of something or somewhere and Student B has the same picture but with a few small differences. The students speak to each other without showing their pictures in order to work out what the differences are. The idea of an information gap also exists in personalisation activities. If two students who do not know each other talk about their families, there is information they can find out from each other to bridge the gap that existed before they started speaking. Similarly, in a group discussion, students do not know their classmates' opinion on the topic of discussion and finding out those opinions and the ideas that support them is a way of bridging an information gap.

Identifying speaking activities in course books

In the Grammar, Vocabulary, Pronunciation and Discourse chapters there are ideas for providing students with spoken practice of language items. In this chapter, we focus on speaking as a skill – as a way of getting students to speak well. In particular, we look at enhancing fluency and getting students to experience the interactive nature of speaking.

Course books have a varied number of ways of signalling speaking activities. Here are some examples:

Cambridge English Empower Speaking is signalled by a heading together with the speech bubble icon as seen next to exercise b.

6 SPEAKING

a Think of some popular films, TV programmes and books. Write six questions about these things. Look at the questions in 5e to help you.

b Ask other students your questions from 6a.

Doff, A., C. Thaine et al. (2015) *Cambridge English Empower A2*, p. 111.

face2face Speaking is usually signalled as a fluency activity when coupled with another language skill, for example:

Speaking and Reading

Redston, C. and G. Cunningham (2012) *face2face Intermediate* (2nd ed.), p. 58.

However, when the aim is freer spoken practice of specific language items, it uses this heading:

Get ready ... Get it right!

Redston, C. and G. Cunningham (2012) *face2face Elementary* (2nd ed.), p. 9.

Interchange This course book uses a variety of headings to indicate speaking – usually when it practises language items.

2 CONVERSATION I'll take it!

5 ROLE PLAY Can I help you?

6 SPEAKING Entertainment survey

6 DISCUSSION What are you doing these days?

Richards, J. C. et al. (2017) *Interchange 1* (5th ed.), pp. 16, 18, 24 and 32.

However, speaking is also signalled with sub-headings that indicate an appropriate interaction pattern for the activity:

C GROUP WORK What do families look like in your country? Do dads stay at home with their children? Do you think that's a good thing or a bad thing? Is it important to you to spend time with your family?

B PAIR WORK Take turns asking the questions in part A. Give your own information when answering.

A: Did you stay home on Sunday?

B: No, I didn't. I went dancing with some friends.

Richards, J. C. et al. (2017) *Interchange 1* (5th ed.), pp. 35 and 45.

Eyes Open This course book has the following phrase in a speech bubble to signal a speaking activity:

Your turn

Goldstein, B. and C. Jones (2015) *Eyes Open* 2, p. 5.

Think Speaking is indicated either by a main heading:

DEVELOPING SPEAKING

Puchta, H., J. Stranks and P. Lewis-Jones (2015) *Think 1*, p. 19.

or by this sub-heading:

SPEAKING

Puchta, H., J. Stranks and P. Lewis-Jones (2015) *Think 1*, p. 20.

and occasionally uses this sub-heading if the speaking activity is a role play:

ROLE PLAY

Puchta, H., J. Stranks and P. Lewis-Jones (2015) *Think 1*, p. 23.

Unlock These course books have a main heading for a series of activities:

SPEAKING

Ostrowska, S., N. Jordan et al. (2019) *Unlock Listening, Speaking & Critical Thinking 3*, p. 29.

and then use different sub-headings for different stages in a speaking activity, for example:

PREPARATION FOR SPEAKING

SPEAKING TASK

Ostrowska, S., N. Jordan et al. (2019) *Unlock Listening, Speaking & Critical Thinking 3*, pp. 32 and 34.

However, speaking is also signalled with the following heading:

DISCUSSION

Ostrowska, S., N. Jordan et al. (2019) *Unlock Listening, Speaking & Critical Thinking 3*, p. 39.

The different ways of signalling speaking in headings illustrates the importance for teachers to identify which activities focus on speaking in the teaching and learning resources they are using, and what terminology is used. However, headings are usually only a signpost, and you also need to look at the nature of the activity in order to determine its aim. Does it practise target language items? Does it aim to get students speaking fluently on a topic? Does it encourage students to interact together? Or does it have more than one learning aim? Then, beyond that, you, the teacher, need to consider what your aims are for your students' learning in light of their needs.

In *Figure 2.0a* is an example of an activity that can be used with differing aims. The speaking activity is the one labelled *B Group Work*. If a teacher completes exercise A first and then moves on to B, the aim of the teacher (and the material) is to practise the vocabulary that focuses on IT. However, a teacher could choose to skip exercise A and just get students to discuss the questions in groups with no prior vocabulary input. In this case, the teacher's aim is more likely to be speaking fluency practice, in other words, encouraging students to express themselves on the topic of IT and communicate with

5 WORD POWER Plugged in

A Complete the chart with words and phrases from the list. Add one more to each category. Then compare with a partner.

✓ computer whiz	hacker	check in for a flight	geek
computer crash	edit photos	download apps	software bugs
flash drive	identity theft	make international phone calls	frozen screen
smart devices	early adopter	solar-powered batteries	phone charger

Problems with technology	Gadgets and devices	People who are "into" technology	Things to do online
		computer whiz	

B **GROUP WORK** Discuss some of the positive and negative consequences of living in a connected world.

- Have you ever had any of the problems mentioned in part A? What happened? What did you do?
- Do you have any smart devices? Which ones? How do they help you? How much do you depend on them?
- Do you have any friends who never put their phone away? Is anyone in your family addicted to new technologies? Are you?
- What is one gadget you would really like to have? Why?
- Is identity theft a problem where you live? What about hackers? How do you protect against them?

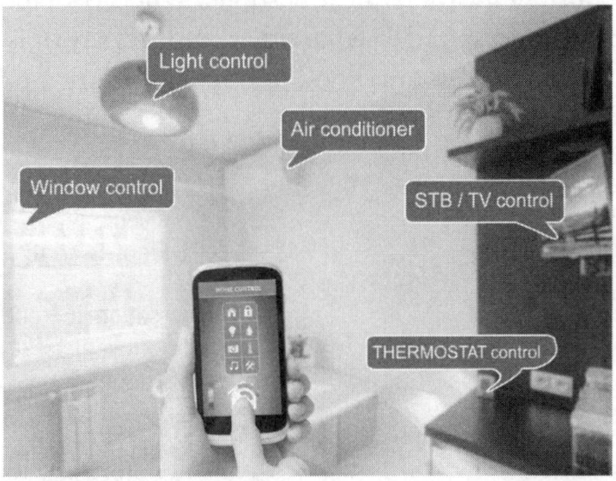

Figure 2.0a: Richards, J. C. et al. (2017) *Interchange 2* (5th ed.), p. 46.

each other by means of spoken language. At the same time, the teacher could listen in to the students' discussion and check whether they are able to use a good range of vocabulary associated with IT. In that case, from the teacher's perspective, the speaking task has a diagnostic aim. If she feels the students' range is limited, she could then go back and do exercise A.

In *Figure 2.0b* (page 46) the speaking activity acts as a lead in to a text about the history of the fast food company *Kentucky Fried Chicken*.

Speaking and Reading

1 Work in groups. Discuss these questions.

1. What fast food companies are there in your country? What food do they sell?
2. What are the good and bad things about fast food?
3. How often do you go to a fast food restaurant? What do you usually have to eat and drink?
4. When you're in a different town or city, how do you decide where to eat?

Figure 2.0b: Redston, C. and G. Cunningham (2012) *face2face Pre-intermediate* (2nd ed.), p. 14.

The speaking aim here is fluency practice, and there are no specific target language items that students should be using. However, there is an associated reading aim – the activity is establishing students' background knowledge on the topic of fast food before they read the text. A teacher could also use this activity diagnostically in terms of evaluating students' interaction skills. While students discuss the questions in groups, she could monitor students' participation in the discussion. She could consider the following questions: Who says a lot? Who says a little? Do they offer each other turns? Do they respond to what other students say or is the discussion like a series of monologues?

This third course book example in *Figure 2.0c* takes a more proactive focus on spoken interaction:

6 SPEAKING

a **Communication 10C** Student A go to 6b below. Student B go to p.133. Do Conversation 1.

Conversation 1. Read your first card. Think about what you want to say. Then start the conversation with Student B.

1 You bought a new phone, but you can't receive text messages on it. Ask Student B for help. Check the instructions he/she gives you.

b **Conversation 2.** Now look at your second card. Think about what you want to say. Then listen to Student B and reply.

2 Student B bought a new mouse for his/her computer, but it isn't working. When he/she asks for help, explain how the mouse works. Here are the instructions:

- Turn on the mouse and wait for the green light.
- Double click on the mouse.
- Wait ten seconds and click again. The mouse is working now.

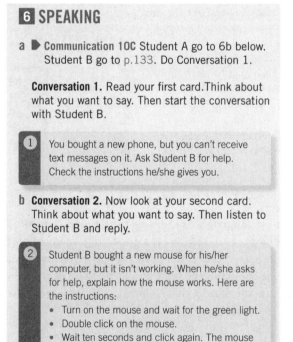

10C Student B

a **Conversation 1.** Read your first card. Think about what you want to say. Then listen to Student A and reply.

> 1 Student A bought a new phone, but he/she can't receive any text messages on it. When he/she asks for help, explain how it works. Here are the instructions:
> - Touch the box that says *Messages*.
> - Wait for a blue screen.
> - Touch the box that says *Receive.* It can receive messages now.

b **Conversation 2.** Now look at your second card. Think about what you want to say. Then start the conversation with Student A.

> 2 You bought a new mouse for your computer, but it isn't working. Ask Student A for help. Check the instructions he/she gives you.

Figure 2.0c: Doff, A., C. Thaine et al. (2015) *Cambridge English Empower A2*, pp. 105 and 133.

This role play could be set up as a speaking fluency activity. However, previously in the lesson, there was a task that focused on interaction strategies for checking instructions (*Figure 2.0d*):

5 CONVERSATION SKILLS
Checking instructions

a Look at the sentences from the conversation. Who says them: Annie (*A*) or Leo (*L*)?

1 **So first** I touch this button?
2 And it takes me to a new screen. **Like this**?
3 And I touch 'Yes'. **Is that right**?

Figure 2.0d: Doff, A., C. Thaine et al. (2015) *Cambridge English Empower A2*, p. 105.

As a result, one of the aims of this speaking activity is to practise the expressions in bold. A teacher can choose the degree to which this is the main aim of the activity and, as a result, how much attention she pays to students' use of this language during the role play.

Managing speaking in the classroom

The success of speaking activities in the classroom is often the result of the way they are managed by the teacher. In *Figures 2.0a* and *2.0b* above, there are questions for students to discuss, and in *Figure 2.0c*, there are instructions that students need to read. In order for these activities to work well, students will need time to prepare for the speaking activity. Even very fluent speakers of English need to think about *what* they are going to say before they begin speaking. Learners need to do this and think about *how* they are going to say it and what language they can use.

Kerr (2017) emphasises the importance of giving students sufficient preparation time for speaking activities. He also suggests getting students to do speaking tasks more than once (see activities 2.3 and 2.9 below). The first time that students do a speaking task, they often feel a sense of challenge, and the result may not be entirely successful and satisfactory from their point of view. If they have the opportunity to repeat the task and work with a different student, they usually feel they have been more successful. This sense of accomplishment can help with their confidence and motivation. Finally, Kerr indicates the value of getting students to reflect on their speaking so they not only practise the skill but develop awareness of it. The *Learner reflection questions* after each activity in this book aim to do just that, as do the activities in *Section C After speaking* in this chapter.

Evaluating speaking in the classroom

Many teachers are asked to evaluate their students' speaking. This can be part of a formal assessment process, or it can be informal and associated with determining students' needs. Institutions often provide teachers with assessment criteria to use, but, in some contexts, teachers may need to come up with their own criteria. If you need to do this, it is useful to look at the Council of Europe's descriptors of spoken language that are included in the Common European Framework of Reference for Languages. They are freely available here: https://rm.coe.int/cefr-companion-volume-with-new-descriptors-2018/1680787989. The descriptors refer to a range of speaking contexts and spoken genre. In an appendix on pages 171 and 172 of the document, there is also a useful overview of the features of spoken language at different levels. Also, in Chapter 9 *Teacher development* of this book, on pages 259 to 260, there is a suggestion for a professional development activity associated with evaluating students' speaking.

Reference

Kerr, P. (2017) *How much time should we give to speaking practice?* Part of the Cambridge Papers in ELT series [pdf], Cambridge: Cambridge University Press.

A Before speaking

2.1 Information trade

Level	A2 and above
Time	10 minutes
Outline	Students do homework research on the topic of a forthcoming lesson and in the next class mingle and exchange information.
Aim	To broaden students' background knowledge on a topic so they have more to talk about.
Preparation	Set a homework task that asks students to research a topic. In *Figure 2.1a* below, students could find out the most important charities in their country and the ways they raise money. It's a good idea to make provision for any students who are unable or opt not to do the homework and prepare visuals and information for them. For *Figure 2.1a* this might include pictures of unusual charities as well as interesting statistics on charity donations in your country.
Rationale	Students often do speaking activities that lead into a topic of the lesson in order to encourage the exchange of information and build background knowledge. However, sometimes topics require more input than students' collective knowledge. Asking students to prepare for the lesson with a homework task is one way around this. While providing for those students that don't do their research homework is an additional task, it does ensure that everyone has information to share for the activity to be effective.

Procedure

1. The day before the lesson, set the homework task of researching the topic of the next lesson.
2. On the day of the lesson, put students who have done the homework into small groups or pairs to share information.
3. Students who didn't do the homework work in one group. Give them each a picture or a statistic that you prepared to look at. They can ask you questions if necessary.
4. Students do a mingle activity. Each student tells another student one piece of information they found out from the homework research and then move on to a new student. (Those who didn't do the homework can share the piece of information they have been given.)
5. Once most students have exchanged information, put students in small groups making sure there is a mix of those who did the homework and those who didn't.
6. Students complete the lead in tasks – exercises 1a and b in *Figure 2.1a* below – and share their information on charities in their home country.

Notes

One of the benefits of this approach is that students get extra speaking fluency practice as they exchange information in the mingle activity. Across a programme, it is probably best used intermittently and perhaps with topics where you know students are likely to have less background knowledge.

Learner reflection questions

1. How much new information did you find out from other students? What information had you found yourself?
2. Did having information about the topic give you more or fewer opportunities to speak? How does doing research about a topic help you in a lesson?

Teacher reflection

What are other ways that you can provide students with background information (e.g. getting them to use their mobile phones in class)? Which activity generated most spoken language – the mingle or the group discussion afterwards? Why do you think this was the case?

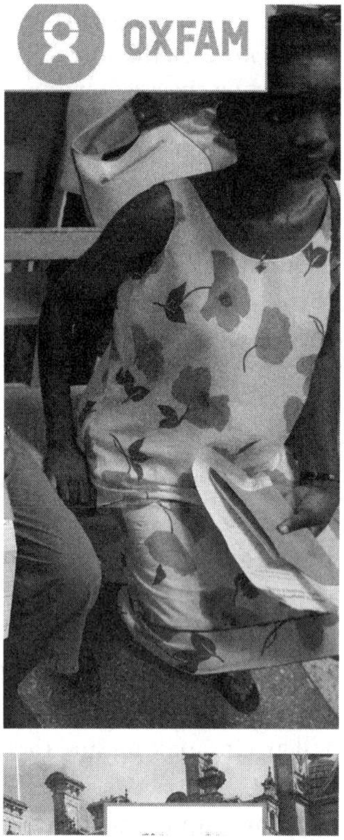

1 LISTENING AND SPEAKING

a Look at the names of the charities. What do you know about the charities? What do they do?

Match the charities with the sentences.

This charity …

1 protects animals and the environment.
2 protects historic buildings, gardens and the countryside.
3 helps people in poorer countries.

What other large charities do you know? What do they do?

b Work in pairs. How do people raise money for charity? Add ideas to the list.

- collect money in the street
- sponsor someone to do a sports event, for example, run a marathon
- make and sell food, e.g. cakes at work or school

Figure 2.1a: Doff, A., C. Thaine et al. (2015) *Cambridge English Empower B1*, p. 34.

While they aren't labelled as speaking activities, exercises 1 and 2 in *Figure 2.1b* aim to provide speaking fluency practice while also developing background knowledge. The homework task could be spread around students: a third of the class research Italy, a third South Africa and a third Madagascar. This would create more opportunities for speaking in the information exchange in the lesson.

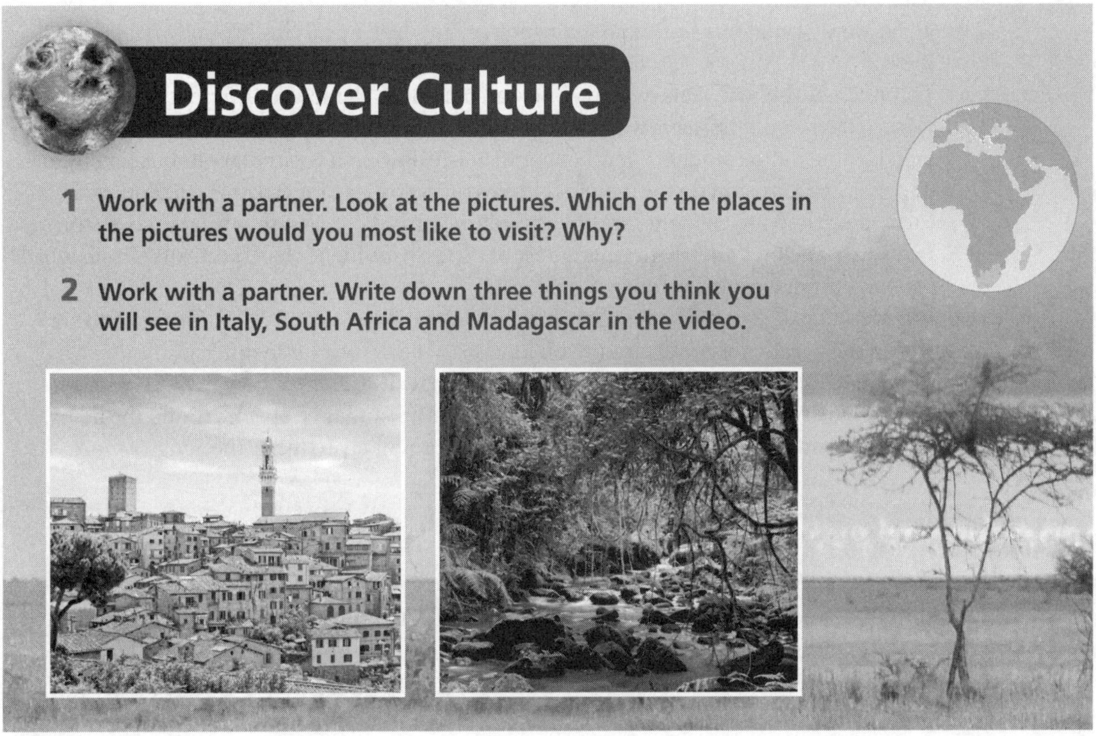

Discover Culture

1 Work with a partner. Look at the pictures. Which of the places in the pictures would you most like to visit? Why?

2 Work with a partner. Write down three things you think you will see in Italy, South Africa and Madagascar in the video.

Figure 2.1b: Goldstein, B. and C. Jones (2015) *Eyes Open 2*, p. 68.

2.2 Language addition

Level	A2 and above
Time	5 to 10 minutes
Outline	Students do a speaking activity involving personalisation or discussion questions trying to hide and detect vocabulary items (words, phrases or expressions) given to them by their teacher.
Aim	To encourage students to extend their spoken language by talking around vocabulary items.
Preparation	Think of vocabulary items that students can include in the speaking activity you are using. They should be items that will fit with the subject or topic of the activity and are manageable for the students' level of competence. Put each vocabulary item on a piece of paper. Students can do the activity in pairs or in groups of up to four students and each pair/group has the same set of vocabulary items. There is a set of eight words for *Figure 2.2a* below (and an alternative set of phrases for higher level students) – two words per student for a group of four.
Rationale	When students personalise the topic of a lesson or discuss aspects of it, they tend to stay within the parameters of the input you have provided. They often don't say as much as they could and make an effort to extend their range. If students know they have to try and include two vocabulary items, they have to think and then speak around the items. It provides students with an extra challenge, but it is likely to make the activity more generative in terms of spoken language produced.

Procedure

1 Students read the questions or prompts for the speaking task. Give each student one or two vocabulary items to use in the discussion. They must not show their words to other students.
2 Give students a few minutes to plan what they're going to say and how they will include their vocabulary items naturally in the discussion. They can write down key ideas, but not whole sentences.
3 Students speak in pairs or small groups. Tell them they should listen carefully to other students to try and identify which words, phrases or expressions you gave them.
4 When students have finished the speaking task, they should guess the target language items.
5 Do class feedback, and check with each pair/group whether they guessed each other's vocabulary items.

Notes

As is the case with many speaking activities, the success of this activity lies in giving students enough thinking and planning time (see the introduction to this chapter). A secondary aim of this activity is that it encourages students to be more active listeners. In order to try and detect the words their classmates have been given, students have to tune into each other.

Learner reflection questions

1 Did you speak more or less when you tried to use your words? Why?
2 Could you use this idea to speak more in class and in the real world? What kind of words can you try to use?

Teacher reflection

What do you think is the greatest strength of the activity in practice – more speaking or better listening? If you do this again, will you give students more or less planning time? Why?

The discussion in *Figure 2.2a* takes place after students have watched a video about the use of codes (e.g. secret words or numbers we use to log into computers and phones) in history.

DISCUSSION

9 Work with a partner. Discuss the questions below.

1 How is learning a language like learning a code?
2 Do you enjoy learning new languages? Why / Why not?
3 What are the secrets of being a good language learner?

Figure 2.2a: O'Neill, R. (2014) *Unlock Reading and Writing Skills 2*, p. 89.

Suggested words for the material in Figure 2.2a

remember	easy	dictionary	understand
fun	culture	practise	hard

The discussion questions above are aimed at A2 level students. However, you could also give the same questions to a group of C1 level students. If so, then the language items you could ask them to include in their discussion could be:

interaction	work out	broken English	be getting at something
slang	interpret	syntax	make yourself understood

The personalisation activity in *Figure 2.2b* comes towards the end of a unit after students have read and listened to texts on the unit topic: music.

SPEAKING

Work in pairs. Answer the questions.

1 Do you play an instrument? If yes, how long have you been playing it? If no, would you like to play an instrument?
2 Which of the instruments in Exercises 1 and 2 do you really like? Which instruments don't you like?
3 What famous musicians can you think of? How long have they been playing music? Have you seen them playing live?

Figure 2.2b: Puchta, H., J. Stranks and P. Lewis-Jones (2015) *Think Level 2*, p. 53.

One option for the vocabulary cards could be to include words from the texts. For example:

punk	perform	saxophone	release an album
keyboards	a hit	fans	drums

2.3 Planning the mingle

Level	A2 and above
Time	10 to 15 minutes
Outline	Students plan who they are going to talk to during a mingle activity according to different criteria that you suggest. You can manage the mingle actively by calling out to students to change partners.
Aim	To encourage more varied interaction in a mingle activity.
Preparation	No preparation of materials is required. There are suggested student choice criteria below, but you may want to think of your own based on what you know about your students.
Rationale	Sometimes mingle activities lose interactive momentum and students don't talk to as many different students as possible. This can be because they are shy or indecisive about who to talk to and/or they get stuck speaking to one person (two students who are friends may stay together and begin talking about other things). This activity aims to get students moving around and interacting with a greater number of students.

Procedure

1 Students plan *what* they are going to say (in *Figure 2.3a* they need to add two activities to the chart) and *who* they are going to talk to – anyone except the students they are sitting beside. Put some criteria on the board, for example:

Find someone who ...

... you don't know very well
... is wearing some clothes you like
... is a different gender
... is taller/shorter than you
... you worked in a pair with last lesson
... lives in a different part of the city

2 Students mingle and try to speak to as many people as possible on their list. Give them a limited time with each person – clap your hands and say 'Move on!', and they have to change partners even if they haven't finished the conversation.

3 When students finish the mingle, they compare their answers with the person sitting beside them.

Notes

Some students may be reluctant to change partners because they feel they need to complete the conversation. However, this needs to be balanced against the fact they will speak to more of their classmates. Having done so makes the follow-up pair discussion more interesting and more generative. Including a time limit means students are more likely to stay on task.

Learner reflection questions

1 What interesting things did you learn about some of your classmates?

2 How did it help you to plan who and what to say to other students? Did you feel less shy?

Teacher reflection

What effect did the planning and the management of the mingle have on the pace of the activity? What other kinds of speaking activities could you set time limits for?

INTERCHANGE 6 What's your talent?

A CLASS ACTIVITY Add two items to the chart. Does anyone in your class do these things? How often and how well? Go around the class and find one person for each activity.

	Name	How often?	How well?
bake cookies			
cook			
cut hair			
do card tricks			
fix things			
play an instrument			
sing			
do yoga			

A: Do you bake cookies?
B: Yes, I do.
A: How often do you bake cookies?
B: Once a month.
A: Really? And how well do you bake?

Figure 2.3a: Richards, J. C. et al. (2017) *Interchange 1* (5th ed.), p. 120.

The activity in *Figure 2.3b* involves students conducting a survey. One variation to the procedure above is to divide the class into two groups to survey each other. Within each group the students decide who in the other group they are going to speak to. During the feedback stage, the main groups could sub-divide into smaller groups of three or four students to collate results and report back to the class.

Your turn

6 Work in groups. Do a music survey. Report your group's information to the class.

- Do you like listening to music?
- What kind of music do you like?
- Do you play a musical instrument?
- Do you ever give money to buskers?

People listen to different kinds of music but ….
Some people listen to music on the bus and ….
Two people always give money to buskers because ….

Figure 2.3b: Goldstein, B. and C. Jones (2015) *Eyes Open 3*, p. 34.

B While speaking

2.4 Discussion group tag

Level	A2 and above
Time	10 to 15 minutes
Outline	Students discuss a topic in groups. At different times during the discussion, one student from each group moves to another group so that ideas and information are spread around the class as a whole.
Aim	To generate more spoken language in a discussion activity.
Preparation	It is not necessary to prepare any materials for this activity, but it is a good idea to plan the groups and the way you will get students to move from one group to another.
Rationale	Sometimes discussions don't take off in the classroom no matter how careful your preparation of students has been. This can be because students quickly run out of things to say, but it might also be because the group dynamic isn't working. By moving students between groups, they can share ideas and augment the discussion. It is also a subtle way of resolving group dynamic problems as students are constantly being remixed into new groupings.

Procedure

1. Students do any preparatory work for the discussion. In *Figure 2.4a* below, they would read the questions, think about them and perhaps note down their answers.
2. Put students in groups of four to six students. Arrange the groups in the room so there is a clear sense of clockwise or anti-clockwise movement. Give each student a number in their group.
3. Teach the words *clockwise* and *anti-clockwise* if students don't know them already.
4. Start the discussion, and when you call a number and direction, the students with that number move either clockwise or anticlockwise e.g. 'Student three – clockwise.'
5. Students find out from the new group member what the other group was talking about and then continue their discussion.
6. Repeat the procedure every two or three minutes or when you sense discussion is flagging in a group.
7. For feedback, ask students what difference it made when a new group member arrived.

Notes and variation

In this activity, a lot of extra speaking is generated when the student who is new to the group reports on what his or her previous group has been saying about the topic. With a smaller class where there are only two or three groups, you could just move students by monitoring, choosing a student and letting them know which group to move to. This approach means the mixing of students can be more targeted in terms of students' strengths and weaknesses.

Learner reflection questions

1 When different students joined a group was there more or less speaking?
2 Did different groups discuss different ideas around the topic? What was an interesting new idea you heard?

Teacher reflection

When a new student joined a group, was there just explanation or a mix of explanation and questioning? How much did group dynamics change when you moved students? What other activities or tasks could you use this idea with?

The discussion in *Figure 2.4a* takes place after students have watched a video about a female race-car driver.

DISCUSSION

8 Work with a partner. Discuss the questions below.

1 What sports are popular in your country?
2 Who are the most famous sportsmen and sportswomen in your country?
3 Are there any sports in your country that are played mainly by men or mainly by women?
4 Is it important to love the sport you do? Why / Why not?

Figure 2.4a: O'Neill, R. (2014) *Unlock Reading and Writing Skills 2*, p. 125.

Students discuss the statements in *Figure 2.4b* after they have completed a survey about online communication. One way to manage this activity is to tell students which statements they should discuss and then report on with each change of students.

Your turn

5 Discuss the following statements. Do you agree or disagree?

Most of my friends …

a communicate through their status updates every day.
b access social networks by phone or tablet.
c have met their virtual friends (on social media, Twitter etc.) in real life.
d don't have a social network account but they would like to have one.

Figure 2.4b: Goldstein, B. and C. Jones (2015) *Eyes Open 3*, p. 54.

2.5 Tell a lie

Level	B1 and above
Time	5 to 10 minutes
Outline	During a personalisation speaking activity, students include some information about themselves that isn't true. After all students have spoken, they question each other and try to guess what each other's lie was.
Aim	To encourage students to say more during personalisation; to ensure students listen to each other carefully.
Preparation	None is necessary for this activity.
Rationale	Personalisation activities can vary in their success depending on the extent to which students have had experience of a topic, and the degree to which they are interested in it. Suggesting that they think of a lie to tell during the personalisation can give them more to talk about. As all students know that the other students are telling a lie, they tend to listen to each other more carefully to try and work out what it is.

Procedure

1 Students prepare for the activity – exercise A in *Figure 2.5* below – and think of one idea that is a lie.
2 Put students in small groups or pairs. They tell each other about their personal experiences and include the lie in their speaking, without telling other students what the lie is.
3 Students listen carefully to see if they can work out what the lie is. They can ask one or two follow up questions to try to identify the lie, but they cannot ask the question 'What was the lie?'.
4 When all students have finished, they guess what the other person's lie was and then reveal their own.
5 In open class feedback, find out how many students were successful liars.

Notes and variation

The level for this idea is B1 and above because students need a reasonable level of competence in order to be able to weave a lie into their spoken language. The idea can also be used in opinion-based discussion activities. The teacher asks students to include a point of view that they don't really agree with and argue in favour of that point of view. After the discussion, group members try to guess which point of view wasn't sincere. Apart from giving students more to talk about, the questioning and answering towards the end of the activity also generates more spoken language.

Learner reflection questions

1 In what different ways did you try to understand if other students were lying?
2 Is it easier to speak when you are saying something that is true or if it is a lie? Why?

Teacher reflection

How attentively did students listen to each other during the activity? Were the successful liars the most competent speakers? Why do you think this was the case?

4 SPEAKING

A **Think about things you've lost or found in your life. They could be your own things or other people's things. Think about:**

when it happened	what the things were
what you did next	where you lost or found them

B GROUP WORK **Talk about the things you lost or found. Ask and answer questions. Then decide which was the most interesting or unusual story you heard.**

So, what did you lose or find?

I lost my wallet in a park a few months ago. It had some money and all my credit cards in it. Unfortunately, I didn't get it back!

Figure 2.5: Hendra, L. A., M. Ibbotson and K. O'Dell (2019) *Evolve 3*, p. 45.

2.6 The Suggesters

Level B1 and above
Time 10 to 15 minutes
Outline As students talk about a topic in pairs, one of the students stands aside and monitors the discussion. When that student feels the discussion isn't going well, she/he feeds in written prompts that aim to keep the discussion going.
Aim To generate more spoken language; to give students a sense of sustaining a discussion over a longer period of time.
Preparation If using *Figure 2.6* below, you will need to photocopy and cut up the worksheet for the students who will take the role of 'suggesters'. If you're using another activity, you will need to create and prepare your own worksheet of suggestions.
Rationale Even though students might prepare in detail for a speaking activity, group discussions will often peter out. Students can find it difficult to think of different ways of directing the discussion and asking questions of their peers that keep things going. This activity can help students understand the kind of interaction that can extend discussions.

Procedure

1 Students work alone and prepare what they are going to say – exercise a in *Figure 2.6*.
2 Put students in groups of three or more. (Note that for the purpose of this activity, the course book task is being done in a pair plus another student. It could also be done in small groups.)
3 Choose one student in each three to be the suggester (the other two will be the speakers).
4 Separately, tell the suggesters that their task is to monitor the discussion and help their speakers to keep going by providing suggestions on pieces of paper (the worksheet for *Figure 2.6*). Explain how they can do this:
   - Listen carefully to the discussion.
   - When the pair has difficulty in keeping the discussion going, they give a student one of the slips of paper – a question they can ask other students.
   - Check that suggesters understand they don't have to say anything themselves.
5 Suggesters read the suggestions while you explain the role of the suggesters to the speakers.
6 Speakers begin the discussion. Monitor and check that the suggesters are making suggestions – you may need to prompt them to help them get started.
7 When most groups have finished speaking, do feedback and ask students how easy or difficult it was to react to the suggestions.

Notes

This activity provides a degree of challenge for students because it means they need to be able to cope with unplanned input in the discussion. At first, the discussion may be a little awkward, but with practice students should become used to dealing with the suggestions. This is good training in managing unexpected spoken language outside the classroom. It pays to choose a confident student to be a suggester the first time you try the activity, and then, as students become familiar with this approach, different students can take on the role.

Learner reflection questions

1 For students having the discussion: what can you do when you get an unexpected question in a discussion or conversation?

2 For students who were making suggestions: how did you know when the speakers were having problems continuing the discussion? What did you learn about the way people speak together?

Teacher reflection

To what degree does this activity develop students' awareness of interaction in group speaking tasks? If doing this activity at higher levels, do you think you need to prepare suggestions or can students think of their own?

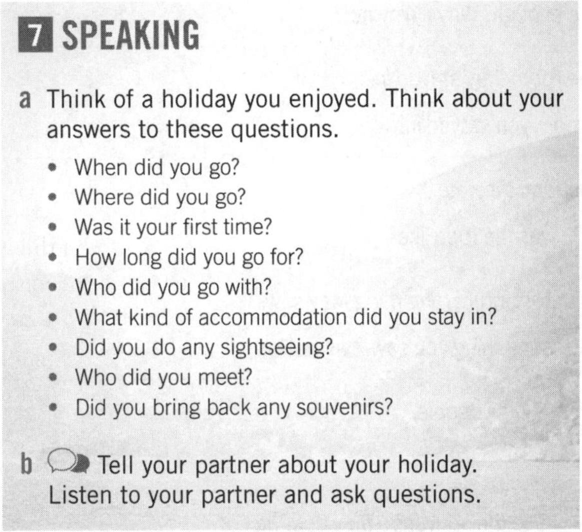

7 SPEAKING

a Think of a holiday you enjoyed. Think about your answers to these questions.

- When did you go?
- Where did you go?
- Was it your first time?
- How long did you go for?
- Who did you go with?
- What kind of accommodation did you stay in?
- Did you do any sightseeing?
- Who did you meet?
- Did you bring back any souvenirs?

b Tell your partner about your holiday. Listen to your partner and ask questions.

Figure 2.6: Doff, A., C. Thaine et al. (2015) *Cambridge English Empower B1*, p. 19.

Worksheet

Ask a student about the time they went on holiday.

Why did you go at that time?

Ask a student why they chose that place to go to.

Why did you go there?

Ask a student if they spent enough time on holiday.

Was the time there long enough? Why / Why not?

Ask a student about the room they stayed in.

Can you describe the room you stayed in?

Ask a student about the food they ate.

Where did you eat? What was the food like?

Ask a student about the most interesting thing they saw.

What was the most interesting thing you saw / visited?

Ask a student how they met new people.

How did you meet … ?

Ask a student why they chose the souvenirs they bought.

Why did you buy a … ? Where did you find it?

2.7 Speaking referee

Level	B1+
Time	10 to 15 minutes
Outline	In a group discussion, one student acts as referee and timekeeper. After one minute, the referee passes the turn to another student who has indicated they are ready to speak. This student begins their turn with a turn-taking expression.
Aim	To develop students' awareness of turn taking in speaking activities and to practise turn-taking expressions.
Preparation	You (or your students) will need to provide an object such as a ball or a stick that the referee can use to pass the turn to another student.
Rationale	Often when students are speaking in groups, one or two students tend to dominate the discussion and some students may say very little. Having a referee to manage the interaction is one way to help spread participation more evenly. It reinforces the idea that discussions need to be inclusive. It also makes taking a turn more manageable for less confident students because they can signal their desire to speak without having to use language. Furthermore, it encourages use of turn-taking expressions which often get forgotten in the heat of a real discussion.

Procedure

1 Students prepare ideas for the discussion – for *Figure 2.7a* they think about questions 1 to 4.
2 Put students in groups of four to six and choose one in each group to act as referee.
3 Explain the rules for the discussion:
- Referees try to ensure all students in the group speak, but don't need to speak themselves.
- No student speaks longer than a minute (referees can use a mobile phone to time speakers).
- Students who want to speak next put up their hand – the referee chooses who speaks next by passing the turn (the ball or stick etc.) to that person.
- The next speaker begins by using a turn-taking expression.
- If no one has put up their hand, the referee can choose the next speaker.

4 Remind students of useful expressions, for example, *I'd like to say / add ... Another point I'd make is ... Another example is ....* Language of agreeing and disagreeing is also useful.
5 Students begin their discussion. Monitor and make sure the referees are managing the discussion and intervene to help if necessary.
6 During feedback on the discussion, ask students their impressions of having a referee.

Notes and variation

The discussion might be a little self-conscious the first time you try this activity. Choose referees carefully – think about someone with a friendly manner who is likely to be supportive of less confident students. You could vary the activity by making the speaking time shorter (30 seconds if your students are lower level or less confident, or time is short) or longer (at least one minute to encourage longer turns). This activity is especially useful for students preparing for an English language exam in which there is a speaking paper that requires them to speak for a longer turn. In effect, the activity is flexible, and you can create as many or as few rules for referees as you like, bearing in mind the needs of your students. Another option is to record the discussion on a mobile phone. Students could then listen back to the recording to evaluate their use of turn-taking expressions.

Learner reflection questions

1 In the discussion, did having a referee mean you had to speak more or less than you normally do?
2 What does this tell you about the way you normally participate in group discussions? Do you need to try doing something different in group discussions?

Teacher reflection

To what extent did this create more balance in terms of student participation in the discussion? Would you change the referee rules in any way the next time you try this activity?

SPEAKING 4 **Discuss your ideas in groups.**

1 What do you do when you're angry with:
• a colleague? • a relative? • a friend? • a child?
2 How do you think conflict should be resolved at work or at home? Give an example from your experience.
3 How do you feel about getting angry in public? Is it acceptable in your country?
4 Is it the same or different in other cultures you know of?

Figure 2.7a: Rea, D., T. Clementson et al. (2011) *English Unlimited B1+*, p. 75.

While the exercise in *Figure 2.7b* suggests it should be done in pairs, it would also work as a group discussion.

2 SPEAKING **Work in pairs. Discuss these questions.**

1 What's the biggest decision you've ever made?
2 Have you ever made the wrong decision? What was it?
3 How good are you at making your mind up about small things?
4 What sort of things do you usually need to think long and hard about?
5 Do you ever reconsider decisions you have made?
6 Who do you ask to help you come to important decisions?

Figure 2.7b: Puchta, H., J. Stranks and P. Lewis-Jones (2015) *Think Level 3*, p. 43.

C After speaking

2.8 Students' self-determined needs

Level	B1 and above
Time	15 to 20 minutes
Outline	After a speaking activity, students reflect on their speaking needs.
Aim	To develop students' awareness of their speaking needs; to encourage independent learning strategies.
Preparation	It may be helpful to look at the Council of Europe's descriptors of spoken language as preparation. This can be viewed here: https://rm.coe.int/cefr-companion-volume-with-new-descriptors-2018/1680787989. On pages 171 and 172 there is a useful overview of the features of spoken language at different levels.
Rationale	Students are often very reliant on teachers for feedback on their spoken language. Given that we cannot listen to all of our students speak all of the time, it helps to pass some of the responsibility of feedback on to them and encourage peer evaluation of spoken language. Students have different strengths and weaknesses and can often provide mutually beneficial support for each other. However, they tend to think of strengths and weaknesses in speaking in terms of language accuracy. This activity shifts the evaluation focus on to other features of spoken language, thereby broadening the evaluation criteria that students use as they determine each other's needs.

Procedure

1 As students plan what they are going to say – exercise A in *Figure 2.8* below – write the following criteria on the board:

How fluent are they?
How accurate are they?
Do they use a good variety of language or do they always use the same words and expressions?
How much interaction is there?
How clear is their pronunciation?
How well is the information organised?

2 Before students begin speaking, point out the criteria above. Tell them you want them to listen to how well other students in their group do these things during the discussion.

3 Students carry out the discussion in groups of three or more learners, then they work alone and choose which three of the criteria on the board need most improvement in their group.

4 Students go back into the same group and share their three criteria and then negotiate and agree on three criteria for the group as a whole.

5 Invite a member of each group to come up to the board and put a tick by the three criteria their group decided on.

6 When all groups have added their three ticks, point out the three criteria with the most ticks. Indicate to students these are key points for them to think about when speaking English.

Notes and variation

A variation to this activity is to mix students into new groups after they have reflected on the three key criteria. This means students report on the performance of the first group. By collating all the ticks at the end of the activity and indicating the needs of the group as a whole, you are indirectly pointing out to students that group needs sometimes differ from individual needs. It can be useful for students to see this difference so they understand why you might focus on a speaking skill that they don't think is relevant to them. Some students may question the criteria you use here and want feedback on grammar mistakes. It's important to point out that speaking well in English isn't just a question of correct grammar and that you will deal with grammar mistakes during grammar lessons.

Learner reflection questions

1 Which of the speaking criteria do you often forget about when speaking?
2 Are your individual needs the same as the group needs? What can you do on your own to address your individual needs?

Teacher reflection

To what extent are students' self-perceived needs in line with your own impressions? Of the three, are there any that you think need prioritising?

12 DISCUSSION Time will tell.

A Think about your dreams and goals for the future. Write down an idea for each category.

an activity you'd like to try
an experience you'd like to have
a skill you'd like to develop
a city where you would like to live
a job you'd like to have
a person you'd like to meet

B GROUP WORK Talk about these questions. Use your ideas from part A.

What do you think you'll be doing a year from now? five years from now?
Do you think you'll still be living in the same city? same country?
What are three things you think you'll have accomplished within the next 10 years?
What are three things you won't have done within the next 10 years?
In what ways do you think you'll have changed by the time you retire?

A: A year from now, I think I'll have a new hobby, like slacklining.
B: I'd like to try that, but I'm more interested in traveling.
C: Me too! I think in five years, I'll be living abroad.

Figure 2.8: Richards, J. C. et al. (2017) *Interchange 3* (5th ed.), p. 68.

2.9 Role play performance

Level	A2 and above
Time	15 to 20 minutes
Outline	Students do a role play in pairs focusing on interaction and fluency. One pair is selected to perform their role play for the class as a model and then new pairs re-do the role play.
Aim	To highlight the interactional nature of role play conversations; to provide students with an opportunity to improve their spoken competence in the role play.
Preparation	No preparation is necessary for this activity. However, you may wish to think carefully which students work in pairs for the first attempt at a role play.
Rationale	Often student role plays seem like two monologues that follow each other. There is little sense of the role play being like a real conversation where two speakers react to what each other says. At lower levels, it's often difficult for students to understand clearly what you mean by *interaction* so it can be useful if they see a demonstration. If this model is provided by their peers, it will seem more achievable than watching a model by very fluent speakers.

Procedure

1 Give instructions for the role play and allow students time to prepare. For *Figure 2.9* below, students will need time to read the news stories and study the reaction expressions.

2 Put the words *fluency* and *interaction* on the board. Tell them you will listen to their conversation and check these aspects of their speaking.

3 Students do the role play. Identify a pair who are fluent and interactive, praise them and ask if they could do an example for the whole class – indicate it is to help their classmates.

4 The example pair perform the role play for the whole class. At the end, point out the strengths and give examples of where they were fluent and interactive.

5 Put students in new A and B pairs and have them re-do the role play.

Notes

In most cases, students will be more successful at the role play the second time, both because they have seen a model, and also because they generally have more confidence and fluency with a second attempt. The evaluation criteria for *Figure 2.9* below are restricted to fluency and interaction. With higher level groups you could introduce other, more sophisticated criteria, for example, the use of a varied range of structures and expressions.

Learner reflection questions

1 What did you learn from watching the example? For students who performed for the class: what did you think worked well with your role play?

2 Do you think the role play was better the first or second time you did it? Why?

Teacher reflection

What was most beneficial for your students: seeing the model role play or having an opportunity to do it again? If you repeat this activity, would you choose the same students or different students to perform an example? Why?

Students don't assume a specific role in the speaking task in *Figure 2.9*, the role play focuses on a situation in which two friends share news. A strength of this particular example is that it provides example expressions that students can use to make their role plays more interactive.

6C **11** p53

a Work on your own. Read about the news stories. Check you understand all the words.

Big storm
Mexico
13 people died

Man who found 1 million dollars
under the kitchen floor
gave money to a hospital

Tourists missing in Africa
Sahara desert
lost for 2 weeks
other tourists found them – they're OK now

Man tries to post m
A woman whc
tioned about t'
on Monday m
in the sleepy v
witness said th
man was in his

b Work with your partner. Take turns to tell each other about the news stories. Use these phrases.

Did you hear/read about … ? No, what happened?
No, where was it? Oh, that's good. Oh no, that's terrible.
Oh, dear. Are they OK? You're joking! Really?

6C **11** p53

a Work on your own. Read about the news stories. Check you understand all the words.

3 students lost in Brazil
Amazon jungle
lost for six days
helicopter found them
they're OK now

Plane crash
in Africa
over 80 people died

Man who won the lottery
dog ate ticket
gave dog to friend

Planes at airp why the
Tuesday morn
a number of k
and have made
to the press at
"I see no reaso
said Mr Dawk

b Work with your partner. Take turns to tell each other about the news stories. Use these phrases.

Did you hear/read about … ? No, what happened?
No, where was it? Oh, that's good. Oh no, that's terrible.
Oh, dear. Are they OK? You're joking! Really?

Figure 2.9: Redston, C. and G. Cunningham (2012) *face2face Elementary* (2nd ed.), pp. 105 and 111.

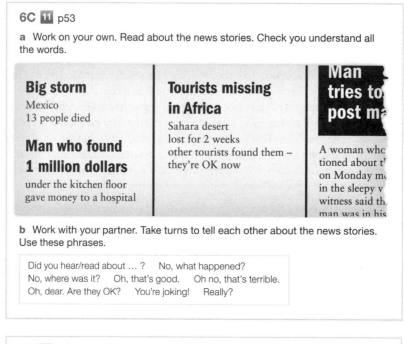

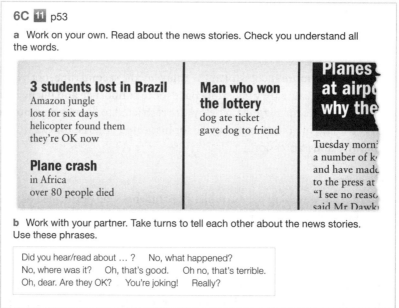

2.10 Pair-to-pair feedback

Level	B1+ and above
Time	15 to 20 minutes
Outline	Students record a pair work speaking activity on a mobile phone and then ask another pair to give them constructive feedback on their speaking.
Aim	To give students practice in self- and peer evaluation of speaking; to encourage independent learning strategies.
Preparation	In the lesson before you do this activity, remind students to bring their mobile phones to class. It may be helpful to look at the Council of Europe's descriptors of spoken language as preparation: https://rm.coe.int/cefr-companion-volume-with-new-descriptors-2018/1680787989. See pages 171 and 172 there for a useful overview of the features of spoken language at different levels.
Rationale	As was the case with activity 2.8, this activity promotes peer evaluation of speaking. The approach here is more direct (student-to-student), and it aims to show students how they can give each other constructive feedback. It helps to record the speaking activity because students will struggle to hear everything if they have only one chance to listen to the speaking activity as is the case in a live presentation.

Procedure

1 Give students time to prepare for the speaking activity. In *Figure 2.10* below, students need to read the instructions and think about what they want to say.
2 Students do the role play and record themselves on a mobile phone.
3 Ask each pair to decide on two or three features of speaking they would like feedback on from another pair. These could be categories referred to in the Council of Europe descriptors for spoken language (see above). However, they could be previously taught target language items.
4 Write the following expressions on the board:
I liked / I liked the way … One / Another thing I would do differently is …
5 Pairs exchange mobile phones, listen to each other's conversations, and choose one or two strengths and one or two needs to give feedback on.
6 Using the expressions on the board, pairs of students give feedback to each other.
7 Allow students an opportunity to ask you any questions and encourage them while they help each other, particularly if this is the first time they've done this activity. Ask them if their feedback was on similar language points.

Notes

Some students may be reluctant to record themselves and if so, let them know they don't have to listen to their own recording if they don't want to. Make sure the pair who listens to the recording is not sitting next to them. You may need to try and convince students of the learning benefit of recording speaking – that it allows other people to evaluate spoken language more carefully.

Learner reflection questions

1 What did you realise about your own speaking when you listened to the recording of the other pair?
2 How can you get other students to help you with your speaking both inside and outside the classroom? Do you always need to get help from the teacher?

Teacher reflection

Did students find it easier to work out strengths or weaknesses in each other's speaking? Why do you think this was the case? In what other ways could you use mobile phones in speaking lessons?

6 SPEAKING

Communication 10C Student A: Read the information below. Student B: Go to p.130.

Student A

You want to talk to Student B about a trip abroad you are going to take (where are you going?).

You are worried because:

- you are scared of flying (what might happen?)
- you are nervous about communicating in a different language (what problems might this cause?)
- you are not very good at trying new food (what food might you have to try?).

Have the conversation. Reassure Student B when he/she tries to talk about a big presentation he/she has to give, but try to bring the conversation back to your trip.

10C SPEAKING Student B

You want to talk to Student A about a big presentation you have to do (where? what is it about?).

You're worried because:

- you don't have much time to prepare (when is it?)
- you don't have any experience of public speaking (what problems might you have?)
- you are worried people might ask difficult questions (what might they ask?).

Have the conversation. Reassure Student A when he/she talks about a trip he/she is going on, but try to bring the conversation back to your presentation.

Figure 2.10: Doff, A., C. Thaine et al. (2015) *Cambridge English Empower B1+*, pp. 123 and 130.

You can find teacher development activities about speaking on pages 257 to 260.

3 Reading

Introduction

Reading activities in course books

English language course books aim to provide interesting and motivating reading texts for students. While these texts are often based on authentic, real-world texts, the language and vocabulary are often simplified to the language level of the course book. Reading plays an important role in English language programmes for a variety of reasons:

- to practise and develop different reading skills;
- to provide a context when new language items are introduced;
- to reinforce previously taught language items by providing students with repeated encounters with them;
- to act as a stimulus and source of ideas for speaking activities;
- to provide a model of a particular writing genre for subsequent writing activities.

More often than not reading texts in course books are used to achieve two or more of these aims in tandem.

Figure 3.0 (page 72) demonstrates typical stages in a course book reading lesson. The stages are very similar to those of a listening lesson (see Chapter 1) and are as follows:

> lead in → initial reading → second, more detailed reading → follow up speaking activity → focus on a language feature

Exercise 1a is a lead in. Pictures and simple, key sentences are used as a stimulus for pair discussion. Apart from practising speaking fluency, the lead in activity gets students thinking about the topic of the reading text and aims to activate any background knowledge and vocabulary they might have associated with it. It does this by getting students to personalise the topic and talk about their own experiences, and then asks them to come up with ideas for solving some typical daily life problems.

Exercise 1b is an initial reading task. Students have to read to match the advice in the text to the problems illustrated in the pictures. Only four of the problems are referred to in the text so students need to discriminate. While it is not explicitly stated, students can also find out whether the advice in the text matches the ideas they discussed in exercise 1a – this gives them a further reason to read. In order to carry out the task in 1b, students do not need to understand the text in a lot of detail. This means they can read the text to get the main ideas and identify the problem being discussed. In other words, it provides students with practice in reading for gist – also known as skim reading.

A teacher would check the answers to exercise 1b, and if satisfied that students have understood the overall gist, would then set exercise 1c as a second reading task. This asks students to read the text in more detail in order to make notes on key points in the text. This means students need to identify the key points in the text, read what information the text provides about these key points, and then write them down in note form. As a result, students need to process information in the text with more thoroughness than they did for exercise 1b.

1 READING

a Look at the problems in the pictures. Does anyone you know have any of these problems? How could you solve them? Tell a partner.

b Read the advice. Which four problems in the pictures is it for? Complete the headings 1–4.

c Read the advice again. What is the advice about these things? Make notes.

1 • music
  • 15 minutes

2 • rules
  • a pile

3 • breaks
  • rewards

4 • screens
  • milk

d Cover the article. Use your notes. Try to remember the advice in the article.

e Do you think the advice in each paragraph is useful? Why / Why not?

How to deal with life's

You don't have any money, you never finish anything you start, your house is dirty, you can't find a good job and your whole life is terrible. Well, maybe it isn't that bad! If you'd like to improve things, we can help. Here are our top ways to deal with some of life's little problems.

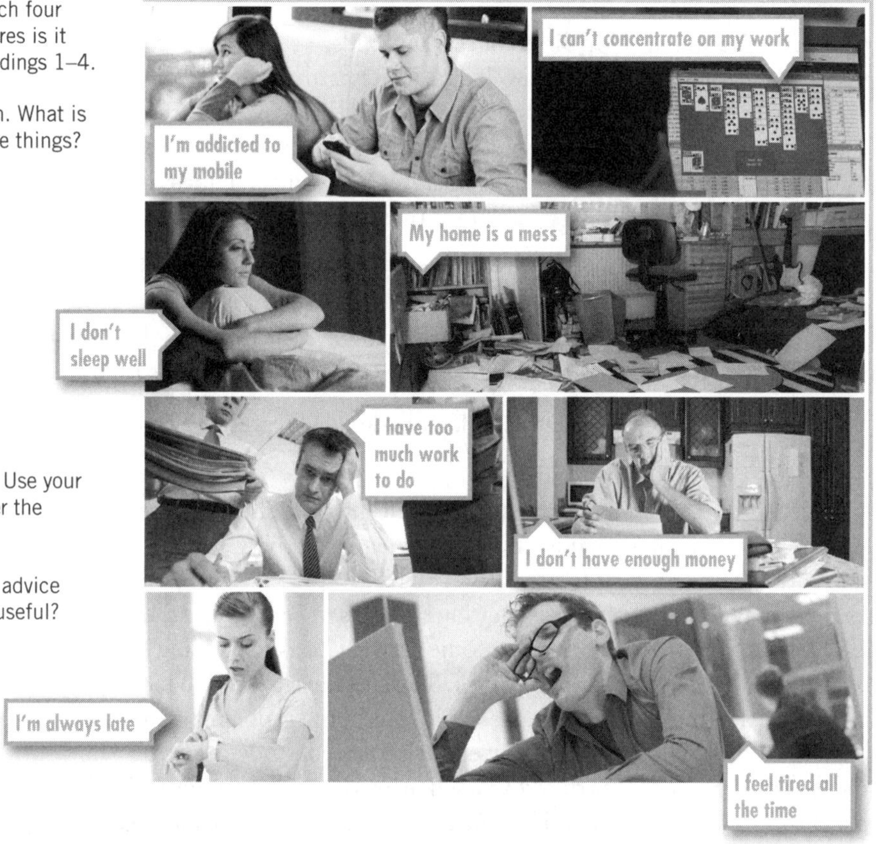
I'm addicted to my mobile
I can't concentrate on my work
I don't sleep well
My home is a mess
I have too much work to do
I don't have enough money
I'm always late
I feel tired all the time

little problems

1

Learn to enjoy cleaning and tidying. People who enjoy this usually have clean homes. Turn on the TV or listen to music while you clean. Start by cleaning every day, but only for fifteen minutes. When the 15 minutes are finished, you should stop. Don't worry if things aren't perfectly clean. Do a little bit of cleaning every day and in a week your place will look great.

2

It's important to give yourself rules. When you go out with friends, decide how many times you will look at your phone – maybe only two or three times in an evening. Ask your friends about how they feel. If they have the same problem as you, put all of your phones together, in a pile and out of the way. That way, no one can look at their phone and you can all enjoy each other's company.

3

The machine we use so much for work – our computer – is the same machine we often use to have fun. So control how you use your computer. If your problem is that you check your email every five minutes, you can get programs that stop the Internet from working for a period of time you choose. Use this time to focus on your work. But you shouldn't work for hours without a break. Work for 25 minutes, and then have a five-minute rest. Rewards are really important, too. Have a biscuit or get some fresh air every hour or so.

4

First think about your body. Exercising regularly will help you to fall asleep more easily. You should try to drink less coffee and smoke less, too. These bad habits keep you awake. Don't use devices with bright screens, for example, your mobile phone, before you go to sleep. They make your brain think that it is daytime, instead of night. Read a book and drink a cup of warm milk or herbal tea in the evening. Then you'll feel ready for sleep.

2 GRAMMAR Imperative; *should*

a Complete the sentences with the correct verbs. Check your answers in the article.

1 Turn on the TV or ____ to music while you clean.
2 You should ____ to drink less coffee and smoke less, too.
3 You shouldn't ____ for hours without a break.
4 Don't ____ devices with bright screens before you go to sleep.

Figure 3.0: Doff, A., C. Thaine et al. (2015) *Cambridge English Empower B1*, pp. 58–59.

It is worth pointing out at this stage that exercises 1b and 1c both provide students with a reason to read. This is a core concept in reading lessons (as it is in listening lessons). A teacher could say to students, 'Just read the text', and a possible reply from a student might be, 'Why should I?'. While most students are unlikely to respond in this way, questioning the teacher's instruction has a certain degree of validity. By providing tasks such as 1b and 1c, this problem is avoided because both tasks give students a reason and some degree of motivation to read.

Exercises 1d and 1e both involve spoken responses to the reading text and show how reading texts can be a source and a stimulus for speaking fluency practice. Exercise 1d links well with 1c because students use the notes they have made to help them recall the information in the text. This activity would be done either in pairs or small groups. Exercise 1e develops this further by asking students to evaluate the usefulness of the advice given in the text. This provides further opportunities for speaking fluency and adds a personal response and a critical thinking dimension to the speaking. As with exercise 1d, this would be carried out in pairs or small groups.

The text in *Figure 3.0* is also context for grammar that students study in the next stage of the lesson. The very beginning of the grammar tasks is shown above. Many course books divide up the reading and the language (grammar or vocabulary) stages of the lesson with separate headings, as is the case with this particular course book.

Not all reading lessons include all these stages. For example, if the text is a screen shot of a cinema webpage and the reading task is to scan to find out times for different films and key information such as the length of a film, then there is likely to be just this one scan task. If the webpage does not include summaries of the film, then there may be no more information to read intensively. Some course books may omit a gist reading stage for a text such as an article. This may be because the text is short and does not warrant it, but there may be other reasons that might not be immediately apparent. Sometimes the lead in to a text involves a focus on vocabulary that appears in the text and there may be no speaking activity. And sometimes a speaking activity or response to the text is not included after the detailed reading. When a stage is perceived as being missing in course book material, teachers often create their own activity to fill the gap. They usually do this because they feel their students would benefit from the extra stage.

Methodological considerations

As noted above, some course book reading lessons begin with a vocabulary stage before the reading. This aims to clarify the meaning of key words in the text and is sometimes in the form of matching words highlighted in example sentences to definitions, or it might involve students using the new words to fill in gaps in sentences. However, often there are only two or three words that students might not know in the text. In this case, the teacher can pre-teach these words to students. Sometimes the Teacher's Book will indicate which words might need pre-teaching, or a teacher will decide on the basis of their awareness of students' language knowledge.

Mention of students' vocabulary knowledge raises the issue of dictionary use while students are reading. One key difference between listening and reading lessons is that, in the latter, the student has more control of the pace of processing the text and can stop to check new words they do not understand. It is generally agreed that this is not the most efficient way of reading, particularly if a reader only needs a gist understanding of a text. Students are usually keen to use bi-lingual dictionaries or translation apps on some kind of digital device and check as they go. This means teachers need to think carefully about how they manage this in light of their reading skills practice aims. At lower levels, bi-lingual dictionaries are efficient and useful. However, at higher levels, there is a strong argument for getting students to use English–English dictionaries so they explore lexical meaning in English. In effect, teachers need to make a decision about how they want students to use dictionaries when they read, and let students know when giving instructions for a reading task. For example, if the aim is to practise gist reading the teacher may tell students they cannot stop to use their dictionaries when reading. However, they can do so once they have finished because at that point the aim of the activity has moved on from practice of reading for gist to that of increasing students' vocabulary knowledge. In effect, dictionary use should ideally be managed in light of the aims of individual activities, and these change during the course of a lesson.

A third methodological consideration concerns the timing of readings. A teacher may have a learning aim of practising skim reading. This suggests that students will read quickly to understand the main ideas in a text. Some students who struggle with reading will often read the text more slowly than they need to in order to get a very general understanding of a text. You may see these students reading word for word with a pen – the pen hovers over each word as they process it. In order to encourage students to increase their reading speed, it helps to set time limits. Time limits need to be achievable for most of the class and, having set a time limit, you may realise it is too strict. If so, you can always give students a bit more time in practice.

As is the case with listening lessons, it is a good idea for students to check reading tasks in pairs before checking the answers as a class. During the pair work, you can monitor and determine how easy or difficult this text is for students. You might also realise there are one or two words or phrases that are problematic, so you could clarify the meaning of these before students read again.

To read aloud or not?

The underlying assumption of most course book reading tasks is that students will read the texts silently to themselves. At lower levels, there can be some benefit in the teacher reading a text aloud with students following. This can be an effective way to help increase the reading speed of some students. In order to follow the teacher's voice, they need to maintain good reading pace.

Some teachers ask their students to take turns reading aloud in class. This can be problematic because it means that students have to process the language forms, try and understand their meaning, and then work out how to pronounce the word. This is quite a complex thing to do and very challenging. It is worth bearing in mind that TV news presenters are paid large sums of money to read aloud in their first language. This suggests it is a very specialised skill and perhaps not suitable for learners of English. A second consideration is that getting students to read aloud is often time-consuming and not the best use of classroom time. When teaching students in a one-to-one situation (or very small groups), there may be some benefit in getting a student to read aloud. However, when teachers do this, the learning aim is often more associated with pronunciation than reading.

Reading skills: practice or development?

In discussing the example material above, reading for gist and detail have been referred to. We say that these are reading subskills. Core reading subskills that relate to course book material are as follows:

- reading for gist (skim reading)
- reading for specific information (scan reading)
- reading for detail (intensive reading)
- reading to increase vocabulary knowledge (including guessing meaning in context)
- reading to infer information (between-the-lines)
- reading to understand text organisation

Another commonly cited reading subskill is reading extensively for pleasure and/or to increase fluency. It is less likely that students read a course book in this way. This subskill tends to be associated with reading longer texts outside the classroom.

Teachers and learners sometimes get confused between what is meant by skim and scan reading. Skim reading involves understanding the most important information in a text, but not the detail. Scan reading involves reading to locate a word or phrase or number. Both can be initial reading tasks and the nature of the text will determine whether one or the other subskill is practised. For example, it is more natural to skim read an article for the main points but scan read a train timetable to locate a destination and a time.

A distinction is often made between practising subskills and developing them. Course books mostly provide practice of different reading subskills. Students need to read in a specific way in order to complete a task. For example, in exercise 1b in *Figure 3.0*, students practise gist reading to match the advice to the questions.

In order to say that students *develop* reading skills, we need to ensure that they are made aware of how they read a text in English. The vast majority of English language learners are already perfectly proficient readers in their first language and have developed skills and strategies to read a range of text types. These skills and strategies do not automatically transfer to their reading of English texts. For some learners, this may be because a lack of vocabulary inhibits their ability to deploy first language strategies while, for other learners who do not have a Roman script in their first language, reading strategies may not work when reading English. Often students feel there is a disconnect between what they do quite naturally in their first language and what teachers encourage them to do when reading in English in class. They see these as two very different activities.

To bridge this gap and develop students' awareness of English language reading skills, the teacher should focus on them in an explicit way. This involves some kind of reflection task that makes the subskills apparent to students. In doing so, it may be useful to make a distinction between a reading *skill* and a reading *strategy*. These two terms are often used synonymously, but they differ slightly. One way of looking at it is that a strategy is something readers and learners use when they have a problem understanding or processing information in a text. They use this in a conscious way. Once they have done this repeatedly, and they deploy this strategy automatically and unconsciously, then we could say that has become a skill. The ultimate aim of developing reading skills is to make strategies automatic and to make reading more efficient.

Course books have fewer reading skill development tasks and teachers often need to create their own. As is the case throughout this book, in this chapter there are learner reflection tasks after each activity. These aim to develop students' awareness of reading subskills and strategies as a first step in their becoming automatic.

A Before reading

3.1 Building the knowledge

Level	A2 and above
Time	15 to 20 minutes
Outline	As a lead in to a reading text, you provide pictures (or video) and have a quiz to equip students with background information on the text.
Aim	To provide background knowledge on a reading text; to motivate students to read.
Preparation	For *Figure 3.1*, you would need to find a range of photos of the three cities mentioned in the reading text to put on the board (or around the classroom). If you are able to show video in the classroom, you can look for video material online. If you don't use the text in *Figure 3.1* below, you will need to write your own quiz questions.
Rationale	Many reading lead in activities in course books ask students to make a note of what they know about the topic of a text. For example, the Teacher's Notes for *Figure 3.1* suggest the teacher check which country the cities are in and then ask the question *What do you know about the weather in those places?* A student studying in Ecuador may have little idea about the weather in Bristol. Seeing pictures of the city and having a short quiz is a motivating way of providing and sharing knowledge that students might not otherwise have. It means that students are likely to be more curious to see the visual material you have brought in. Showing pictures or video on its own can be motivating, but linking the visual input to the information will probably increase interest.

Procedure

1 Put students into two or three teams and tell them they are going to have a quiz about three cities. Tell them the names of the cities and where they are located.

2 Point out the pictures around the room and give students a couple of minutes to move around and look at them (or show any video material you have found).

3 Ask the first team a question and give students fifteen seconds to confer and answer. The team wins a point if they get the answer right. If they don't get the answer right, the next team can try and answer. If the second team gets it wrong, give the correct answer.

4 Move on to the next team and ask another question and continue in this vein. Ask as many questions as you need to reach a winning team or a draw.

5 Then mix the students from the different teams into pairs or small groups. Ask them to recall as much information from the quiz as they can remember and tell each other which city they would like to visit and why.

Notes and variation

Students could answer the questions on a worksheet, but managing this activity as a competition is more active and likely to be more motivating for students. By asking each team in turn, you prevent students from shouting out and allowing one team to dominate the quiz. With different levels and in light of what you imagine students' background knowledge is in relation to the topic of a text, you can vary the kind of quiz questions you ask, for example, you could make them more open-ended. The recap is important so that all students pool the information from the quiz to build their background knowledge.

Learner reflection questions

1. How much information in the quiz did you know and how much did you guess?
2. Is it more interesting to look at the pictures/video before the quiz? Why?
3. How does the information help you read?

Teacher reflection

How was building background knowledge different from trying to activate students' knowledge? Is it possible to build background knowledge with all genres? In what other ways can you help students build background knowledge?

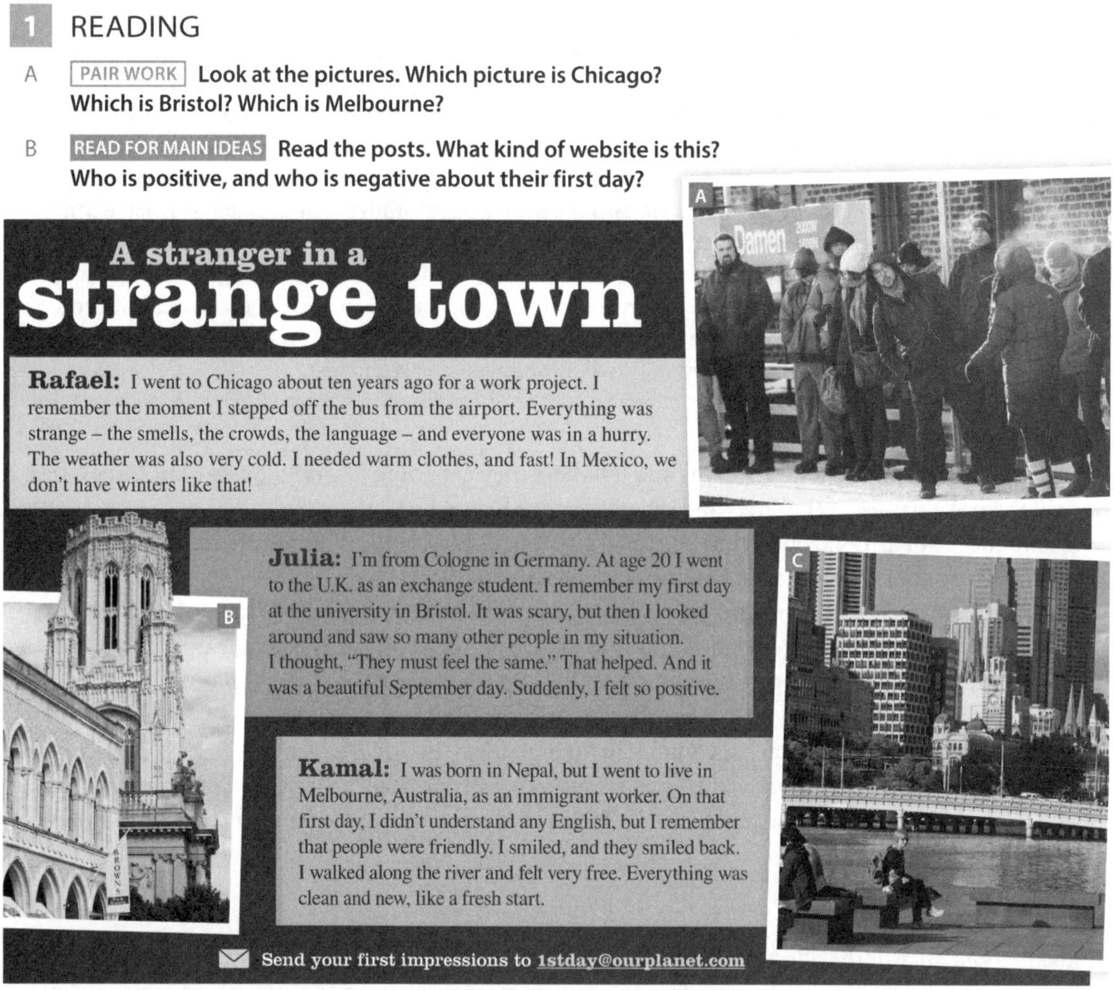

1 READING

A PAIR WORK **Look at the pictures. Which picture is Chicago? Which is Bristol? Which is Melbourne?**

B READ FOR MAIN IDEAS **Read the posts. What kind of website is this? Who is positive, and who is negative about their first day?**

A stranger in a strange town

Rafael: I went to Chicago about ten years ago for a work project. I remember the moment I stepped off the bus from the airport. Everything was strange – the smells, the crowds, the language – and everyone was in a hurry. The weather was also very cold. I needed warm clothes, and fast! In Mexico, we don't have winters like that!

Julia: I'm from Cologne in Germany. At age 20 I went to the U.K. as an exchange student. I remember my first day at the university in Bristol. It was scary, but then I looked around and saw so many other people in my situation. I thought, "They must feel the same." That helped. And it was a beautiful September day. Suddenly, I felt so positive.

Kamal: I was born in Nepal, but I went to live in Melbourne, Australia, as an immigrant worker. On that first day, I didn't understand any English, but I remember that people were friendly. I smiled, and they smiled back. I walked along the river and felt very free. Everything was clean and new, like a fresh start.

Send your first impressions to 1stday@ourplanet.com

Figure 3.1: Clandfield, L., B. Goldstein et al. (2019) *Evolve 2*, p. 50.

Worksheet – quiz questions and answers

1 Which city had a very cold winter temperature of minus 27 degrees? (Chicago)
2 Which city sits on two rivers? (Bristol – Avon & Frome Rivers)
3 Which city has a subway transport system? (Chicago)
4 Which city had a very hot summer temperature of 46 degrees? (Melbourne)
5 Which city is famous for being very kind? (Bristol)
6 Which city has a very large number of cafes and restaurants? (Melbourne)
7 Which city sits on a lake? (Chicago – Lake Michigan)
8 Which city has over 400 parks and gardens? (Bristol)
9 Which city sits on the Yarra River? (Melbourne)
10 Which city has a lot of rain in November? (Bristol)

3.2 Vocabulary pre-teach by example

Level A2 and above

Time 15 to 20 minutes

Outline In pairs, students work together to ascertain meaning of target vocabulary items in sentences and, in new pairs, students peer teach the new vocabulary.

Aim To clarify the meaning of unfamiliar vocabulary in the text in a student-centred way; to show how these words are used in the text.

Preparation If you use *Figure 3.2a* below, you need to copy and cut up the sentences that illustrate the meaning as well as the gapped sentences from the text on worksheet one. If you are using a different reading text with different vocabulary, you will need to write sentences that contextualise and give the meaning of the new words. You will also need to word process gapped sentences with the words from the reading text.

Rationale Typical ways for vocabulary to be pre-taught are by means of teacher elicitation and checking of the new words, or by some kind of word-to-meaning matching task. The elicitation approach works well for one or two words, but can have a negative impact on the pace of a lesson if there are too many words. A matching task is more student-centred, but definitions don't show meaning in context. This activity encourages students to engage more fully with new vocabulary, and the gapped sentences from the text allow students to preview how the word appears in the text. Note that in some cases, the gapped sentences only include part of a sentence where the new word appears so that students don't preview too much of the text.

Procedure

1. Divide the class into two groups – Student As and Student Bs – and give out the example sentences and gapped sentences to the two groups of students – one set for each student. Tell them the gapped sentences are from the reading, but they don't fill these in now.
2. In their groups, students work in pairs, read the examples and decide what words go in the gaps without writing in the answers. Monitor and confirm students' answers (pairs who finish quickly can help other students). Students can also think of more example sentences that help explain the meaning of their words.
3. Then put students into A and B pairs and get them to explain their words to each other – they give a definition and use the example in the sentence as well as the ones they've thought of.
4. Students then exchange the worksheets with examples and gap fill sentences and write in the answers – they can check each other's work.
5. If necessary, re-elicit any words you think are a problem or go straight into the reading.

Notes and variation

In a mono-lingual setting, translation could be used as a final check of understanding of the words. However, students get more speaking practice if the activity is done only in English. At higher levels, you could give the gapped sentences from the text and just the words without examples. Students could guess and use English–English dictionaries to check their guesses and then think of examples for the peer teaching.

Learner reflection questions

1 How is this activity different from looking up the meaning of a word in the dictionary?
2 How did example sentences from the text with gaps help you when you read the text for the first time?

Teacher reflection

Did you feel you needed to elicit and double check any words at the end of this activity? Why / Why not? By providing students with some sentences from the text, what reading subskill do students (unconsciously) practise?

The words on the worksheet are indicated in the Teacher's Book as being worth pre-teaching.

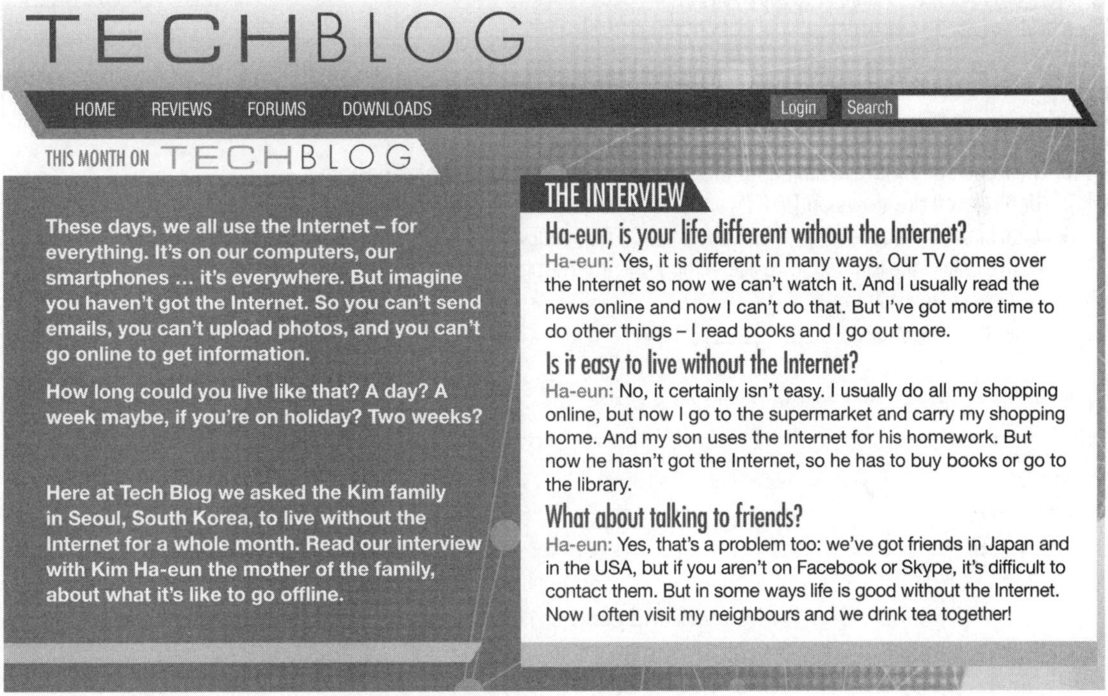

TECHBLOG

HOME REVIEWS FORUMS DOWNLOADS Login Search

THIS MONTH ON TECHBLOG

These days, we all use the Internet – for everything. It's on our computers, our smartphones ... it's everywhere. But imagine you haven't got the Internet. So you can't send emails, you can't upload photos, and you can't go online to get information.

How long could you live like that? A day? A week maybe, if you're on holiday? Two weeks?

Here at Tech Blog we asked the Kim family in Seoul, South Korea, to live without the Internet for a whole month. Read our interview with Kim Ha-eun the mother of the family, about what it's like to go offline.

THE INTERVIEW

Ha-eun, is your life different without the Internet?

Ha-eun: Yes, it is different in many ways. Our TV comes over the Internet so now we can't watch it. And I usually read the news online and now I can't do that. But I've got more time to do other things – I read books and I go out more.

Is it easy to live without the Internet?

Ha-eun: No, it certainly isn't easy. I usually do all my shopping online, but now I go to the supermarket and carry my shopping home. And my son uses the Internet for his homework. But now he hasn't got the Internet, so he has to buy books or go to the library.

What about talking to friends?

Ha-eun: Yes, that's a problem too: we've got friends in Japan and in the USA, but if you aren't on Facebook or Skype, it's difficult to contact them. But in some ways life is good without the Internet. Now I often visit my neighbours and we drink tea together!

Figure 3.2a: Doff, A., C. Thaine et al. (2015) *Cambridge English Empower A2*, p. 32.

Worksheet
Contextualising sentences 1–3 with new word in **bold.** *Gapped sentences from the text a–c.*

Student A

1 There was an **interview** with Ariana Grande on TV. Some of her answers were really interesting.
2 I always **contact** my friends by text or social media messaging. I never phone them.
3 It's fun to **imagine** winning Lotto, but I know it will never happen.
a If you aren't on Facebook or Skype, it's difficult to ______________ them.
b But ______________ you haven't got the internet.
c Read our ______________ with Kim Ha-eun the mother of the family.

Student B

1 The Robinsons who live next door are really nice – they're great **neighbours**.
2 I don't watch **the news** on TV. If I want to know what's happening in the world I look online.
3 I didn't use my mobile phone at all last week. It was really difficult not to have it for a **whole** week.
a We asked the Kim family to live without the internet for a ______________ month.
b Now I often visit my ______________.
c And I usually read ______________ online.

3.3 Summary prediction

Level	B1 and above
Time	5 to 10 minutes
Outline	Before reading a text, students listen to you give an oral summary of it. They then ask you questions about the summary, and predict the content and the structure of the text.
Aim	To give students practice predicting both the content and structure of a reading text; to provide a link between listening and reading.
Preparation	For *Figure 3.3* below, there is no preparation. If you use a different text, you will need to write your own lead in questions and summary to read out to students.
Rationale	Providing a summary gives students more information on which to base their predictions. Students could simply read the summary, but this means reading in order to read. Reading the summary aloud to students gives listening practice and then provides a speaking opportunity when they ask questions. This activity also gets students to focus on the genre and the way it's organised.

Procedure

1 For *Figure 3.3* write the following questions on the board (see *Additional notes* below for ideas):
What kind of problems can you have when booking a private car?
How are online advice columns usually organised?
Do you think the language in the text will be informal or formal?
2 Read the text summary below aloud, or use it as a basis to tell students about the text, and let students know they can ask you questions about the summary – but not the text.
3 In pairs, students discuss the questions on the board.
4 Do open class feedback on the questions and write up ideas the students give.
5 Students open their course books and read the text quickly to check their predictions.
6 Do feedback on the initial reading by checking the accuracy of students' predictions on the board.

Notes

This activity is suitable for texts that adhere to a recognisable genre with distinguishing characteristics, for example, social media posts, formal letters etc. It's particularly useful for students in exam and EAP classes who need to be able to recognise the discourse organisation of texts efficiently when they read.

Learner reflection questions

1 In this activity, you thought about the information in the text and the way it's organised. Why is it a good idea to do both?
2 Are texts in your first language organised in a similar way to texts written in English? What is similar and what is different?

Teacher reflection

Were your students better at predicting the organisation of the text or the kind of language it contained? To what extent do you point out text organisation in reading lessons?

A Skim the advice column. What problem did the reader have? How does the writer suggest solving the problem?

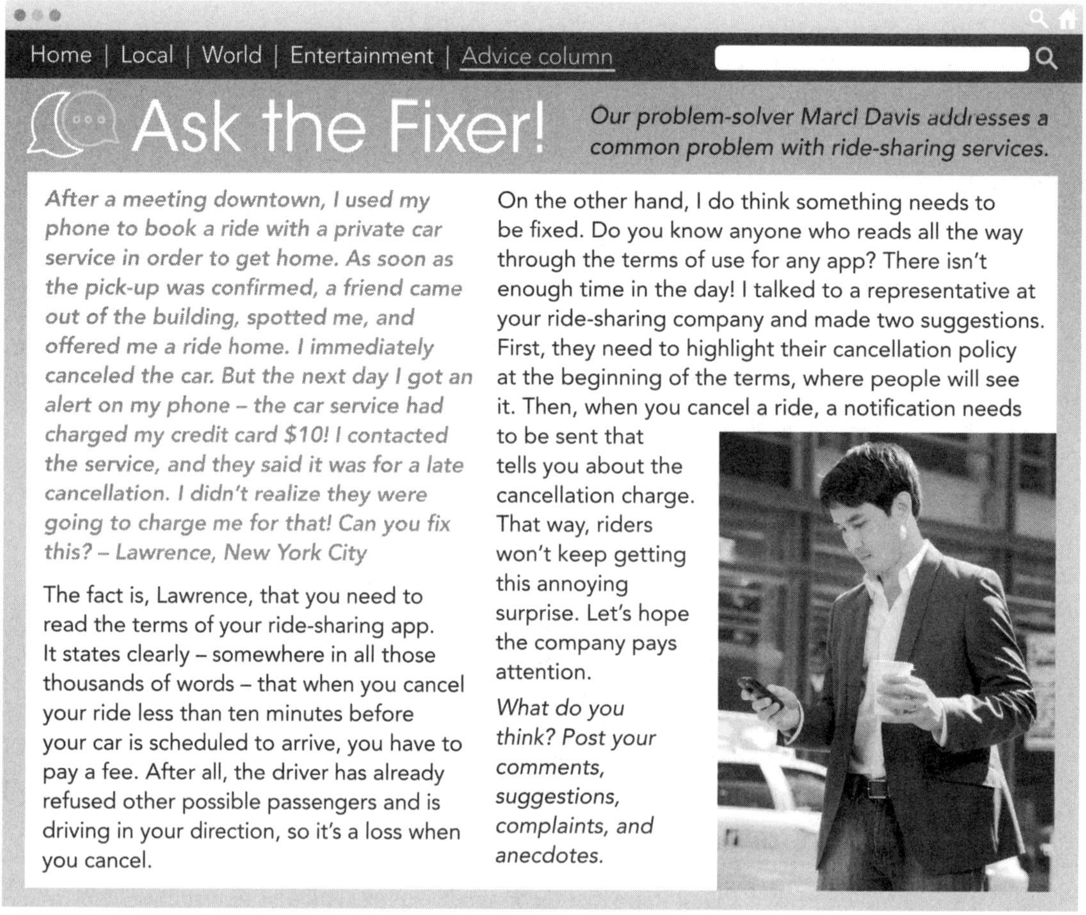

Home | Local | World | Entertainment | Advice column

Ask the Fixer!

Our problem-solver Marci Davis addresses a common problem with ride-sharing services.

After a meeting downtown, I used my phone to book a ride with a private car service in order to get home. As soon as the pick-up was confirmed, a friend came out of the building, spotted me, and offered me a ride home. I immediately canceled the car. But the next day I got an alert on my phone – the car service had charged my credit card $10! I contacted the service, and they said it was for a late cancellation. I didn't realize they were going to charge me for that! Can you fix this? – Lawrence, New York City

The fact is, Lawrence, that you need to read the terms of your ride-sharing app. It states clearly – somewhere in all those thousands of words – that when you cancel your ride less than ten minutes before your car is scheduled to arrive, you have to pay a fee. After all, the driver has already refused other possible passengers and is driving in your direction, so it's a loss when you cancel.

On the other hand, I do think something needs to be fixed. Do you know anyone who reads all the way through the terms of use for any app? There isn't enough time in the day! I talked to a representative at your ride-sharing company and made two suggestions. First, they need to highlight their cancellation policy at the beginning of the terms, where people will see it. Then, when you cancel a ride, a notification needs to be sent that tells you about the cancellation charge. That way, riders won't keep getting this annoying surprise. Let's hope the company pays attention.

What do you think? Post your comments, suggestions, complaints, and anecdotes.

Figure 3.3: Richards, J. C. et al. (2017) *Interchange 3* (5th ed.), p. 41.

Text summary to read aloud

A man in New York had a problem when he booked a ride with a private car company. He had to pay ten dollars that he didn't want to pay. He wrote to an online advice column because he wanted to know if the problem could be fixed. The answer he received talks about terms and conditions of the app the man used to book the car.

Additional notes

Advice columns often begin with a message that gives background information, explains the problem and requests help/advice, followed by a reply evaluating the problem and giving suggestions. Language is less formal and more typical of spoken language, e.g. in *Figure 3.3*, use of dashes and exclamation marks, and *spotted* rather than *saw*. The phrases in the reply *the fact is, after all* and *that way* suggest spoken language.

B While reading

3.4 What's different?

Level	A1–A2
Time	10 to 15 minutes
Outline	Before the lesson change some words in the text. Read the text aloud for students to follow and underline the words that have changed.
Aim	To encourage fluency in reading for lower level students; to give students practice reading at a faster rate.
Preparation	There is no preparation if you decide to use the suggested word changes in *Figure 3.4* below. These can be changed according to the needs of your students. If you use a different text, you will need to decide on word changes in that text.
Rationale	At low levels, some students will read a text very slowly, word-by-word. If they follow you as you read aloud, they need to keep their eyes moving along the line of the text. This activity introduces a task element to engage students a little more.

Procedure

1 In pairs, students predict the content of the text from the photos – elicit their ideas and write them on the board.
2 Read the text aloud. Students follow and check their predictions, then discuss in pairs. Ask them how many were correct.
3 Read the text aloud again and students listen for words that are different in your reading from what's written in the text and underline them.
4 Students check their answers in pairs.
5 Check answers to changed words. Read each sentence with the changed word aloud – students call out the correct answer.
6 Students read the text again silently to answer a more detailed comprehension task.

Notes

The example material below is aimed at younger learners, but this activity can work with lower level adults. The task element is a way of mitigating the idea that being read aloud to is for children. Adult students at higher levels may not enjoy being read aloud to for this reason, but it does depend on individual groups.

Learner reflection questions

1 Did listening and reading make you read faster or slower?
2 In your own time, you can practise this kind of reading with a reading book that has audio. How can this help make you a better reader?

Teacher reflection

What did this reveal about the reading speed of different students in your group? Note the suggestion in the second learner reflection question – how could you set this up as an on-going homework activity?

Erin and Tonk to the rescue

Erin Bolster and Tonk

Erin Bolster was a guide in Glacier Park in Montana, USA. In July 2011, she took a group of eight people on horses for a ride in the woods. Erin was on a big white horse called Tonk.

Everyone was ready to have fun, and the ride started well. Erin knew there were bears in the woods, but they didn't usually go near people.

Suddenly, an angry, 300 kilogram grizzly bear came out from the trees. It was very near to an eight-year-old boy who was on his horse. The boy's horse saw the bear and got very scared. It ran away with the boy on its back. The bear ran after them.

Tonk was scared, too. He didn't want to move. But Erin needed to help the boy. She didn't stop to think. She gave Tonk a kick and they went after the bear.

She found the bear near the boy and his horse. Then the boy fell off the horse and the bear started to go towards him! Erin put Tonk between the bear and the boy. Together they ran at the bear three times. The bear made a terrible noise – but then it went away. Erin picked the boy up and took him back to his father and the other riders.

The boy's father was very happy and Erin and Tonk were heroes!

Figure 3.4: Puchta, H., J. Stranks and P. Lewis-Jones (2015) *Think Starter*, p. 103.

Suggested word changes – one per paragraph

1 eight → eighteen
2 go → come
3 near → close
4 needed → had
5 ran → rode
6 father → mother

3.5 Step-by-step interactive read

Level A2 and above
Time 10 to 15 minutes
Outline In small groups, students progressively read a text and react to it as they read.
Aim To provide practice in reading longer texts for meaning and interest; to encourage co-operative reading strategies in students.
Preparation If you use *Figure 3.5a* below, there is no preparation for this activity. If you use a different text, you may want to slightly change the criteria for responding to the text.
Rationale When people read in their first language, and there is another person nearby, they often pause in their reading to comment on something they've read about. This activity formalises this scenario in a classroom setting. The criteria that students use to react are generic and suitable for a variety of text types[1]. The reading stages aren't timed, so each student is able to read at their own pace. The group discussion at each step means students share information, so slower, less competent readers get support from stronger students.

Procedure

1 Put students in small groups of three or four students and write the following criteria on the board:
 ✓ *I already know this.*
 × *I didn't know this*
 ✶ *This is interesting / surprising.*
 ⅄ *I don't like this idea.*
 ? *I'm not sure what this means.*
2 Students read for about a minute. As they read, they make notes next to the information in line with the board criteria.
3 Tell students to stop reading and for one student in each group to comment on something in the text using the board criteria for the group to discuss. Ensure that students take turns to comment.
4 Continue in this way until the reading is complete and then do feedback by asking the whole class for examples from the criteria on the board.
5 You could now get students to do a course book comprehension task, but if you feel the students have understood the text well, you could just move on to the next activity.

Notes and variation

This activity is suitable for longer texts that can be read in stages. You can change the criteria according to the kind of text, the information in it and the level of students. For example, at upper intermediate and advanced levels, you could include criteria that encourage students to infer meaning (e.g. *What is the writer really saying here?*). The amount of time you let students read for each stage can be flexible depending on the reading ability of your students.

Learner reflection questions

1 What did you learn about the text from other students when you stopped to talk about it?
2 How could you use this idea when you read outside the classroom?

[1] The use of such symbols and criteria are suggested by the activity 'Using symbols' from *Teaching and Developing Reading Skills* by Peter Watkins (Cambridge University Press, 2017).

Teacher reflection

What effect did this activity have on more and less competent readers in your class? If you do this activity again, would you think a bit more carefully about the composition of the groups? What other language skill do students get good practice of when doing this activity?

Exercising your brain

READING

1 What do you think is good for your brain? What's bad for your brain?

I think sleeping's good for the brain.

2 Read the article about exercising the brain. Were your ideas the same?

Keep your brain in top condition

Your brain needs exercise in the same way as your body does. But using your brain doesn't need to be hard work. Have a look at these ideas.

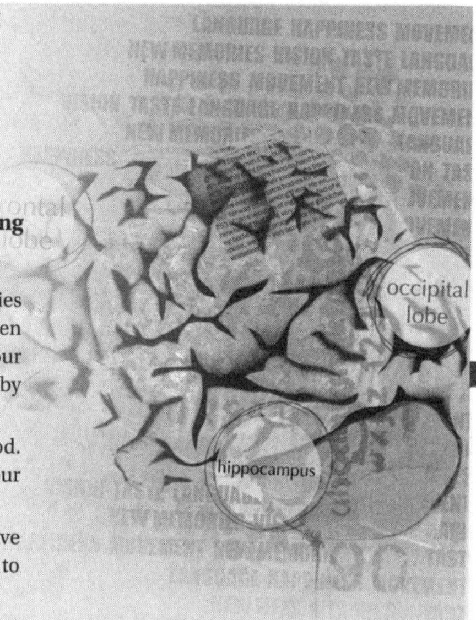

1 Try writing backwards, or writing with your other hand. This makes new connections in your brain and helps you to get new ideas. The great thinker and artist Leonardo da Vinci often used mirror-writing.

2 Start using new parts of your brain. Take up new hobbies, like tennis, chess or dancing the tango.

3 Sleep. If you don't get enough sleep, it's harder for the brain to do some activities, like producing language and new ideas.

4 Chew gum. This exercises the hippocampus, a part of the brain that's important for making new memories.

5 Ask your brain to do old activities in new ways. For example, when you're on a train or bus, close your eyes and guess where you are by listening.

6 Don't eat too much junk food. Cholesterol is bad for both your heart and your brain.

7 Think young! Experiments have shown that when people start to believe they're old, they act old.

8 Play memory games. This keeps your brain young. Games like remembering long lists of words can take ten to fourteen years off the mental age of older people.

9 Learn a new language. This is one of the most difficult things your brain can do, so it's great exercise. It's good for your brain's frontal lobes, which usually get smaller with age.

10 Eat lots of fish. The omega 3 oils in fish like salmon and tuna are good for the brain.

11 Get enough exercise. The right amount of exercise can give people 30% less chance of developing Alzheimer's.

12 Relax. Too much stress is bad for the brain. The hippocampus is about 14% smaller in people who are always stressed.

Figure 3.5a: Tilbury, A., T. Clementson et al. (2010) *English Unlimited A2*, p. 114.

The reading in *Figure 3.5b* could be staged one paragraph at a time.

UNIT 6

Superstitions? Who needs them!

Superstitions have been around for thousands of years. A lot of people never walk under ladders or they believe that black cats bring **good** (or bad) luck. Some people think one magpie is bad luck but two together is good luck. Other superstitions are more modern, like football players who don't change their socks or who always enter the pitch with their right foot.

Lots of people, however, believe strongly that superstitions are **silly**. They say that superstitions are based on **old** habits, customs or beliefs. How could you have bad luck by opening an umbrella inside? Why is the number thirteen more **dangerous** than other numbers?

To prove their point, they have 'Anti-Superstition Parties', usually on Friday the thirteenth, a date that many people think brings bad luck. At these parties, people break mirrors and dance with open umbrellas. And nothing bad happens!

Peter Moore, a dentist, has been to several anti-superstition parties. He says, 'People must be crazy to believe that the number seven is **lucky** or that they could be more **successful** by putting a horseshoe outside their house.' Chelsea Evans, a chef, agrees. 'I love the parties. I've broken lots of mirrors and my life is going well!'

FACT! *Fear of the number 13 is called Triskaidekaphobia and fear of Friday the Thirteenth is called Friggatriskaidekaphobia.*

Figure 3.5b: Goldstein, B. and C. Jones (2015) *Eyes Open 3*, p. 69.

3.6 Student-centred comprehension

Level	B1+ and above
Time	15 to 20 minutes
Outline	After reading a text, in pairs, students write questions about what they've read. Pairs exchange questions and answer them before having a group discussion.
Aim	To encourage students to read in more detail as well as analysing and evaluating information in texts.
Preparation	There is no preparation necessary for this activity.
Rationale	At higher levels, students should begin to develop the ability to read texts critically. This often means they need to infer (between-the-lines) meaning and formulate their opinions about it. Many course books include reading tasks that focus on the skill of inferring meaning, but may not focus on the critical evaluation that students feel is important. This activity gives control back to students and gets them to formulate their own questions.

Procedure

1 This activity can be done after either a gist or a more detailed reading of text.
2 Put students in pairs to write three to four questions about the text to give to another pair.
3 Give students criteria for the questions, for example:
- *some detailed information*
- *something that you think happened, but it's not completely clear*
- *the opinion of the writer*
- *something that is not clearly stated in the text, but is a relevant point*
- *an evaluation of an event / point of view*
- *a possible result of something that is talked about in the text*

4 Explain that questions need to be about specific information in the text. For example, for *Figure 3.6*: *What's your opinion of Intangible Cultural Heritage?* is too general; *Why does the writer have some doubts about Intangible Cultural Heritage?* is more specific.
5 Students write questions together in pairs and then exchange with another pair.
6 Each pair answers the questions, then discuss their answers as a group of four.
7 Do open class feedback and ask each group for an interesting point about the text.

Notes

The first time you do this activity, it may pay to limit the questions to two or three. Actively monitor and help students where necessary. This activity is particularly useful if your students are studying for some kind of exam that has a reading paper or if they are or are about to study academic English.

Learner reflection questions

1 What kind of reading do you need to do to write the questions?
2 What do you understand by the term 'read between-the-lines'? When do you need to do this?

Teacher reflection

Did students focus on meaning in the text you hadn't noticed? Were their questions specific enough? Does it matter if some students infer too much? Why / Why not?

Protecting our intangible[1] cultural heritage[2]

by Linda Barker

1 In today's ever-changing global landscape, most of us recognize the importance of preserving our own unique cultural heritage. But what do we save? A magnificent building which is under threat? A historical part of a city? An important work of art? All of these are significant, but what about our songs, stories, **ceremonies** and traditional practices? These intangible aspects of our culture can be just as meaningful as anything we build or create. Shouldn't they also be **preserved** for future generations to experience and enjoy?

2 The answer, according to UNESCO (United Nations Educational, Scientific and Cultural Organization), is yes. That is why in 2008 it published its first Intangible Cultural Heritage (ICH) list. You may already know of UNESCO's famous list of World Heritage Sites, consisting of places selected for special **protection** because of their value to the world, such as the Pyramids of Giza in Egypt or the Great Barrier Reef in Australia. However, the ICH list is different. Its purpose is to record *living* customs and **traditions** which are **endangered** by globalization. These include languages and spoken traditions (such as storytelling and poetry), performing arts, traditional crafts and local knowledge and **beliefs**.

3 Today, there are more than 400 customs and traditions on the ICH list. Two recent entries show us just how rich and varied are the practices selected for protection. The culture of the Jeju Haenyeo, the women divers of Jeju Island in South Korea, was added to the list in 2016. These amazing women dive 10 m under the sea to get food – without the use of breathing equipment. They do this for up to seven hours a day, 90 days of the year, holding their breath for about one minute every dive. Knowledge about diving practices is passed down from **generation** to generation within families. Yet today, most of the divers are in their 60s, 70s or 80s. As they have become older, younger women have not stepped in to take their place, meaning the practice is in danger of disappearing.

4 Another cultural practice added to the ICH list in the same year is falconry. This is the ancient custom of hunting with trained birds of prey, such as falcons and hawks. Regarded as both an art form and a sport, it requires years of training and discipline. Falconry is practised around the world from France to Mongolia to the United Arab Emirates, which is home to the world's first falcon hospital and each year hosts a falcon 'beauty contest'. Sadly, falconry is now threatened by the growth of cities and the loss of natural habitats. There are fears that the practice may disappear unless efforts to preserve it are successful.

5 Both Jeju Haenyeo and falconry illustrate the tremendous range of cultural practices which the ICH list was created to preserve. And yet, while most of us would agree that UNESCO's efforts are valuable, I find myself questioning the fairness and usefulness of the ICH list. Why are some customs and practices included while others are not? Who decides this? Does inclusion on the list make a difference in the long term? In this age of rapid globalization, when fewer young people are interested in learning about the customs of their ancestors, it may already be too late to preserve much of our diverse and precious cultural heritage. But for the benefit of future generations, I believe we must never stop trying.

[1]**intangible** (adj) something which exists although you cannot touch it

[2]**heritage** (n) traditions, languages or buildings belonging to the culture of a particular society which were created in the past and still have importance

Figure 3.6: Westbrook, C., L. Baker et al. (2019) *Unlock Reading, Writing & Critical Thinking 3*, p. 90.

C After reading

3.7 Recall the text

Level A2 and above
Time 5 to 10 minutes
Outline After completing the reading and comprehension tasks, students recall information around some key sentences without looking back at the text.
Aim To check that students have a good understanding of the text as a whole; to provide speaking fluency practice.
Preparation If you use *Figure 3.7* below, you will need to make one copy of cut up sentences for each pair/group. If you use a different text, you will need to choose the sentences you will use and then copy and cut them up.
Rationale Often post-reading speaking tasks focus on students' personalisation of the text. Sometimes the topic of a text may not be appropriate for your students to personalise or it may not generate many ideas for them. Getting students to recall information in the text is an alternative way of providing spoken fluency practice. It can encourage students to focus on the way pronouns are used in texts, as in the example sentences below where students need to explain what *it* and *this illness* refer to.

Procedure

1 Students close their course books after the final reading activity.
2 Put students in pairs or groups of three and hand out the sentences face down.
3 Students take turns to turn over a sentence, read it and then together try to remember all the information in the text that relates to this sentence. They can also say if they agree or disagree with the information or if they can relate it to other things they know.
4 Students do the same for each sentence, working at their own pace.
5 Do feedback and ask students what they think were the most important ideas in the text.
6 If you feel their recall of the text wasn't good, you could ask them to read it again.

Notes and variation

Students are often quite motivated to read the text again after this activity. Inevitably, there is some information they are unable to recall and the desire to refresh their memories gives them a good reason to read. At higher levels, you might give students only words or phrases. If you have an English for Academic Purposes class, you could provide students with the topic sentences of each paragraph of an essay as the basis for their recall. You can also revisit texts in later lessons. Ask students to recall and summarise the text and try to recall key new vocabulary.

Learner reflection questions

1 What information in the text was difficult to remember? Why do you think this was so?
2 When you try to remember and explain a text in this way, what skill do you practise? If you study English with another student outside class, how can you use this idea?

Teacher reflection

How does this activity help students with new language items they might have found in the text? In pairs/groups, was there one student who remembered more and dominated? What can you do to make sure all students contribute?

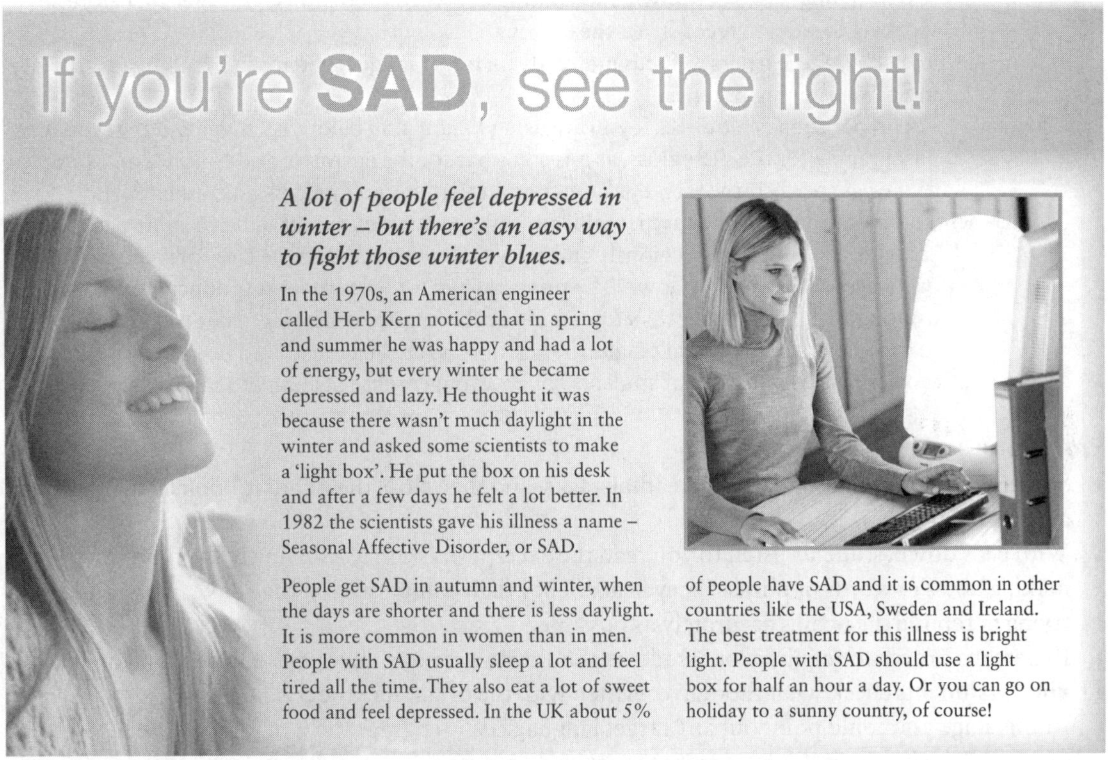

If you're **SAD**, see the light!

A lot of people feel depressed in winter – but there's an easy way to fight those winter blues.

In the 1970s, an American engineer called Herb Kern noticed that in spring and summer he was happy and had a lot of energy, but every winter he became depressed and lazy. He thought it was because there wasn't much daylight in the winter and asked some scientists to make a 'light box'. He put the box on his desk and after a few days he felt a lot better. In 1982 the scientists gave his illness a name – Seasonal Affective Disorder, or SAD.

People get SAD in autumn and winter, when the days are shorter and there is less daylight. It is more common in women than in men. People with SAD usually sleep a lot and feel tired all the time. They also eat a lot of sweet food and feel depressed. In the UK about 5% of people have SAD and it is common in other countries like the USA, Sweden and Ireland. The best treatment for this illness is bright light. People with SAD should use a light box for half an hour a day. Or you can go on holiday to a sunny country, of course!

Figure 3.7: Redston, C. and G. Cunningham (2012) *face2face Elementary* (2nd ed.), p. 86.

Sentences to talk about

He put the box on his desk and after a few days he felt a lot better.

It is more common in women than in men.

The best treatment for this illness is bright light.

3.8 Dictogloss excerpt

Level B1 and above

Time 10 to 15 minutes

Outline After reading a text for comprehension, students do a dictogloss of an excerpt from the text, listening with pens down, then noting key words and phrases they recall, before working in pairs to reconstruct the excerpt.

Aim To encourage learners to focus indirectly on target language items in a reading text; to give intensive listening practice.

Preparation No preparation is required. If you are using *Figure 3.8a* below, it's suggested that you read paragraph 4 for the dictogloss, as it is a key part of the narrative and contains an example of the past perfect (the target grammar point that this text provides a context for).

Rationale Traditional dictogloss activities typically involve a complete text (albeit a short one) that students have not read previously and are asked to re-create on the basis of some key words or phrases that they note down. The principal aim is to get students producing language using a range of grammar structures and vocabulary items. The fact that students have read the text already doesn't make the activity less challenging than a normal dictogloss. However, it does mean that students have a stronger sense of context for the excerpt.

Procedure

1 Students complete the course book reading tasks, and then close their course books. Students need a piece of paper.

2 With pens down, students listen to you read the excerpt. As soon as you finish, they can start making notes of words or phrases they heard. They then compare what they have in pairs and start trying to rebuild the text as accurately as possible.

3 Repeat the process if required, but students should always have their pens down when you read.

4 Finally, students check what they have written with the original in the course book.

5 At this stage you could point out any target language. With paragraph 4 of *Figure 3.8a* below you can ask: *Which tense is different from the others?* This would then move on to checking meaning and form of the past perfect.

Notes

This post-reading activity is a useful diagnostic tool for new language. If, in your monitoring, you can see that all students heard and wrote down the past perfect, this would suggest that your subsequent focus on it could be brief. You may just be able to check the meaning quickly and then move on. At higher levels, there is little you need to change in terms of the methodology. The texts that students read will have more complex language so this increases the level of challenge.

Learner reflection questions

1 What did you use more to try and write the text you listened to – your memory or thinking about grammar and vocabulary you could use?

2 What were the differences between the text you wrote and the text in the course book? Does this give you an idea of something you need to study more outside of class?

Teacher reflection

What is the benefit of using this approach to getting students to identify new language in a text? Did students' writing show up other language needs you weren't expecting?

The reading task in *Figure 3.8a* asks students to read the paragraphs in the correct order. Students predict what happens next after each one.

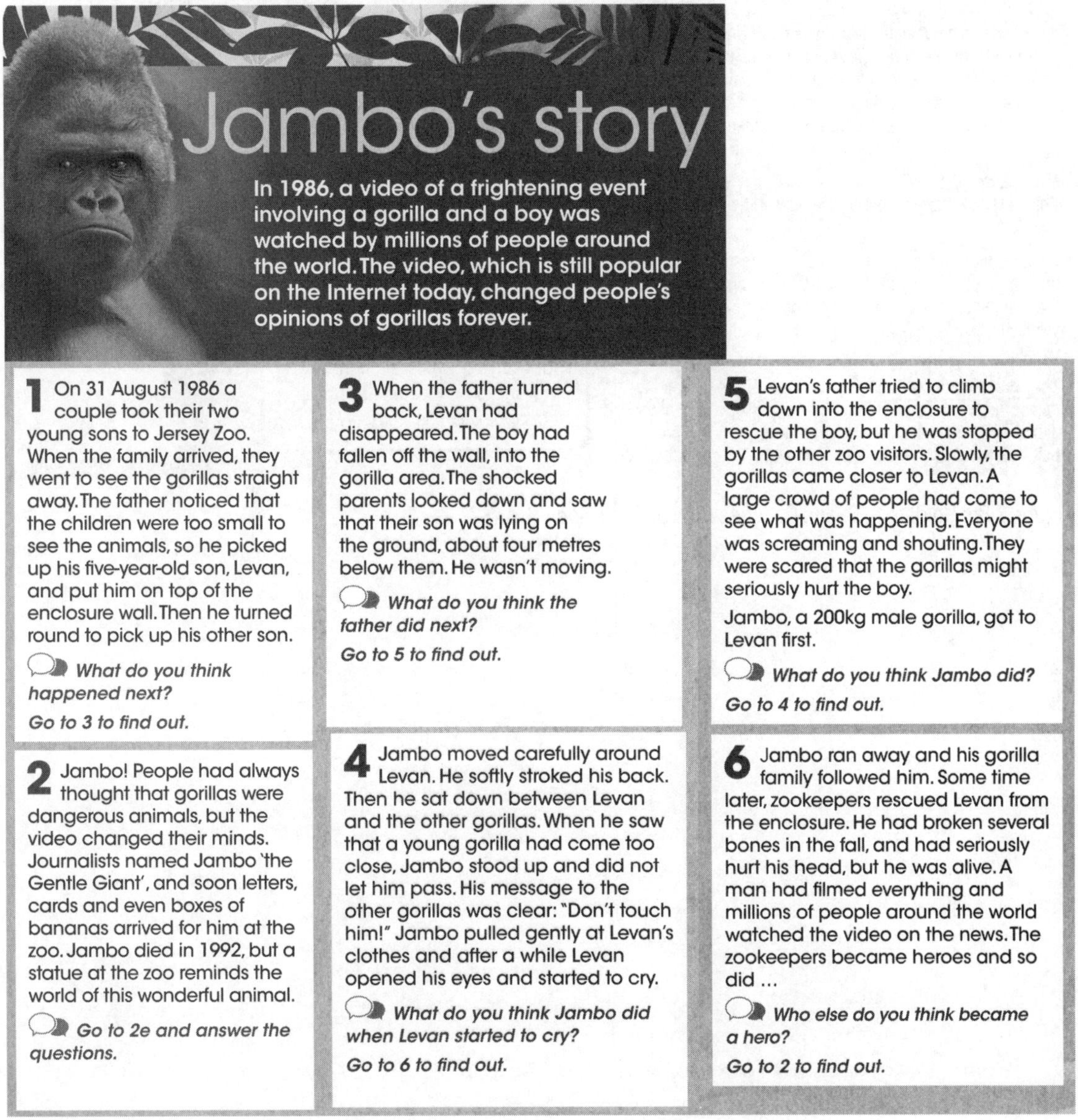

Jambo's story

In 1986, a video of a frightening event involving a gorilla and a boy was watched by millions of people around the world. The video, which is still popular on the Internet today, changed people's opinions of gorillas forever.

1 On 31 August 1986 a couple took their two young sons to Jersey Zoo. When the family arrived, they went to see the gorillas straight away. The father noticed that the children were too small to see the animals, so he picked up his five-year-old son, Levan, and put him on top of the enclosure wall. Then he turned round to pick up his other son.

What do you think happened next?

Go to 3 to find out.

2 Jambo! People had always thought that gorillas were dangerous animals, but the video changed their minds. Journalists named Jambo 'the Gentle Giant', and soon letters, cards and even boxes of bananas arrived for him at the zoo. Jambo died in 1992, but a statue at the zoo reminds the world of this wonderful animal.

Go to 2e and answer the questions.

3 When the father turned back, Levan had disappeared. The boy had fallen off the wall, into the gorilla area. The shocked parents looked down and saw that their son was lying on the ground, about four metres below them. He wasn't moving.

What do you think the father did next?

Go to 5 to find out.

4 Jambo moved carefully around Levan. He softly stroked his back. Then he sat down between Levan and the other gorillas. When he saw that a young gorilla had come too close, Jambo stood up and did not let him pass. His message to the other gorillas was clear: "Don't touch him!" Jambo pulled gently at Levan's clothes and after a while Levan opened his eyes and started to cry.

What do you think Jambo did when Levan started to cry?

Go to 6 to find out.

5 Levan's father tried to climb down into the enclosure to rescue the boy, but he was stopped by the other zoo visitors. Slowly, the gorillas came closer to Levan. A large crowd of people had come to see what was happening. Everyone was screaming and shouting. They were scared that the gorillas might seriously hurt the boy.

Jambo, a 200kg male gorilla, got to Levan first.

What do you think Jambo did?

Go to 4 to find out.

6 Jambo ran away and his gorilla family followed him. Some time later, zookeepers rescued Levan from the enclosure. He had broken several bones in the fall, and had seriously hurt his head, but he was alive. A man had filmed everything and millions of people around the world watched the video on the news. The zookeepers became heroes and so did ...

Who else do you think became a hero?

Go to 2 to find out.

Figure 3.8a: Doff, A., C. Thaine et al. (2015) *Cambridge English Empower B1*, p. 118.

The main reading task in *Figure 3.8b* is matching headings to paragraphs. This text contextualises multi-word verbs. Paragraph 4 would work well as a dictogloss activity.

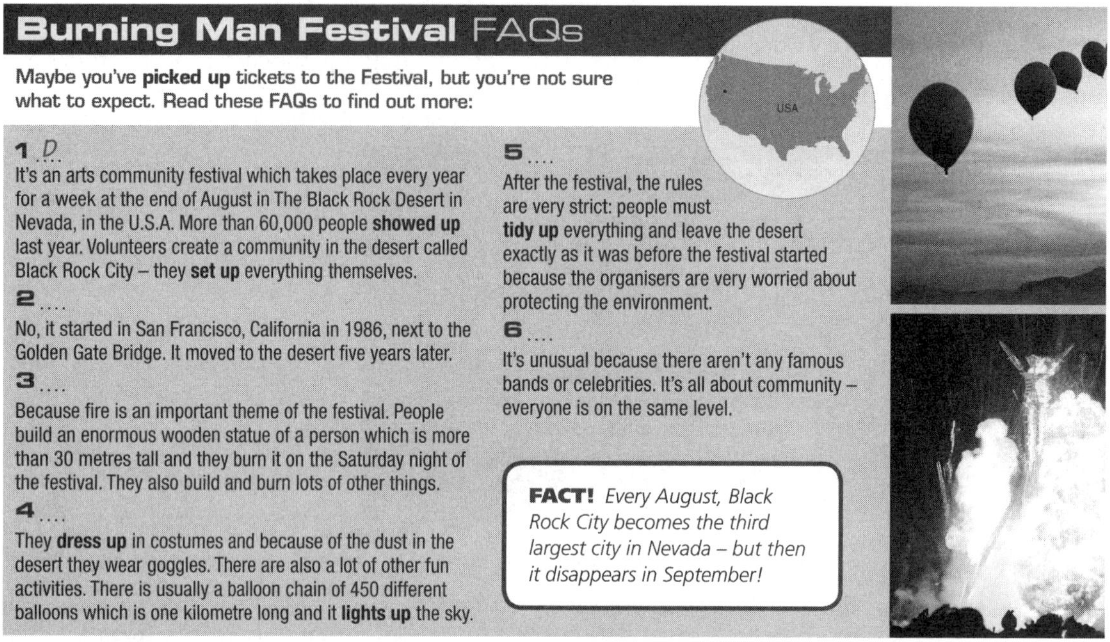

Burning Man Festival FAQs

Maybe you've **picked up** tickets to the Festival, but you're not sure what to expect. Read these FAQs to find out more:

1 D

It's an arts community festival which takes place every year for a week at the end of August in The Black Rock Desert in Nevada, in the U.S.A. More than 60,000 people **showed up** last year. Volunteers create a community in the desert called Black Rock City – they **set up** everything themselves.

2 ....

No, it started in San Francisco, California in 1986, next to the Golden Gate Bridge. It moved to the desert five years later.

3 ....

Because fire is an important theme of the festival. People build an enormous wooden statue of a person which is more than 30 metres tall and they burn it on the Saturday night of the festival. They also build and burn lots of other things.

4 ....

They **dress up** in costumes and because of the dust in the desert they wear goggles. There are also a lot of other fun activities. There is usually a balloon chain of 450 different balloons which is one kilometre long and it **lights up** the sky.

5 ....

After the festival, the rules are very strict: people must **tidy up** everything and leave the desert exactly as it was before the festival started because the organisers are very worried about protecting the environment.

6 ....

It's unusual because there aren't any famous bands or celebrities. It's all about community – everyone is on the same level.

FACT! *Every August, Black Rock City becomes the third largest city in Nevada – but then it disappears in September!*

Figure 3.8b: Goldstein, B. and C. Jones (2015) *Eyes Open 3*, p. 37.

3.9 Homework reading extension

Level	A2 and above
Time	5 to 10 minutes
Outline	For a homework extension task, students read a text online on a topic related to the text they read in class. They then complete a form to record what they read and any new vocabulary.
Aim	To provide practice in extensive reading; to encourage students to read outside the classroom; to help increase students' vocabulary knowledge.
Preparation	Make a copy of the reading task form below. If you don't use *Figure 3.9a* below, you will need to think of useful internet search terms (see *Procedure*) for the text students have read.
Rationale	Reading is the one language skill that is easily practised outside the classroom. The internet is a valuable source of reading texts and is likely to be the place that learners do a lot of reading in their first language. This activity means that you aren't reliant on your institution having a set of simplified reading books (graded readers). While some of the texts students encounter might be difficult, they are likely to find something that balances their interest with their level of competence.

Procedure

1 After students have completed the reading comprehension tasks in the course book, explain that you want them to find and read a text on a similar topic online for homework.
2 Hand out the form for students to complete and suggest search terms. For *Figure 3.9a* they could be: *new foods, healthy foods, vegetarian/vegan foods, easy to produce foods*. Make it clear that the text doesn't need to be very long.
3 Explain that in the next lesson students are going to feed back to each other (in pairs/groups) on their reading and share vocabulary.
4 In the next class, each group discusses what they have read and comes up with a list of five or six useful words resulting from their combined lists to write on the board and share with the class.

Notes and variation

Providing the form to complete gives students more of a sense of focus. When students feed back to each other, it pays to monitor and help students articulate the way in which they read their text. An alternative is for students to bring a copy of their text to class to exchange in pairs and gist read.

Learner reflection questions

1 Do you read all texts in exactly the same way? Why / Why not?
2 How does reading a lot help improve your English?

Teacher reflection

What connections can you make for students between the kind of text they read and the way they read it? To what degree do you think you need to take responsibility for students' reading practice and to what extent do you think students themselves need to take responsibility? How can you negotiate this with your students?

1 READING

A **PREDICT** **Look at the picture in the article. Why do you think this is called the Impossible Burger?**

B **Read the article. Were you right? Read the article again and write the headings in the correct places.**

1 In a restaurant near you

2 Meat from plants

3 Good for the future

4 The secret ingredient

C PAIR WORK **THINK CRITICALLY** **Read the article again. Are Impossible Burgers the best thing to happen to food in years? Discuss the positives and negatives of green food with your partner.**

The new and wonderful world of Impossible Foods

A ______________________

Impossible Foods is a company in Silicon Valley, California. They make burgers and other delicious meat and dairy products. There's something very unusual about their food: Their meat and dairy don't come from animals, but from plants. Yes, plants! I didn't believe it at first, but it's true. Thanks to Impossible Foods, you can eat a delicious burger that looks like meat and tastes like meat but is made with only plants.

B ______________________

How does the Impossible Burger look and taste so real? The secret is something called heme. It's an ingredient that exists in both plants and animals. Heme gives raw beef its red color and meat flavor. Impossible Foods uses the heme found in plants, not animals, to make the Impossible Burger. It's healthy, and the plant ingredients don't hurt the environment. Clever, isn't it?

C ______________________

So, why is Impossible Foods doing this? Well, animal farming uses about 50% of the Earth's land and 25% of the Earth's water. That's a very expensive way to produce food. So, it seems to me that the Impossible Burger is a great example of a food of the future – good for the planet and good for your health. Soon it'll be cheap to eat, too!

D ______________________

Maybe you think all of this is science fiction, but it's not. Twenty restaurants in the U.S. now sell the Impossible Burger. Soon these delicious burgers will be everywhere. In my opinion, it's the best thing to happen to food in years!

GLOSSARY

dairy (*adj*) milk products, or food made from milk

Figure 3.9a: Clandfield, L., B. Goldstein et al. (2019) *Evolve 2*, p. 72.

Homework form

Reading Homework Record

Kind of text (for example, article, email, social media posting, ad):

Topic of text:

Way(s) you read the text (for example: quickly to understand the most important ideas; slowly to understand details):

New vocabulary:

Easy / OK / Difficult – why?

Interest / enjoy?

Internet search terms for the text in *Figure 3.9b* (page 100) could relate to Naples, Pompeii and Mt Vesuvius, mosaics or, more generally, archaeology. This material is aimed at young learners and any extension could incorporate a CLIL (Content and Language Integrated Learning) dimension.

READING

1 Read Jenny's holiday blog and complete the sentences with a word or a number.

DAY 5

Dad gets it right! (finally)

Day five of the Italian adventure and we're in Naples. We arrived here early yesterday morning, but as usual we were only at the hotel for about five minutes before Dad wanted to take us somewhere. This time it was to the ancient city of Pompeii near Naples. I didn't really want to go. I wanted to go shopping for shoes.

We travelled there by train. The journey didn't take long – but long enough for Dad to tell us a bit about the history. Many years ago, Pompeii was a large Italian city near a volcano called Mount Vesuvius – then on 24 August 79 CE – the volcano erupted and completely covered the city in ash. It killed about 20,000 people. But the ash didn't destroy the buildings and now, 2,000 years later, you can walk around the city and see how people lived all those years ago.

2,000-year-old houses: thanks, Dad – really boring, I thought, but I was wrong! The houses were very interesting. Most of them were really big with lots of rooms (so lots of space to get away from annoying brothers and sisters!) There were paintings and mosaics all over the walls. I'd love a Roman mosaic of One Direction on my bedroom wall. Also, I was amazed at the bathrooms. I'd love a big bathroom in our house – ours is so small!

I got really interested in Pompeii. I wasn't bored at all. In fact, I've got lots of ideas for our house when we get home!

Mount Vesuvius – a real [1]__________ . (I hope it doesn't erupt!)

More than [2]__________ people died here, all of them covered in ash.

The paintings and [3]__________ are really beautiful.

The houses in this ancient city are more than [4]__________ years old.

2 Answer the questions.

1. Where is Jenny's family staying at the moment?
2. How did they go to Pompeii?
3. What did Jenny's dad tell them about on the way there?
4. When did Vesuvius erupt?
5. What did Jenny like about the Pompeii houses?
6. What was Jenny's overall opinion of Pompeii?

Figure 3.9b: Puchta, H., J. Stranks and P. Lewis-Jones (2015) *Think Level 1*, p. 52.

You can find teacher development activities about reading on pages 261 to 264.

4 Writing

Introduction

Writing skills

Before looking at how writing skills are dealt with in course books, it is important to determine the ways in which course books represent writing skills. One way is associated with the 'process writing' approach. When someone writes a text in their first language, they might follow some, if not all, of the following steps. They will think about what they want to include in the text, they might then consider how these ideas can be organised in a logical sequence. At this point, they are probably ready to write a first draft, which they could then revise and polish. They may ask another person to read what they have written to get feedback on the content or to check the language. The extent to which a writer follows these steps will obviously depend on the text and its importance. Someone writing an academic paper is more likely to follow all of these steps very carefully while someone writing a tweet may not bother with any of them. Typically, labels for the different steps are: brainstorming, planning, drafting, revising, editing, polishing and seeking feedback. We call these 'process writing skills', and this is *often* what is being referred to when you see the term 'writing skills' in course books.

Conversely, when some course books talk about 'writing skills' they are referring to language features of writing such as: spelling, punctuation, paragraphing, sentence co-ordination, reason or result linkers, narrative tenses, subordination, essay structure etc. This way of representing writing skills always involves a focus on some aspect of language found in written texts.

Writers deploy three language systems when writing:

- Vocabulary is important in terms of correct spelling and the lexical choices that writers make.
- Grammar is central in conveying ideas clearly in writing. It also allows writers to express themselves with a degree of complexity.
- Discourse is a core element of writing given the extended nature of much written text. This might include a focus on, for example, genre features or paragraphing. Cohesion, another feature of written discourse, includes the use of linking words and phrases to make a text clear to a reader. (See Chapter 8 for more discussion and examples of discourse and writing.)

Clearly, the fourth language system, pronunciation, is not used in writing. Writing skills that focus on vocabulary, grammar and discourse can be labelled as 'language-focused writing skills' and this is what some course books mean when they indicate 'writing skills'. Both process and language-focused writing skills are included in this chapter.

Writing activities in course books

Before focusing on examples of specific writing exercises, it is worth acknowledging that students often do a lot of incidental writing when they use a course book. This may be associated with written language practice, particularly of vocabulary and grammar, for example, filling in gap fills or transforming the grammar of sentences, but it can also involve activities such as notetaking or writing answers to reading comprehension tasks. In this chapter, we focus on writing that aims to develop students' ability to write texts even if sometimes these texts can be very short, for example, a text message.

Some writing exercises in course books ask students to write a text without reading and analysing a model. In *Figure 4.0a*, for example, students write a summary of the text they have read without doing any kind of analysis of summary writing or reading a model text summary. Activities such as these are useful because, as is the case with speaking, it is sometimes helpful for students to practise written fluency. Furthermore, a freer activity of this nature can act as a diagnosis of students' strengths and needs in terms of written language.

> **WRITING**
>
> **Use your answers in Exercise 2 to write a summary of the text in no more than 100 words.**
>
> *Jenny didn't want to go to Pompeii and ...*

Figure 4.0a: Puchta, H., J. Stranks and P. Lewis-Jones (2015) *Think Level 1*, p. 52.

Alternatively, course books might adopt a simple input → output approach to writing skills. For example, as in *Figure 4.0b*:

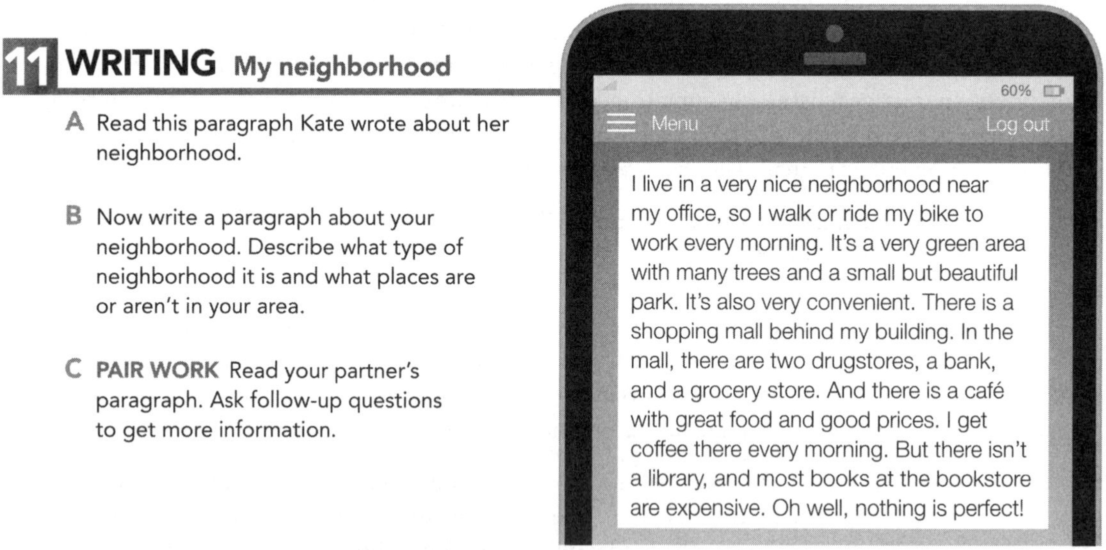
11 WRITING My neighborhood
A Read this paragraph Kate wrote about her neighborhood.
B Now write a paragraph about your neighborhood. Describe what type of neighborhood it is and what places are or aren't in your area.
C PAIR WORK Read your partner's paragraph. Ask follow-up questions to get more information.
60%
Menu
Log out
I live in a very nice neighborhood near my office, so I walk or ride my bike to work every morning. It's a very green area with many trees and a small but beautiful park. It's also very convenient. There is a shopping mall behind my building. In the mall, there are two drugstores, a bank, and a grocery store. And there is a café with great food and good prices. I get coffee there every morning. But there isn't a library, and most books at the bookstore are expensive. Oh well, nothing is perfect!

Figure 4.0b: Richards, J. C. et al. (2017) *Interchange 1* (5th ed.), p. 54.

In this exercise, students are given a model text and then prompted to write a similar one by personalising the information in the text. In both these examples, process and language-focused writing skills are not focused on in any explicit way during the process of writing.

Figure 4.0c is an example of a more structured input → output approach that does incorporate both approaches to writing skills.

2 READING

a Read the posts on the *Things I hate* discussion board. Tick (✓) who sometimes get annoyed by people who use their phones.

☐ Genji ☐ MadMax ☐ Lars2
☐ Meepe ☐ AdamB ☐ Rainbows

b Read the posts again. Who thinks these things?

[1]People who send texts often have nothing to say.
[2]It can be good fun to send texts to friends.
[3]People shouldn't send texts when they're eating with other people.
[4]It's rude not to look at someone when they're talking to you.
[5]I don't like people who go online in the middle of a conversation.

c Underline all the adjectives in the posts. Which five are negative?

d Look at the posts again and find:

1 three ways to agree
2 one way to disagree.

Things I hate

Genji
I hate it when people look at their phone when they're talking to you. It's quite clear that if you're talking to somebody, they should look at you, not at their phone. It's the worst thing you can do if you're with someone. I've got a friend who does that.

Meepe
Yes, I agree. I've also got a friend who's like that. You're talking to him and he starts surfing the Internet on his phone! It's so annoying.

MadMax
Yes, you're right, it's really rude. People go online in the middle of a conversation, and some people also send texts while you're talking to them. I hate that.

AdamB
Yes, my sister does that too. We're having dinner and she starts sending texts to all her friends. It's awful.

Lars2
Yes, I feel the same way. And texting is so boring as well. People say the most boring things when they text – they never say anything important. It's like 'I'm on the bus. What are you doing?' or 'I'm at home'.

Rainbows
I don't agree. It can be useful if you want to meet a friend. Also, my friends send really funny texts, so we have a good laugh.

3 WRITING SKILLS

Linking ideas with *also*, *too*, and *as well*

a Look at the sentences and answer the question.

MADMAX Some people also send texts while you're talking to them.
MEEPE I've also got a friend who's like that.
RAINBOWS It can be useful if you want to meet a friend. Also, my friends send really funny texts.

Where does the word *also* come in each sentence? Underline the correct answer.

1 *before / after* a main verb (*get, send, live* …)
2 *before / after* an auxiliary verb (*be, have, can* …)
3 at the *beginning / end* of a new sentence.

b Look at the sentences below and underline words or phrases that mean the same as *also*. Then answer the question.

1 **ADAMB** Yes, my sister does that too.
2 **LARS2** Yes, I feel the same way. And texting is so boring as well.

Where do they come in the sentence: at the beginning, in the middle or at the end?

c Add *also*, *too* or *as well* to these sentences.

1 I've got a new PC and I've got a new laptop.
2 We had a satnav in the car and we took a street map.
3 She works for a mobile phone company and she knows a lot about computers.
4 Tablets are very light to carry. They have a large screen so they are easy to read.

4 WRITING AND SPEAKING

a Plan a post about something that annoys you. Use these ideas or your own. Make notes.

- another form of technology (not phones)
- people's bad habits
- an activity you hate doing.

b Write your post. Use the ones on the discussion board to help you. Give your post to another student.

c Agree or disagree with another student's post, and try to add a sentence with *also*, *too* or *as well*. Then pass your post to the next student.

d Check the linking words in other students' posts. Did they use *also*, *too* and *as well* correctly?

e Compare posts. Which do you think is the most interesting? Why?

Figure 4.0c: Doff, A., C. Thaine et al. (2015) *Cambridge English Empower A2*, p. 107.

The broad outline of this sequence of activities is as follows:

reading of an example text → language-focused writing skill analysis → practice of writing skill → writing of text

Exercises 2a and b focus on reading and understanding the information in the model text – 2a practises gist reading skills and 2b practises reading for more detail. Although not labelled as such, exercises 2c and d analyse language-focused writing skills, firstly looking at useful vocabulary for this kind of blog post, and then focusing on language of agreement used to respond to the posts of other writers.

Exercise 3 is more clearly signalled as analysis and practice of a language-focused writing skill, that of linkers of addition. Both exercises 3a and b involve analysis with a focus on word order while exercise 3c provides controlled written practice of the linkers. Exercise 4 moves on to the productive part of the process, getting students to write their own blog post. The context of writing aims to replicate that of writing a real blog post, so students write their post, pass it to another student, who then writes a reply. This provides students with a sense of audience for their writing (see the teacher development activity on writing in Chapter 9, p. 267 for more on this). Embedded in the instructions for exercise 4a and d are elements of process writing skills. In 4a, students are encouraged to make notes and plan their post, and in 4d they get feedback on their language use in the post. Overall, the example above shows how language-focused writing skills and process writing skills work in tandem and complement each other in order to help students produce a communicative piece of writing.

Genres and information technology

An important part of developing students' language-focused writing skills is increasing their awareness of how different genres are organised in English. Typical genres that are found in course books are: personal profiles, job application emails, restaurant or film reviews, reports, blog posts, social media posts, essays. There are sometimes differences in terms of how we structure these genres in English when compared to other languages, for example, some language cultures find the typical for-and-against essay overly schematic and lacking depth. Genres are seen as being socially constructed, in other words, they have developed or evolved in line with their social purposes and the expectations of readers.

It is interesting to note the degree to which course books now focus on genres associated with information technology (IT). While it could be argued that some of these genres, for example tweets, are similar to spoken language, they do have their own conventions. As such, in order to write an effective tweet, students need to observe the word limit. This means they need to understand what language they can leave out of a tweet so that it conveys a message clearly and succinctly.

While some people worry that the advent of IT has resulted in an impoverishment of writing skills, it can be argued that we are, in fact, writing far more using IT tools than people did 30 years ago. IT also offers more opportunities for students to find a real audience for their writing in English. While, 30 years ago, a student's teacher or an examiner were the most likely readers of student writing, nowadays, students can publish online for all the world to see. This opportunity to reach a real and far-reaching audience is potentially very motivating. Of course, once something is published online it is often there to stay and means students need to develop an ability to craft their written message as effectively as they can.

A Before writing

4.1 Pin an idea

Level	A2 and above
Time	5 to 10 minutes
Outline	Prior to the writing task, in pairs, students contribute ideas in a class brainstorm on the topic.
Aim	To provide students with a wide range of ideas prior to writing.
Preparation	Each pair or small group of students will need a piece of blank paper they can write their idea on. You will also need sticky tack to stick these ideas on the board.
Rationale	It is quite common to get students to brainstorm the content of a piece of writing in pairs before they write. This activity, however, aims to broaden the range of ideas by including the whole class. While it might be more straightforward to get students to write their ideas on the board, that can have a negative impact, leading some students to discard ideas because they think they're too similar. Having the pieces of paper ensures students don't self-censor and all ideas are represented. It doesn't matter if some ideas are similar.

Procedure

1. Students read example texts and/or do any analysis – exercise A in *Figure 4.1a* below.
2. Put students in pairs or groups of three and give each a piece of paper. Then write the following rubric on the board:

   I think that a good way of ... is ... because ...
3. Ask each pair/group to complete the rubric with one idea that could be included in the text they are going to write – a suggestion for a relaxing life to be included in a blog post if you're using *Figure 4.1a* below.
4. When everyone has finished, students come to the board and stick up the piece of paper with their idea. (They can read aloud any that are difficult to see from a distance.)
5. Establish which ideas are similar and group them together on the board.
6. Students write their blog post using the ideas from the board.
7. If you want to set the writing as homework, students can take a photo of the board with their phones (or you could take a photo and email the image to them).

Notes and variation

With different genres, different rubrics will need to be given, for example, for a discursive essay, *I think one of the benefits of ... is ... On the other hand, a drawback is ...* might be more appropriate. A variation of this is to ask students to do some research as homework and contribute two ideas on a piece of paper in the next class. At higher levels with more complex texts, some pairs/groups can brainstorm part of the text and others a different part. For example, if students are writing a for or against essay, half the class can brainstorm arguments for and the other half arguments against.

Learner reflection questions

1. Was it easier to write the blog post after seeing different ideas? Why / Why not?
2. Is it better to just start writing or is it better to think and make notes first? Why?

Teacher reflection

How quickly did students get on with writing after the brainstorming? How well did students identify similar ideas and organise others? How can you make sure students do this kind of preparation for writing systematically, rather than just start writing without preparation?

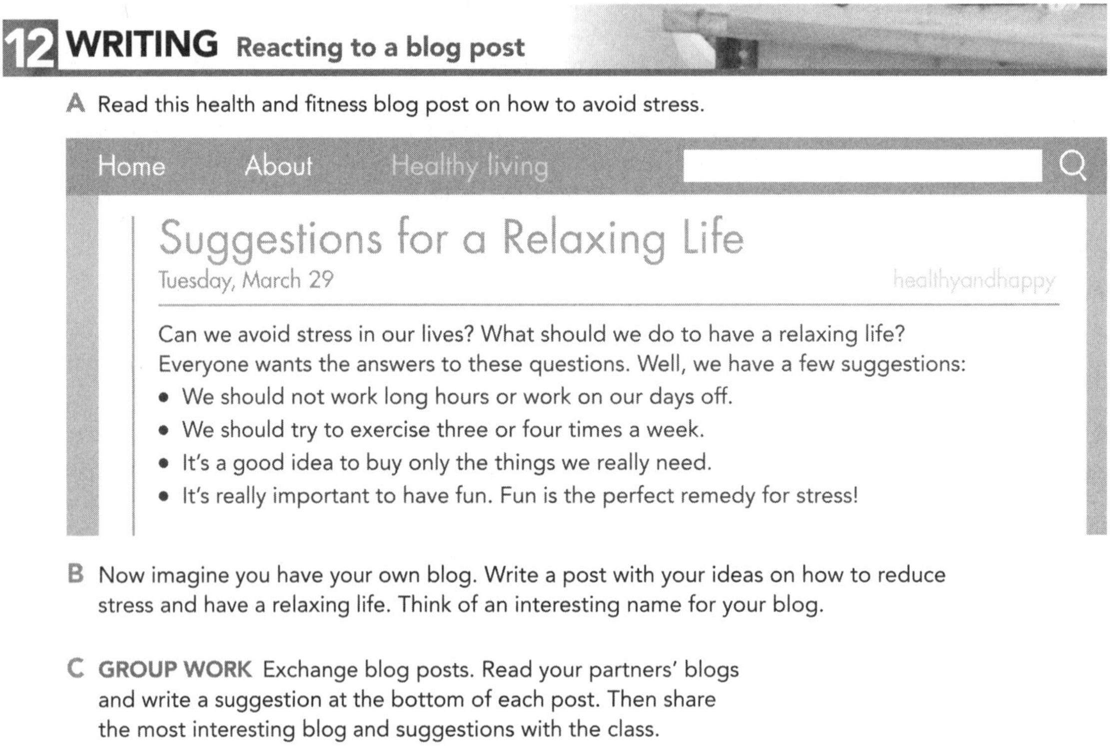

12 WRITING Reacting to a blog post

A Read this health and fitness blog post on how to avoid stress.

Home About Healthy living

Suggestions for a Relaxing Life

Tuesday, March 29 healthyandhappy

Can we avoid stress in our lives? What should we do to have a relaxing life? Everyone wants the answers to these questions. Well, we have a few suggestions:

- We should not work long hours or work on our days off.
- We should try to exercise three or four times a week.
- It's a good idea to buy only the things we really need.
- It's really important to have fun. Fun is the perfect remedy for stress!

B Now imagine you have your own blog. Write a post with your ideas on how to reduce stress and have a relaxing life. Think of an interesting name for your blog.

C **GROUP WORK** Exchange blog posts. Read your partners' blogs and write a suggestion at the bottom of each post. Then share the most interesting blog and suggestions with the class.

Figure 4.1a: Richards, J. C. et al. (2017) *Interchange 1* (5th ed.), p. 82.

With the example in *Figure 4.1b*, you could give students the following framework for each pair/ group to make notes:

> *Environmental problem ...*
> *What's happening now?*
> *What could happen in the future?*
> *Possible solutions ...*

Pairs/groups that choose the same problem can read each other's ideas before writing a first draft.

WRITING
An article for the school magazine

The sad story of a once beautiful river

The Quiller River was once so beautiful that there is even a song about it. And now?

The situation is alarming. There are lots of factories along the river. Newspapers have recently reported that the water in the river is totally polluted. There are hardly any fish left, and the water itself smells terrible. The situation will be even worse in a few years unless factories stop polluting the water. So I really think politicians should do something about it. We need stricter laws to protect our river.

And just look at the river banks. They are covered in litter. It seems that there are lots of people who throw their waste into the river. This must stop! We should all get together and help clean up the river banks.

If politicians wake up and we all do something, we might once again be able to enjoy the beauty of the river. Let's hope it's not too late.

5 Choose one of these environmental problems and make notes about what the situation is now, possible consequences and what should be done.

a one of the problems mentioned in this unit, for example, deforestation in the Amazon
b an environmental issue in your town or country

6 Write an article for your school magazine raising awareness about the environmental issue you have chosen.

- Find a good title.
- Write an introduction that catches the reader's interest.
- Describe what the problems are, what you think the consequences might be and what should be done.

Figure 4.1b: Puchta, H., J. Stranks and P. Lewis-Jones (2015) *Think Level 2*, p. 63.

4.2 Prefabricated language

Level	A2 and above
Time	10 to 15 minutes
Outline	In pairs, students decide on the accuracy of both student-written and teacher-written example sentences that could be used in a piece of writing.
Aim	To provide students with language examples to help them with their writing; to provide some feedback on language accuracy before students write a text.
Preparation	If you use *Figure 4.2a* below, you will need to copy and cut up the sentences on the worksheet for each pair. You will also need to cut up pieces of blank paper for students to write example sentences on. If you don't use *Figure 4.2a*, you will need to write your own three correct and three incorrect sentences.
Rationale	When students are writing a text, they are often more concerned with language accuracy because writing is more permanent than speech and may be widely read. This activity focuses on some key language examples that are typically used in the kind of text they will write. Students also get an opportunity to try out some language of their own and receive feedback. By getting students to evaluate the examples of another pair, students aren't made to feel uncomfortable if the sentence they wrote contains errors.

Procedure

1 Students complete any language analysis and/or practice tasks – exercises 3a to 3c in *Figure 4.2a* (students have just read an example email from a student in Dubai to a host family in Sydney).

2 Put students in pairs and hand out a blank piece of paper to each student.

3 Students work alone to write two example sentences that can be used in an email of introduction to a home stay family in an English-speaking country.

4 Each pair combines their sentences and then swaps these with another pair. You add in the six teacher-written sentences (see worksheet below). Let students know that some of your sentences are correct and others contain errors.

5 Students discuss all the sentences and decide which ones are correct and then correct the others. At this stage, you should only confirm the correction of student-generated sentences.

6 When all the pairs have finished, they return the student-generated sentences. In open class, check corrections to the worksheet sentences. Students then work alone and begin planning and writing the email.

Notes and variation

If students ask you to check the accuracy of sentences, make sure they have considered them to some degree and don't just ask what's right and wrong. At higher levels, you could use only student-generated examples and perhaps specify target structures you want them to write, for example, one sentence using *although* and another using a reason or result linking word. Another variation for high levels is to include sentences with different levels of formality, or those that are relevant to a particular genre, and students have to identify which sentences are most appropriate for the text they will write.

Learner reflection questions

1 Was your example sentence correct? What did you learn from writing it?
2 Before you begin writing, you can think about the language as well as ideas for the actual text you're going to write. Why is this a good idea?

Teacher reflection

To what degree did you have to prompt students to think about language accuracy for themselves? Having tried this activity, was there any difference in the way students approached the actual writing? Why do you think this was the case?

3 WRITING SKILLS
Linking ideas with *after*, *when* and *while*

a Underline the word in each sentence that's different from Ahmed's email.

1 Thank you for offering to be my homestay family while I'm in Sydney.
2 I want to become a marine biologist when I finish university.
3 I'm looking forward to meeting you after I arrive.
4 When I'm in Sydney, I really want to study hard.

b Look at the sentences in 3a and complete the rules with the words in the box.

after beginning while

1 We use *when* and ________ to join two activities that happen at the same time.
2 We use *when* and ________ to join two activities that happen at different times.
3 If the linking word is at the ________ of the sentence, we use a comma (,) between the two parts.

c Underline the correct words. There is more than one possible answer.

1 *After / When / While* I finish my English course, I'd like to go to Canada for a holiday.
2 I'd like to go skiing in the mountains *after / when / while* I'm on holiday.
3 I often play basketball with my colleagues *after / when / while* I finish work.
4 *After / When / While* I watch a game of football, I usually want to play a game myself.
5 My English improved *after / when / while* I was in Sydney.

4 SPEAKING AND WRITING

a Make a list of English-speaking countries you know.

b Which country in 4a would you like to visit? Why?

I'd like to go to …
I like warm places.
They say the people are friendly.

c Plan an email about yourself to a homestay family in that country. Make notes about:

- your age
- free-time interests
- study / job
- family
- what you'd like to do in that country

d Write your email. Tick (✓) each box.

- ☐ Start the letter with *Dear*
- ☐ Say thank you
- ☐ Say who you are
- ☐ Talk about study / work / free time
- ☐ Talk about your family
- ☐ Say what you want to do in the country
- ☐ Include *I'm looking forward …*
- ☐ Finish the letter with *Best wishes*
- ☐ Use ***after***, *when* and *while* to link your ideas

e Swap emails with another student and check the ideas in 4d.

Figure 4.2a: Doff, A., C. Thaine et al. (2015) *Cambridge English Empower A2*, p. 77.

Worksheet
Possible corrections for the three incorrect sentences:

I want to meet lots of new people ~~while~~ when I arrive.
My name is Toni and ~~I'm coming~~ I come from Mexico.
I'm looking forward to ~~meet~~ meeting you.

I want to become an English language teacher after I graduate.
While I'm in London I want to practise speaking English a lot.
I like going to the cinema and meeting my friends at the weekend.
I want to meet lots of new people while I arrive.
My name is Toni and I'm coming from Mexico.
I'm looking forward to meet you.

Prior to doing the exercises in *Figure 4.2b*, students have read a blog post description of a concert. The examples that you give to students can include the focus on the indefinite pronoun as well as other grammar items included in the example text – the present perfect, *there was/were*, or the zero conditional.

Useful language

Avoiding repetition (2)
We use *one* (singular) and *ones* (plural) to refer to something we mentioned earlier in a text.

- *There were lots of bands but for me the best* **one** *was The Hurricane from Manchester.*
- *Their first songs were folk and blues but the last* **ones** *sounded more like reggae and rock.*

3 Look at the Useful language box. What kind of words do *one* and *ones* replace?

4 Complete the sentences with *one* or *ones*.

1 I really liked the last band. The first ......*ones*...... weren't as good.
2 There are two boys in the band. The tall .... plays the drums.
3 They sang two songs. Which .... did you like best?
4 I've seen them in concert twice. The last .... was in the park last summer.
5 I like all their songs but the earlier .... are great to dance to.
6 Dave's got three guitars: a red .... and two black .... .

Get writing

PLAN

5 Plan a blog post about a concert you've been to. Use Exercise 2 to help you. Decide what order to put them in.

WRITE

6 Write your blog post about the concert. Use your notes from Exercise 5 and the model text to help you.

Figure 4.2b: Goldstein, B. and C. Jones (2015) *Eyes Open 3*, p. 39.

4.3 Talk about it first

Level	B1 and above
Time	10 to 15 minutes
Outline	After making notes on what they are going to write, students talk to two or three classmates to exchange ideas.
Aim	To give students an opportunity to get feedback on the content of their writing before they write the text; to allow them to collect more content ideas from their classmates.
Preparation	There is no preparation necessary for this activity.
Rationale	This activity is suitable for B1 level and higher because it focuses on written texts that are longer and more complex. Many writing activities in course books encourage students to brainstorm ideas for their writing and make notes. If the piece of writing is neutral in its focus, students can do this together. However, if the nature of the writing is more personal (it's about them or expresses a personal opinion or argument) we generally encourage students to, initially at least, produce their own ideas. This activity encourages students to exchange their ideas and get feedback. When talking about what they are going to write, students may also get further inspiration and new ideas might occur to them.

Procedure

1. Before students begin writing, get them to make notes alone on what they will write. In *Figure 4.3* below, students make notes in response to the instruction in exercise E.
2. Put students in an onion-ring formation – an inner circle facing outwards and an outer circle facing inwards.
3. Students move around and talk to two to four other students.
4. Encourage students to ask questions, give feedback on ideas and make suggestions – you could do an open class example with a student.
5. After sharing their ideas, students write their first draft.

Notes and variation

For a more complex piece of writing at a higher level, students could first do research as a homework task and, in the onion ring, talk about what they have found out. If you are teaching an English for Academic Purposes (EAP) class, you could suggest that students evaluate each other's ideas critically in order to put critical thinking skills into practice.

Learner reflection questions

1. Did you get ideas from other students or did you think of new ideas as you were talking?
2. What is the value of talking about what you're going to write before you begin writing?

Teacher reflection

This activity combines speaking and writing. Why is it useful to include speaking in writing classes? How else can you do this?

2 WRITING

A **Manuela is applying to be a volunteer for the Street Beats Festival. Read her personal statement in the application below. Answer the questions.**

1 What language skills does Manuela have?

2 What experience does she have with events? What volunteer experiences does she have?

3 How well does she know the city?

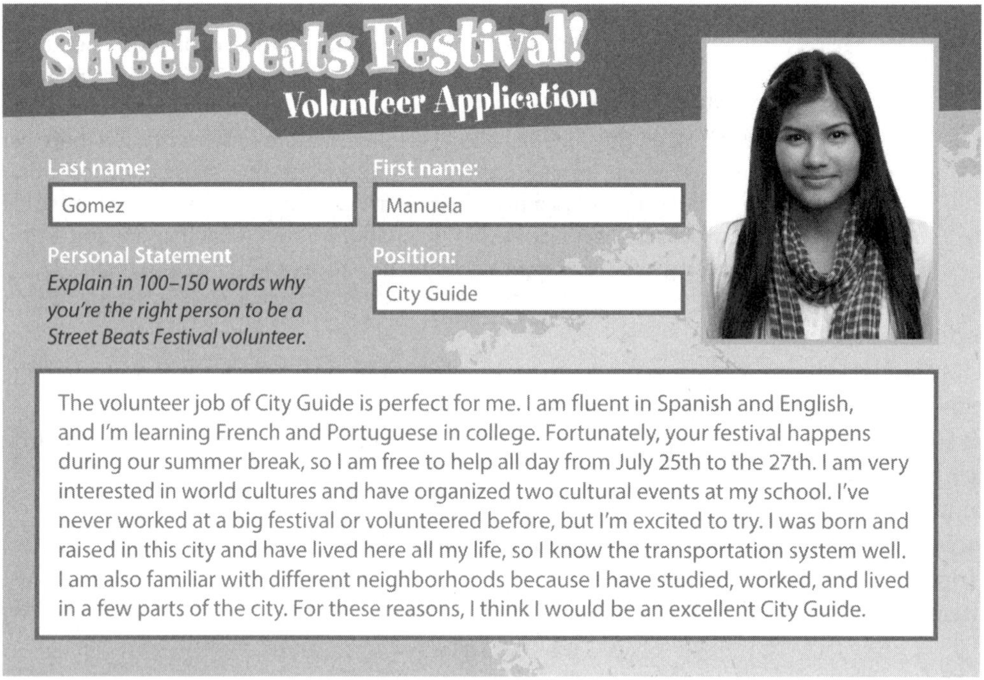

Street Beats Festival!
Volunteer Application

Last name: Gomez

First name: Manuela

Personal Statement
Explain in 100–150 words why you're the right person to be a Street Beats Festival volunteer.

Position: City Guide

The volunteer job of City Guide is perfect for me. I am fluent in Spanish and English, and I'm learning French and Portuguese in college. Fortunately, your festival happens during our summer break, so I am free to help all day from July 25th to the 27th. I am very interested in world cultures and have organized two cultural events at my school. I've never worked at a big festival or volunteered before, but I'm excited to try. I was born and raised in this city and have lived here all my life, so I know the transportation system well. I am also familiar with different neighborhoods because I have studied, worked, and lived in a few parts of the city. For these reasons, I think I would be an excellent City Guide.

WRITE IT

D **Imagine you're applying to be a City Guide or Cast Helper. Write a personal statement for the volunteer application. You can use your own information or make it up. Check your writing after you are finished.**

E PAIR WORK **Exchange personal statements with a partner. What was the best reason your partner gave for wanting the job?**

Figure 4.3: Hendra, L. A., M. Ibbotson and K. O'Dell (2019) *Evolve 3*, p. 29.

B While writing

4.4 Word count competition

Level	A1 and above
Time	5 to 10 minutes
Outline	Students write a text on a topic that is familiar to them and then try and write as many words as they can within a set time period.
Aim	To give students practice in writing fluency; to develop students' ability to write at a good pace.
Preparation	There is no preparation for this activity.
Rationale	While a number of course book writing tasks necessarily involve writing drafts and improving them, this can be a time-consuming process. Students can get overly focused on accuracy and this inhibits their ability to produce a text. It can be a liberating experience, therefore, for students to do a freer writing such as this. Having to produce a written text within a strict time limit, may be something that students at lower levels rarely, if ever, have to do. However, it is appropriate practice for students preparing to sit a written examination. Some students, as part of their work, may need to write texts in English to a deadline. Asking students to comment on an interesting idea in the text they read is one way of linking fluency to communication. The implicit message is that although you wrote quickly, and perhaps not accurately, you still managed to communicate ideas.

Procedure

1 Do any reading and analysis tasks associated with the text you want students to write – exercises a and b in *Figure 4.4a* below.

2 Put students in groups of four to eight. Students close their books and individually, for one minute, think about the topic (they should not make notes) – for *Figure 4.4a* the topic might be: *A day in my life*.

3 Tell students they now have three minutes to write as much as possible for the task. Explain that they should not worry about making errors, and that the winner in each group is the one who writes the most number of words. (You can be flexible about the time allowed depending on your students' ability, but be firm and stop the writing after the time limit.)

4 Students then swap their writing with another person in the group. Each student counts the number of words and reads to find interesting information in the writing. Pairs give feedback to each other followed by a group check of word counts.

5 The student who has written the most words is the winner in each group.

6 In feedback, ask who the winners were and how many words they wrote. Also ask what interesting ideas they found out about.

Notes and variation

At very low levels, it's preferable not to focus on accuracy in any way. Students can do this activity using a digital device with autocorrection tools. The aim is writing fluency and the production of as much language as possible, so it doesn't matter if the device helps with accuracy. However, at B2 and above, the element of competition could be about balancing fluency and accuracy, in which case the writing should be paper-based.

Learner reflection questions

1 Was it important to think about writing correctly for this activity? Why / Why not?
2 After you write quickly in this way, can you revise your writing and correct it?

Teacher reflection

To what extent is this activity similar to activities that aim to practise spoken fluency? Which students were motivated to write more by the competitive element in this activity? With your students, how much should planning for writing be balanced by just getting ideas down on paper?

6 WRITING

a Read part of an email from Sophia to her sister. She writes about a day in her life in London. Where do Sophia and Megan have coffee? Why?

I walk to work every day because my flat is near the office. I start work at 8:30 and I finish at 5:30. I work with Megan. We go out to a café for coffee every day because the coffee machine in the office isn't very good. We also have lunch there. They have nice sandwiches and chocolate cake – my favourite! Megan always says, 'I'll pay.' She's very nice.

b ▶ Now go to Writing Plus 6C on p.156 for *because* and *also*.

c Write about a day in your life. Use *because* and *also*.

d Read about your partner's day. Do you do the same?

Figure 4.4a: Doff, A., C. Thaine et al. (2015) *Cambridge English Empower A1*, p. 53.

With the example in *Figure 4.4b*, students could be given double points if they manage to use one of the expressions in exercise 6 correctly in their fluency writing. Before they start writing, give students between 30 and 60 seconds to study the expressions before closing their books.

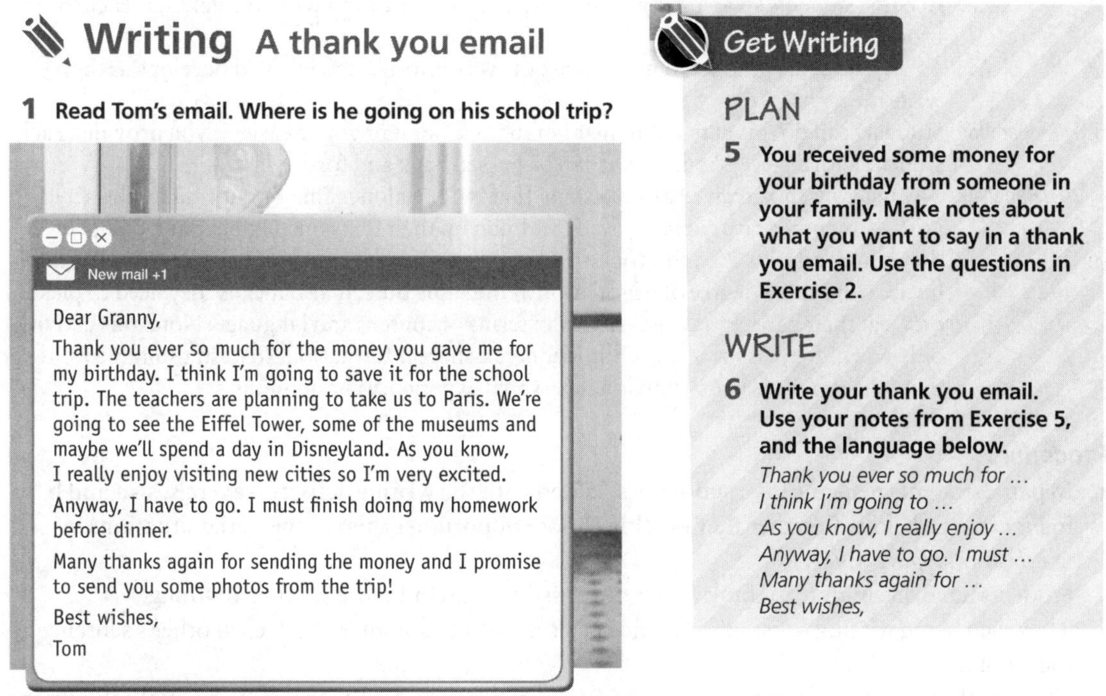

Writing A thank you email

1 Read Tom's email. Where is he going on his school trip?

New mail +1

Dear Granny,

Thank you ever so much for the money you gave me for my birthday. I think I'm going to save it for the school trip. The teachers are planning to take us to Paris. We're going to see the Eiffel Tower, some of the museums and maybe we'll spend a day in Disneyland. As you know, I really enjoy visiting new cities so I'm very excited.

Anyway, I have to go. I must finish doing my homework before dinner.

Many thanks again for sending the money and I promise to send you some photos from the trip!

Best wishes,

Tom

Get Writing

PLAN

5 You received some money for your birthday from someone in your family. Make notes about what you want to say in a thank you email. Use the questions in Exercise 2.

WRITE

6 Write your thank you email. Use your notes from Exercise 5, and the language below.

Thank you ever so much for …
I think I'm going to …
As you know, I really enjoy …
Anyway, I have to go. I must …
Many thanks again for …
Best wishes,

Figure 4.4b: Goldstein, B. and C. Jones (2015) *Eyes Open 2*, p. 71.

4.5 Sentence turn about

Level A2 and above
Time 10 to 15 minutes
Outline In pairs, students swap their writing after each sentence and write the next sentence to produce two joint texts.
Aim To give students practice in monitoring the way information in a text develops as they write it.
Preparation Students can do this activity in their notebooks, but it might be easier if you provided each student with a piece of paper that can be passed back and forth.
Rationale Writing is often perceived as something that is done alone. This activity makes the act of writing an interactive exercise. Students build up their texts one sentence at a time, but they constantly have to monitor and respond to what their partner has just written. This is likely to involve a degree of negotiation at the same time. It also means they need to pick up on what their partner has just written in terms of content and language. Note: this activity only works for texts where both students can share information, so it isn't suitable for texts that talk about students' individual personal experiences or opinions.

Procedure

1 In pairs, students read any instructions associated with the writing activity – exercises 5a and b in *Figure 4.5a* below. Together they quickly choose important criteria (one of the situations in exercise 5a, *Figure 4.5a*).
2 Students have one minute to think about the possible content before writing anything.
3 They then begin writing – just one sentence at a time – but shouldn't check each other's sentence as they write.
4 When both students have completed a sentence, they swap and write the next one, making sure the ideas and the grammar are connected to what has already been written. They can ask their partner questions about her/his sentence if they aren't sure of something.
5 Students continue swapping the writing back and forth until the two texts are completed.
6 The pairs then read both texts and decide which one they prefer and why. This can be reported back to the class.

Notes and variation

The fact that their partner is waiting gives a sense of urgency for students to maintain a good writing pace. This activity is similar to a pass-it-on writing activity (sometimes called *Consequences*) where each student in a group adds a sentence to a text, only reading the previous sentence. The result is often amusing because of odd connections and sudden changes in direction of the text. By contrast, in *Sentence turn about*, students can see the whole text as it evolves, and need to make sure it continues to make sense. This idea can also be used for writing dialogues.

Learner reflection questions

1 What did you have to think about when you read your partner's sentence and wrote your own?
2 Do you find it easier to write together with another person or on your own? Why?

Teacher reflection

Were some pairs more interactive and co-operative than others? Why do you think this was the case? What do you think students found most challenging about this activity?

write an email or note apologising

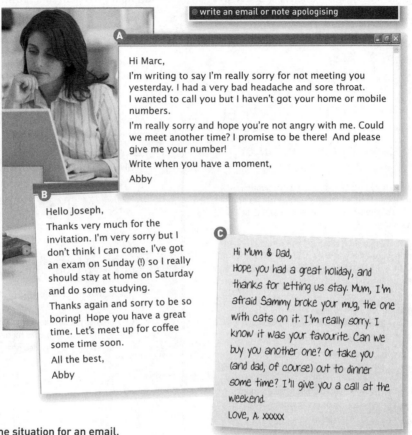

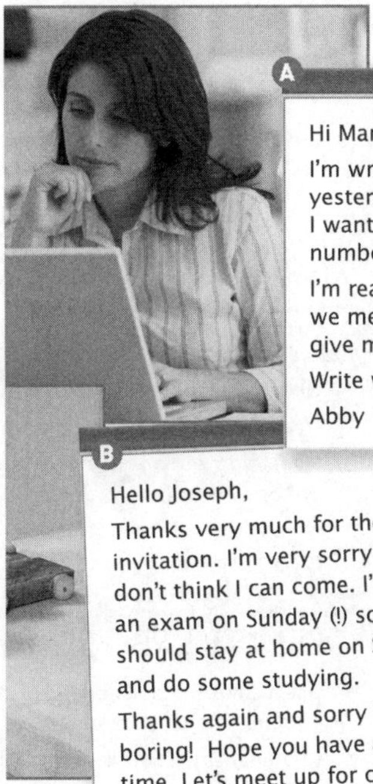

A

Hi Marc,

I'm writing to say I'm really sorry for not meeting you yesterday. I had a very bad headache and sore throat. I wanted to call you but I haven't got your home or mobile numbers.

I'm really sorry and hope you're not angry with me. Could we meet another time? I promise to be there! And please give me your number!

Write when you have a moment,

Abby

B

Hello Joseph,

Thanks very much for the invitation. I'm very sorry but I don't think I can come. I've got an exam on Sunday (!) so I really should stay at home on Saturday and do some studying.

Thanks again and sorry to be so boring! Hope you have a great time. Let's meet up for coffee some time soon.

All the best,

Abby

C

Hi Mum & Dad,

Hope you had a great holiday, and thanks for letting us stay. Mum, I'm afraid Sammy broke your mug, the one with cats on it. I'm really sorry. I know it was your favourite. Can we buy you another one? or take you (and dad, of course) out to dinner some time? I'll give you a call at the weekend.

Love, A. xxxxx

5 a Choose one situation for an email.

It's Sunday afternoon. You have a very bad cold. Tomorrow you have a meeting with a colleague at work, but you think you should stay in bed.

You're on holiday and you're using your friend's car. Yesterday you had a small accident. You broke one of the lights at the back of the car. Your friend loves his car.

You visited a friend in another city at the weekend. On Monday morning, you remember that another friend had her birthday party on Saturday.

b Discuss ideas for your emails in pairs.

1 Who are you writing to?
2 How can you say sorry?
3 What reasons can you give?
4 Can you use any expressions from 2 and 4?

6 a Work alone and write your email.

Figure 4.5a: Tilbury, A., T. Clementson et al. (2010) *English Unlimited A2*, p. 104.

With the example in *Figure 4.5b*, the writing turns could be more structured, with students only focusing on the bullet point suggestions. Each student writes an imperative and a first sentence, then passes it to their partner to write a second sentence. They then write the next imperative and sentence and swap again. This gives students practice in writing a main idea (first sentence) followed by a supporting idea (second sentence).

WRITING
A web page giving advice

How to use a public computer – safety tips

There are times when you may want to use a public computer, for example in an Internet café, a library or at an airport. That's when it's especially important to be smart and safe.

- Don't save! When you want to log into a social networking website or your web mail, the system will ask you, 'Do you want to save this password?' Don't click 'Yes' when you are working on a public computer.
- Log out! Make sure you do not simply close the browser when you want to leave a site. You should always "log out" of the site when you finish your session.
- Close windows! If you need to walk away from the computer for any reason, you should close all the windows on the computer first. Don't leave any information on the screen that other people shouldn't see.
- Watch out! Be careful about people looking at the screen over your shoulder. Ask them politely to go somewhere else so you can use the computer in private.

5 What would be important advice for good online behaviour? Make notes.

Here are some ideas:
- what (not) to share on social networks
- creating secure passwords and how to keep them safe
- what to do when you receive offensive comments on social websites
- what you should know about uploading photos on social networks

6 Write the text for a web page giving advice on good online behaviour (about 200 words).
- Use an introduction and bullet points to structure your text.
- Use language from Exercises 2 and 3 to give advice, and make sure your readers understand what situations your advice refers to.

Figure 4.5b: Puchta, H., J. Stranks and P. Lewis-Jones (2015) *Think Level 2*, p. 45.

4.6 Making improvements

Level	A2 to B1+
Time	15 to 20 minutes
Outline	Students write a paragraph and deliberately avoid using a language-focused writing skill (in this case punctuation) before exchanging with their partner for improvement.
Aim	To give students practice using accurate punctuation.
Preparation	There is no preparation for this activity.
Rationale	This activity is particularly useful for texts where written accuracy is important, for example, job applications, formal invitations, essays, etc. It provides double practice of an aspect of language-focused writing, as students first need to think as carefully to omit punctuation in their writing, as they do when improving their partner's work.

Procedure

1. Students complete any analysis and/or practice tasks associated with the writing skill focus of the lesson – exercise 1 in *Figure 4.6a* below.
2. Students write one paragraph of their description of a place without using punctuation. It's a good idea if they write on alternate lines.
3. Students swap their paragraph with another student, and they improve each other's work by adding appropriate punctuation.
4. Students work in pairs showing each other the improvements they have made. Monitor and answer any questions students have.

Notes and variation

This activity can be used for lower-level language-focused writing skills, for example, spelling, tense use, paragraphing etc. At a lower level, it helps to keep the focus quite specific in terms of what language-focused writing skill is ignored and has to be improved. However, at higher levels you could ask students to focus on the writing skill that is the main focus of the writing lesson as well as any other language that could be improved.

Learner reflection questions

1. What was harder – writing the paragraph without punctuation or improving your partner's paragraph? Why?
2. Is it good to think about punctuation when you are writing? What's another time you should check punctuation?

Teacher reflection

When did students need more help – writing their unpunctuated paragraph or when they corrected and discussed their paragraphs in pairs? What other accuracy issues did you notice during this activity?

1 Work with a partner. Correct the punctuation and capital letters in the paragraph.

PLUS

I
~~i~~ live in montreal it is a city in canada it is a beautiful city there are many shops and restaurants the people are friendly there is an art festival in june people in montreal speak both french and english it is very crowded with tourists in the summer in the winter people like to ice skate cross-country ski and play ice hockey

WRITING TASK

Describe the place where you live. Write about its positives and its negatives.

Figure 4.6a: O'Neill, R., M. Lewis et al. (2019) *Unlock Reading, Writing & Critical Thinking 2*, p. 33.

C After writing

4.7 Content development

Level	A2 and above
Time	5 to 10 minutes
Outline	Students write a text in pairs and then swap with another pair to analyse and suggest a content addition or development.
Aim	To improve the content of students' writing and signal the importance of developing ideas.
Preparation	There is no preparation for this activity.
Rationale	A lot of writing feedback activities are based on specific language-focused writing skills (see activity 4.8 below), but the content ideas are often not considered. This activity not only focuses on the content but also gets students thinking about how they can develop ideas (sometimes a struggle for some students who say that they don't know what to write about).

Procedure

1 In pairs, students write their text together – in *Figure 4.7a*, this is a vlog script.
2 On the board write:
an extra idea, an idea that's not clear, something to add to an idea that's in the script
3 Pairs swap their scripts, read each other's ideas and think of suggestions they can make to improve the content using the prompts on the board.
4 The pairs work as a group of four and give feedback on their suggestions.
5 Each pair revises their first draft.

Notes and variation

This activity works best with texts where there is no personal content and can be written collaboratively. The implicit message is that students can get support from their peers in terms of developing ideas for text content. Students also get useful speaking practice in the final phase of the activity when they give feedback to each other. At higher levels, where the content is more complex, and in English for Academic Purposes (EAP) classes, where the content might involve research, the editing could be done as a homework activity and pairs give each other feedback in the next class. You would need to make copies of each piece of writing or ensure that there is an accessible online copy, so both students in a pair have the text.

Learner reflection questions

1 When you read the other pair's script, did you get any additional ideas for your own script?
2 When you write in your first language do you sometimes get ideas from other people? Who can you get ideas from when you write in English?

Teacher reflection

What were your students more capable of doing – adding ideas or developing ones that were already suggested? Given the collaborative nature of this activity, how much speaking did students do throughout the lesson? Were they aware they were getting speaking fluency practice?

For the lesson in *Figure 4.7a*, before writing the text students read a model advice text on how to save money. The language writing skill focused on is pronoun substitution.

WRITE IT

E **Imagine you have a vlog. In today's vlog, you are going to make suggestions for saving money on the two topics below. Write your script. Don't forget to use *one* and *them* when you can.**

phone transportation

F **Work with a partner and film your vlog. Watch the vlogs in class and say what the best advice is.**

Figure 4.7a: Clandfield, L., B. Goldstein, C. Jones and P. Kerr (2019) *Evolve 2*, p. 61.

In *Figure 4.7b* students read an example competition entry before writing. Note how exercise 2 provides a useful content check list.

Writing A competition entry

2 Look back at Jon's competition entry again. What does Jon write about?

- favourite activities (daytime / at night)
- the monitors / other campers
- the daily routine
- why he liked it
- the food
- the weather

Get writing

PLAN

5 Plan your competition entry for the camp website. Include information from Exercise 2 to help you. Decide what order you are going to put them in.

WRITE

6 Write your competition entry for the camp website. Use your notes from Exercise 5 and the model text to help you.

Figure 4.7b: Goldstein, B. and C. Jones (2015) *Eyes Open 3*, p. 27.

4.8 Language edit

Level	B1 and above
Time	10 to 15 minutes
Outline	After completing a piece of writing, each student writes questions that they would like answered related to language-focused writing skills in their text.
Aim	To give students practice editing for language accuracy; to develop learner autonomy by encouraging students to determine their language-focused writing skill needs.
Preparation	There is no preparation for this activity.
Rationale	Polishing or improving the language in a piece of writing is an important part of the process of producing a text. While teachers encourage students to check their own work, this is often done only superficially. By getting students to look at their peers' writing, they are more likely to focus. It helps to do this activity in small groups so each text is checked by two or more students. The activity works better at level B1 and above, by which time students have developed more awareness of language-focused writing skills.

Procedure

1 Students have already completed a first draft of their text – exercise b in *Figure 4.8a* below.

2 Put the following criteria on the board:

spelling, punctuation, paragraphs, correct use of (target grammar point) *linking words/expressions, complex sentences, variety of vocabulary*

3 Students choose two or three language-focused writing skills they would like feedback on in their text and write relevant questions.

4 Put students in groups of three. Each student passes their text on, reads their peer's text and their questions and thinks of answers. They can make their own notes if they wish.

5 Each text is then passed on a second time for the next student to read and think about answers to the questions.

6 Monitor and be available to help students, but encourage students to work out as much as possible on their own.

7 After reading the texts, students give feedback, answering the questions and suggesting relevant language improvements.

Notes and variation

Getting students to choose the skills they would like feedback on themselves is a good way of getting them to consider what their writing skill needs might be. It also encourages learner autonomy. You can vary the criteria that you put on the board. The writing skills focus for the text in *Figure 4.8a* was reason and result linkers, so these could be specifically listed on the board. The grammar points you list could be related to specific needs you know your group of students has, or a review of recently studied points.

Learner reflection questions

1 Having received feedback on the writing skills you selected for your questions, do you feel you need to practise these skills more?

2 What writing skill that is <u>not</u> related to grammar do you think you need to focus on more in the future?

Teacher reflection

How relevant were students' choices about writing skills they asked to have feedback on? If you feel they chose skills that don't match what you perceive as their needs, what can you do to help students?

4 WRITING

a Choose one of these inventions to write about or use your own idea.

- cars
- the aeroplane
- glass
- photography
- boats
- TV

Think about the questions below and make notes. Walk around the class and collect ideas from other students.

- Why is the invention important?
- What good or bad results has it had?
- How was life different before?
- What other things have changed because of it?

b Write a web post for the website. Remember to explain results and reasons using *as, because, because of* and *as a result of.*

Figure 4.8a: Doff, A., C. Thaine et al. (2015) *Cambridge English Empower B1*, p. 115.

Figure 4.8b is a lesson from a B2 level course book and has a longer text. The writing task could be set as homework and language edit could be done in class.

WRITING TASK

Write an essay which provides both short- and long-term solutions to an environmental problem and takes the costs into consideration. Refer to a specific case study in your essay.

PLAN

1 Look back at your notes about the case study you chose and the diagram in Critical thinking. Create an outline for your essay using this structure.

1 Introductory paragraph: description of the problem and main purpose of report
2 Recommended solution #1
3 Recommended solution #2
4 Recommended solution #3
5 Concluding paragraph: summary and evaluation of key points

Figure 4.8b: Sowton, C., A. S. Kennedy et al. (2019) *Unlock Reading, Writing & Critical Thinking 4*, p. 94.

4.9 Writing competition

Level	A2 and above
Time	60 to 90 minutes
Outline	Students write a text that is entered in a class competition which is judged by the students themselves in groups.
Aim	To develop students' awareness of writing for an audience and with a sense of communicative purpose.
Preparation	There is no preparation for this activity unless you want to organise some kind of prize for the winners.
Rationale	Much of the student writing that is done in English language classes is read only by the teacher (or not read at all). By setting up a competition framework, students are given a sense of writing for a purpose and for a specific readership, their peers. It helps to provide competition criteria that are straightforward and don't have too strong an emphasis on specific language-focused writing skills. The criteria can be as simple as *the most interesting ..., the most exciting ..., the clearest ...* etc.

Procedure

1 Students complete any analysis and/or practice exercises before they begin writing.
2 Tell students their piece of writing will enter a competition – for *Figure 4.9* this could be *the most interesting profile*.
3 Set a strict time limit for the writing. (In the interests of time management, it doesn't matter if some are not fully completed.)
4 Put students into groups of between four and six students. Redistribute the texts so that no one in a group is evaluating their own.
5 Students pass around and read all the texts, then decide together which was the most interesting – the winner for their group.
6 In open class, the winners are announced. The winning texts can then be read aloud to the group as a whole.

Notes

This is quite a long activity, but it's preferable to do this in class so the playing field is even for the competition. It could also be done with a very short text like a tweet, for example. Although some students may be sensitive about having their work judged by their peers, conducted in a collaborative and fun environment this can be a rewarding experience. Given that they are both participants and judges, the competitive element is mitigated at the least to some degree. This activity works better with texts that communicate an idea or tell a story (narratives, profiles, essays etc.) rather than those with an instrumental function (invitations, apologies etc.).

Learner reflection questions

1 What was it that made the winning piece of writing in your group interesting for you? Did the other group members agree?
2 How important was the language the writer used to make their writing interesting?

Teacher reflection

Did you agree with the students' decisions? What aspects of writing did they talk about as they were reaching their decision? What did this tell you about the writing strengths and needs of students in your class?

WRITING

Someone I admire

4 Think of someone that you admire: a famous person; or someone you know in your own life; or someone you invent.

For the person, think about:

- facts about their life (when they were born, etc.)
- what they do, where and how, when they started
- what they want to do in the future
- why you admire them

5 Write an essay called 'Someone I admire' in about 150 words. Use the example essay and language above to help you.

Figure 4.9: Puchta, H., J. Stranks and P. Lewis-Jones (2015) *Think Level 1*, p.117.

You can find teacher development activities about writing on pages 265 to 268.

5 Grammar

Introduction

The presentation of grammar in course books

In many course books, grammar forms the backbone of the syllabus with vocabulary, pronunciation and the four language skills working in support of grammar. A strength of modern course books is that they usually present or clarify grammar in some kind of context. Typically, this is a reading or listening text that includes examples of the grammar to be taught. *Figure 5.0a* is an example that shows the way in which grammar lessons are often ordered.

Oliver and Kirsten Foster left the UK in 2009. In three years they travelled to Mexico, Peru, the USA, Thailand, China, Dubai and Germany before arriving at their latest home in Egypt. They're both photographers, so they can work anywhere in the world. They now have a three-year-old daughter, Liona, so they have to make plans more carefully. But they don't want to change their lives. Next year they are going to live in Ecuador and then South Africa.

OLIVER SAYS: I love meeting new people, but you shouldn't forget your family back home. I phone my mum every week.

KIRSTEN SAYS: You should live like the local people and try to make friends with people from the country.

3 GRAMMAR *should / shouldn't*

a Look at the sentences. Underline the correct words. Then check in the texts.

1 You *should / shouldn't* try to learn the local language too.
2 You *should / shouldn't* forget your family back home.
3 You *should / shouldn't* live like the local people.

b Choose the correct answer to complete the rules.

You should means:
a you have to do it b it's a good idea.
After *should* and *shouldn't* we use:
a *to* + infinitive b infinitive without *to*.

c 3.81 **Pronunciation** Listen to sentences 2 and 3 in 3a.

1 Is there a /l/ sound in *should* and *shouldn't*?
2 Is the vowel long or short?

d Now go to Grammar Focus 12B on p.158

e Read the advice about living abroad. Change the verbs in blue by adding *should* or *shouldn't*.

WOULD YOU LIKE TO LIVE ABROAD?
TAKE OUR ADVICE!

1 **Don't stay** at home all the time. **Go out** and meet people.
You shouldn't stay at home all the time. You should …
2 **Try** to visit a new place every weekend. **Don't wait** until the last few weeks of your stay.
3 **Read** about the country before you go there.
4 **Don't get** angry when things go wrong.
5 **Remember** that things work differently in other countries.

12B *should / shouldn't*

a Complete the sentences with the verb in brackets and *should* or *shouldn't*.

1 **A** He feels tired all the time.
B He *should go* (go) to the doctor.
2 You ______ (drink) a lot of water when you run.
3 You ______ (bring) a lot of books. We're only going for three days.
4 You ______ (drive) all night. Stop and get some sleep.
5 It's going to be cold so you ______ (take) some warm clothes.
6 The children ______ (come) into the house – it's getting dark.
7 We ______ (pay) for the meal. The food was horrible.
8 I ______ (say) sorry to him. I broke his cup.

Figure 5.0a: Doff, A., C. Thaine et al. (2015) *Cambridge English Empower A2*, pp. 122–123 and 158.

This lesson is the final grammar lesson in a course book for A2 level learners. The target grammar point is the modal verb *should / shouldn't* used to give advice. The grammar structure is contextualised in the reading text where experienced travellers give advice about travel abroad (there are, in fact, three mini texts like the one in the example in *Figure 5.0a* in the full lesson).

Exercise 3 follows a typical sequence for presenting a grammar structure:

> identify the target grammar point → clarify the meaning → clarify the form → highlight pronunciation → do controlled written practice → do less controlled (spoken or written) practice.

We can now break this down in relation to the specific course book activities. Exercise 3a highlights the target language. It is a way of signalling to students that this is the language focus of the lesson. It also aims to make a connection between the grammar point and the context – the reading text.

Exercise 3b checks both meaning and form. The first question in the box asks students to think about what *should* means in order to give them an understanding of how it is used in spoken and written language. The second question in the box encourages students to think about the grammatical patterns associated with *should*. This is what we call its grammatical form. For some grammar structures, for example tenses with more than one verb like the present continuous (e.g. *I'm working part-time this week*), the form task will look at what main and auxiliary verbs are used and their order.

Exercise 3c asks students to listen to the pronunciation of *should* and *shouldn't* and highlights the short vowel sound and the silent 'l'. Students are then directed to controlled written practice activities at the back of the book: 12B, exercise a, in the example above. For this particular lesson, there are another two practice activities on the page (but not included in Figure 5.0a). Students then return to the main lesson and do exercise 3e. This is freer practice of the target grammar point and could be done as both a speaking and writing activity.

The nature of grammar lessons and variations

The example above is typical not only of the sequence but also of the overall approach to presenting grammar. The activities are created to provide a student-centred focus in the lesson. In other words, there are tasks for students to do alone, and then discuss in pairs, before checking their answers with the teacher. This gives students time to process the new language, think about it and connect it with existing knowledge. It means students are not completely dependent on understanding a teacher's explanation of the grammar point.

In the example above, meaning, form and pronunciation are dealt with systematically. In some course book lessons, one step in the process may be missing. For example, there will be a task that checks the meaning of the grammar point, but there is nothing that checks the form. Sometimes tasks that focus on grammar form are given in a special grammar section at the back of the course book. With the example above, the controlled written gap fill in 12B, exercise a, comes from the grammar section at the back of the course book. If a step in the process outlined above is missing, and you feel your students would benefit from it, you can create your own task to supplement the course book material.

One criticism of the type of approach in the example is that students spend a lot of time with their heads down doing tasks and thinking about the answers to the questions. This can result in a very passive learning environment that is not motivating for many learners. One way that teachers can intervene and add value to these micro steps of a grammar lesson is by asking extra questions when they check the answers to the meaning and form tasks. Rather than just asking 'do you understand?', a teacher would use a question that focuses more specifically on *should / shouldn't*. For example, she could ask 'Do I use *should* if I think my idea is really important or quite important?'. Alternatively, if the teacher knows that students understand the modal verb *must*, she might ask whether *should* is stronger or weaker than *must*.

These kinds of questions help back up exercise 3b in the example and also aim to involve students in the lesson a little more actively. Having completed exercise 3c, some teachers may choose to drill example sentences from the text so students have the opportunity to try out the pronunciation. All these teaching techniques are initial ways of getting the grammar off the page. The activities in this chapter give more ideas of ways you can do this.

Meaning and form

When teaching a grammar structure, it helps to bear in mind the relationship between meaning and form. More often than not, course books deal with meaning and form separately, particularly at lower levels. However, proficiency in a language means being able to choose the form that best matches the intended meaning (when speaking or writing) or identifying the meaning that best matches the perceived form (when listening or reading). This is an instantaneous process that is sometimes called 'form–meaning mapping'.

An alternative approach

The approach to teaching grammar outlined above is commonly known as PPP (Presentation → Practice → Production). This approach can be reassuring for many students because it follows a logical progression and gives them a sense of dealing with grammar points thoroughly in a step-by-step fashion. However, other students may find this approach overly systematic and might prefer something that is initially more communicative and meaning-focused.

One way to cater to these students is to begin at the end of a course book lesson. More often than not, the final activity in a course book lesson will give students an opportunity to use the target grammar structure in a meaningful context. *Figure 5.0b* shows the final production activity that comes after the grammar lesson we have analysed in the example above (the complete lesson also includes vocabulary input and listening practice).

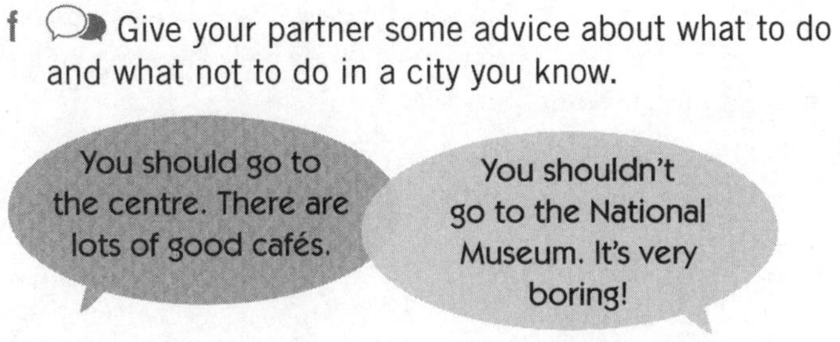

Figure 5.0b: Doff, A., C. Thaine et al. (2015) *Cambridge English Empower A2*, p. 123.

Off the Page

The teacher could ask students to do this activity first without having presented *should / shouldn't* and without pointing out the use in the speech bubble examples (or perhaps writing up the task on the board without any examples). The teacher monitors and listens for use of *should / shouldn't*. If students are using the target grammar well, then there is no need to teach it. However, if they are not, the teacher can write down some of the incorrect examples she hears and use these as a springboard for teaching *should / shouldn't*. In effect, the grammar lesson begins with feedback and correction on the language students have produced. The teacher then shows students a better way of expressing their ideas using the target grammar. Students would then look for examples of *should / shouldn't* in the reading texts and follow the grammar tasks. In the end, students could repeat the speaking task in exercise f above or do a similar one to practise using *should / shouldn't*. This approach is commonly known as Task-Teach-Task (TTT) and can be very useful at higher levels where students may know the target grammar, but still have difficulty in using it correctly.

A Focus on meaning

5.1 Shopping for meaning

Level	A2 and above
Time	15 to 20 minutes
Outline	Using imaginary money, students go around the class buying examples of a grammar structure that relates to a particular meaning.
Aim	To give students practice evaluating grammar examples in relation to areas of meaning.
Preparation	Make correct and incorrect examples of the target grammar structure to give to 'shopkeepers'. Copy and cut these up. Find something that can act as money, for example, counters, matchsticks or small pieces of coloured paper.
Rationale	Getting students to consider grammatical meaning typically involves a degree of passive sitting and thinking. This activity aims to liven up the process by turning it into a game that gets students moving around the classroom. It can be done after a course book task that focuses on grammatical meaning, for example, exercise 6a in *Figure 5.1* below.

Procedure

1 Choose three pairs of students. Each of these pairs will be the shopkeepers that sell grammar examples – some correct and some incorrect. See the worksheet below for *Figure 5.1*. Don't tell students which examples are correct or incorrect.

2 The remaining students, the 'shoppers', work in pairs. Half the pairs look for sentences that match one area of meaning, examples that *talk about things that happen every day/week/month*, and the other half look for examples that *talk about things that are happening now.* Avoid using the tense names – for *Figure 5.1* the present simple and present continuous – so students focus on meaning and not form.

3 Give each pair of shoppers a limited amount of money, for example, 10 counters. Shoppers then go around the shopkeepers trying to buy correct examples for their area of meaning, negotiating the price. (Shopkeepers will also need money so they can give change.)

4 Shopkeepers should try to get a good price for their examples, even the ones they think are incorrect, but they cannot charge more than five counters for any one example.

5 Set a time limit of about 10 minutes and let the shopping begin.

6 The shopkeepers who have sold the most correct examples are the winning shopkeepers, and the pair who have bought the most correct examples are the winning shoppers.

7 In open class, go through all the examples and point out which are correct and which are incorrect.

Notes

You can give all the shopkeepers all of the grammar examples, or you can spread the examples amongst the shopkeepers – it depends on the size of your class and how much time you want to spend on the activity. At higher levels, this activity can work well with a tense that has a variety of meanings, for example, different conditional structures.

Learner reflection questions

1 Why wasn't it a good idea to just look for examples of one of the tenses?
2 When you read or hear examples of a grammar structure, how does it help you understand the meaning?

Teacher reflection

Did some students try and identify examples just by tense name? What does this tell you about the way they think about grammar? How can you address this in future lessons?

HELP WITH GRAMMAR
Present Simple or Present Continuous

6 **a** Look at this sentence. Then complete the rules with *Present Simple* or *Present Continuous*.

I usually go by train, but I'm taking the bus today.

- We use the ______________ to talk about things that happen every day/week/month, etc.
- We use the ______________ to talk about things that are happening now.

Figure 5.1: Redston, C. and G. Cunningham (2012) *face2face Elementary* (2nd ed.), p. 67.

Worksheet
Correct sentences for cutting up

She gets up every day at 7.00 am.	I'm working quite hard at the moment.
They visit their grandmother once a month.	She's not here, she's playing tennis with Maria.
We do our food shopping at the weekend.	They're saving money to buy a new car.
The concerts always begin at 8.30 pm.	We're having a great holiday in Spain.
He sometimes catches the tram to work.	It isn't raining hard right now.
They don't go to the cinema very often.	He's studying for his final exams.
We don't usually go to bed late during the week.	They're having a good time at the party.
I don't often see friends during the week, only at the weekend.	I'm reading a really interesting book at the moment.

Incorrect sentences for cutting up

It snows heavily outside.
He's not free now, he speaks to a customer.
We stay with friends just for two days.
I watch a great series on TV at the moment.
They have a party next door, it's very noisy.
The bus is always leaving at 8.15 am.
Every day they're having lunch in a café.
I'm hardly ever seeing my friends from school.
They aren't often going to the theatre.
He isn't normally arriving late to work.

5.2 Meaning call outs

Level	A2 and above
Time	10 to 15 minutes
Outline	The teacher calls out course book grammar meaning rules and, in response, students write example sentences.
Aim	To give students practice writing meaning-based examples to check their understanding.
Preparation	Think of a series of meaning call outs for the grammar point you are teaching. Suggestions for the *Figure 5.2a* course book lesson are given below. However, you may think of extra rules to call out that include a topic that you know will interest your students.
Rationale	Many course book grammar exercises get students to say or write examples and label the grammar with the correct tense name. By contrast, this activity avoids using the tense name and asks students to write examples based on meaning explanations in association with different topics.

Procedure

1 Students complete the task that focuses on meaning (exercise 3A in *Figure 5.2a* below) and close their books – they will write sentences in their notebooks.

2 Tell students the kind of sentence or question you want them to write, but to use their own information. They should use 'I' for sentences and 'you' for questions.

3 Do an open class example with the class.

4 Say each call out sentence two or three times and give students sufficient time to write. For now, don't get them to check with a partner. Call outs for *Figure 5.2a* below might be:

Write a sentence about a hobby you always do.
Write a question about another person's activity at this moment.
Write a sentence about food or drink – now.
Write a question about something a person does every day.

5 Do four or five call outs and then get students to compare their examples in pairs. Monitor, help and tell each pair they can check one or two examples with you that they're not sure about.

Notes

Once you have done this activity a couple of times, it will require less explanation. You can make it more challenging by offering less information in the call out. For instance, the open class example could be reduced down to 'sports activity – now'. At higher levels, this could be used as a meaning-focused revision activity for a variety of tenses.

Learner reflection questions

1 Was it harder to think of an example of the correct grammar when you wrote the sentences and questions? Why do you think so?

2 How similar were your examples to your partner's?

Teacher reflection

How is this activity different from asking students to complete an example using the correct verb form' – as suggested in exercise 3C of *Figure 5.2a*? Which students were more successful at doing this activity? Why do you think that was the case?

3 GRAMMAR: Simple present and present continuous

A **Circle the correct options to complete the rules. Use the sentences in the grammar box to help you.**
Use the simple present when actions happen **usually / at the time of speaking**.
Use the present continuous when actions happen **usually / at the time of speaking**.

Simple present and present continuous

Do you **exercise** much?	**I'm lifting** my coffee cup.
I stretch every morning	He's **jumping** right now.

ACCURACY CHECK

Use the *-ing* form of the verb with the present continuous.
I'm ~~watch~~ the game now. ✗
I'm watching the game now. ✓

B **Now go to page 132. Do the grammar exercise for 3.2.**

C **Put the verbs in the correct form. Then check your accuracy.**
A I _'m thinking_ (think) of a famous soccer player.
B Where [1] ______ (he / come) from?
A He [2] ______ (come) from Brazil, but right now he [3] ______ (live) in Spain.
B [4] ______ (he / play) in the game on TV right now?
A No, he [5] ______ (not be).

D PAIR WORK **Think of a famous athlete, but don't tell your partner. Ask questions to guess your partner's famous athlete.**

Figure 5.2a: Clandfield, L., B. Goldstein, C. Jones and P. Kerr (2019) *Evolve 2*, p. 25.

For *Figure 5.2b*, the activity call outs could just refer to the topic of the sentence, for example: 'exercise', 'food', 'study', together with the key concept: 'good idea' or 'necessary'. The call out 'exercise – good idea' would mean students write: *You should go to the gym more often.*

Language focus 1
should/must

1 Complete the examples from the text on page 20. Then complete the rules in the box.

1 You .... get enough sleep.
2 You .... get between eight and nine hours of sleep each night.
3 You .... watch TV before you go to bed.

We use [1].... to say what we think is a good idea and [2].... to say what we think is necessary.

Figure 5.2b: Goldstein, B. and C. Jones (2015) *Eyes Open 3*, p. 21.

5.3 Find the poster

Level B1+ and above

Time 10 to 15 minutes

Outline In pairs, students are given example sentences of a grammar structure with different uses, before moving around the classroom and sticking them onto the correct 'meaning poster'.

Aim To help students distinguish different ways in which some grammar structures can be used.

Preparation Prepare three or four meaning posters on sheets of A3 paper with a graphic or an appropriate heading for each one. Copy and cut up sentences containing the target grammar point (see those given below for the modal verbs of speculation in *Figure 5.3*). Each pair of students will need sticky tack or something they can use to stick their sentences to the posters. If you are focusing on a different grammar structure from *Figure 5.3* you will need to create your own examples.

Rationale At higher levels, students often have to understand how similar grammar structures can be used to express different meanings. A typical example is modal verbs used to express different levels of certainty when speculating. Students also need to understand how a single grammar structure can be used to express different meanings: the present perfect, for example, can describe a recently completed action, or an activity that began in the past and is still happening. A simple matching task worksheet might provide students some practice of such points, but the approach in this activity is to get students up and moving around and considering other students' choices.

Procedure

1. Students complete the meaning task in the course book – exercises 1a and b in *Figure 5.3*.
2. If your grammar structure can be represented by some kind of graphic, draw it on the board and elicit the meaning and an example from the course book – see the example continuum lines of certainty below.
3. Hand out three or four cut up sentences to each pair of students.
4. In pairs, students move around the room and stick their sentences on the meaning poster that corresponds to the grammar in each sentence. Encourage students to check other sentences placed by other students and to challenge them if they think they're incorrect.
5. When students have finished, collect in all the posters and check the answers in open class.

Notes and variation

An extension to this activity would be to give each pair blank pieces of paper on which they write their own example sentences for each of the meaning posters.

Learner reflection questions

1. Was it helpful to read the grammar examples that other students placed on the posters before adding yours? Why / Why not?
2. In your first language, do you sometimes use the same grammar structure to talk about different ideas? What's an example?

Teacher reflection

How clear were students about different uses of the grammar structure? Is there one specific meaning that students find difficult to grasp? Did some students find the graphic representations of meaning easier than written definitions?

Lost

GRAMMAR
Modals of deduction and speculation

1 a Look at the sentences from the conversations. Which highlighted modal verbs can you use to say:

1 you're sure something is true?
2 something is possible? (x2)
3 you're sure something is not true?

The train must go from here.
There might be a local bus that goes past.
Oh, no. This can't be our train!
There could be one further along.

b Find one more example of each modal verb in the scripts on p154.

2 a During their car journey, Alice, Javier and Donna got lost. Complete their conversation with appropriate modal verbs from 1a.

ALICE This [1]______ be the right road. None of the signs say Beauville on them.
DONNA You're right. Sorry, guys. I think we're lost.
JAVIER Well, maybe we should head towards the nearest town. I'm sure there [2]______ be a shop with a map there.
DONNA Maybe. But we're not near any towns at the moment.
ALICE Oh, look, there's a garage coming up. It [3]______ sell maps.
DONNA I'll stop so you can go in and ask.
...
JAVIER No, no maps. And he's never heard of Beauville!
ALICE What! Let's call Andy. She lived round here. She [4]______ know the area pretty well.
JAVIER OK, you can use my phone. I haven't got her number though.
ALICE Oh no! Er, I think it's 0151 ...
JAVIER No, it [5]______ be that. It's the wrong area code.
ALICE Oh, no. What are we going to do?

Grammar reference and practice, p140

b 2.22 Listen to check.

Figure 5.3: Rea, D. and T. Clementson (2011) *English Unlimited B1+*, p. 65.

Continuum lines to put on posters

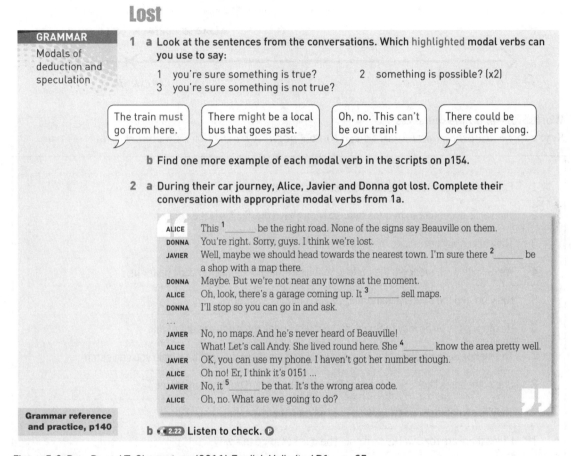

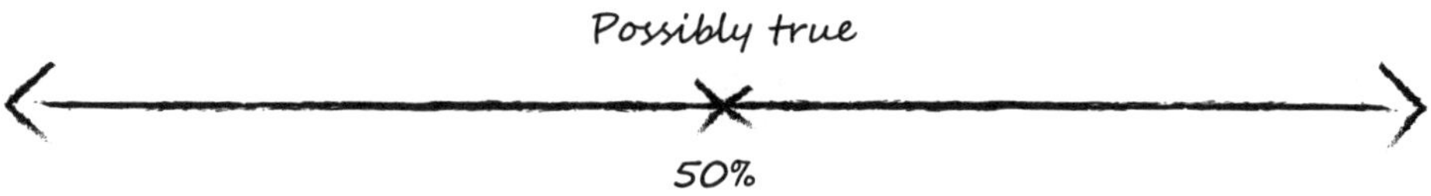

Worksheet – example sentences
Key: 1 to 5 = almost certain it's not true; 6 to 10 = possibly true; 11 to 15 = almost certain it's true

1 Emma's away on holiday. It can't be her knocking at the door.

2 I had a 'flu injection two months ago, so I can't have the 'flu. It's just a cold.

3 They never buy tickets, so they can't be the Lotto winners.

4 We definitely put money in the parking machine – the parking ticket can't be for us.

5 I only posted the parcel this morning. It can't be there already.

6 He often goes on holiday to Spain, so he might speak the language quite well.

7 The station is sometimes closed at the weekend, so there may not be a train you can catch.

8 She sometimes likes crime stories. This could be a good book to buy for her.

9 They're sometimes late to work so they might not arrive before nine o'clock.

10 I think there are road works so it could be quicker to go this way.

11 I checked an online map – this must be the right place.

12 Buses pass by really frequently, there must be one soon.

13 We paid online two days ago, you must have the money by now.

14 She's by far the hardest worker – she must win the prize this year.

15 I heard someone moving around upstairs. He must be home from holiday.

B Focus on form

5.4 Students' form questions

Level	B1 and above
Time	20 to 25 minutes
Outline	After completing a task that checks the form of a grammar structure, students write questions about the form to ask the teacher.
Aim	To encourage students to think more comprehensively about the form of grammar; to identify aspects of the form of a grammar item that needs clarification.
Preparation	There are no materials to prepare, but it would be useful to think of question prompts for students similar to those suggested in the *Procedure*.
Rationale	Course books often provide some kind of task that focuses on the form of grammar items, using a range of task types: labelling parts of a structure, completing gapped sentences, filling in tables, choosing the correct word in a summary of the form. In *Figure 5.4a* below, exercise 7b uses gapped form summaries while exercise 7c asks students to answer questions. These are all useful activities, but sometimes they may not be sufficient to deal fully with students' understanding about form and how to use the grammar structure. This activity gives students an opportunity to consider more closely the form of the target grammar and to ask about anything they are unsure of.

Procedure

1 Students complete the course book grammar task – exercise 7 in *Figure 5.4a* below.
2 Ask students to look at the text (reading or listening audio script) that the grammar came from. Students underline more examples.
3 Put students in small groups of three or four to think of questions to ask you, the teacher, about the form of the grammar point. They can also think of examples to check whether they are correct or not.
4 On the board, give students some question prompts, for example:
  What's the correct order for ... ?
  Which verb changes when ... ?
  Is this example correct?
5 You can also put some key words that are relevant to the grammar point on the board, for example: *main verb / auxiliary / question form / negative form / regular / irregular* etc. If you teach a monolingual group and you speak the students' first language, they could ask if the grammar point is the same as or similar to a grammar structure in their language.
6 Allow students at least 10 minutes to work in their groups, then let them ask you their questions.

Notes and variation

The group discussion provides an opportunity for speaking practice and some peer-to-peer teaching, with stronger students likely able to answer questions from weaker learners. This activity would probably be challenging for very low level learners unless they are able to do it in their first language. Students need a small degree of knowledge of grammar terminology in order to carry it out. It is also possible to do this activity with a focus on meaning. For example, in groups, students come up with questions that focus on how to use the grammar structure correctly. Some useful board prompts might be: *finished / unfinished / in progress / sure / not sure / countable / uncountable / real / imaginary* etc. The success of the activity assumes that you, the teacher, have researched the grammar point thoroughly so you are able to deal with students' questions.

Learner reflection questions

1 What did you learn about the grammar from other students when you were talking in groups?
2 Why is it useful to find or create examples to help you understand the meaning of some grammar points?

Teacher reflection

What aspects of the form of the grammar structure emerged from the students' questions? Was this covered by the course book? How correct were students' examples?

HELP WITH GRAMMAR Present Perfect for life experiences (1): positive and negative

7 **a** Look at these sentences. Then choose the correct verb form in the rules.

Present Perfect	He**'s done** a lot of work for charity.
Past Simple	Danny **started** acting at the age of seven.

- We use the *Present Perfect/Past Simple* for experiences that happened some time before now. We don't know or don't say when they happened.
- We use the *Present Perfect/Past Simple* if we say exactly when something happened.

b Fill in the gaps for the Present Perfect with *'ve*, *haven't*, *'s* or *hasn't*.

POSITIVE

I/you/we/they + ... (= have) + past participle
he/she/it + ... (= has) + past participle

NEGATIVE

I/you/we/they + ... + past participle
he/she/it + ... + past participle

TIP • We often use *never* with the Present Perfect: *I've never met Johnny Depp.*

c How do we make past participles of regular verbs? Is there a rule for past participles of irregular verbs?

d Check in GRAMMAR 4.1 p135.

Figure 5.4a: Redston, C. and G. Cunningham (2012) *face2face Pre-intermediate* (2nd ed.), p. 31.

In the example in *Figure 5.4b*, the questions students have about form are likely to also lead to questions about meaning – particularly around the time reference.

Language focus 1 Second conditional

1 Complete the examples from the text on page 76. Then complete the rules.

imaginary situation	possible consequence
If I .... until the end of a class,	I .... in detention!
If you .... to start a new school magazine,	you .... it to the teachers.

1 We use .... + past simple and .... + infinitive to form the second conditional.
2 We use the second conditional to talk about unreal situations in the present or **future / past**.

Figure 5.4b: Goldstein, B. and C. Jones (2015) *Eyes Open 3*, p. 77.

5.5 Table assembly

Level	A2 and above
Time	5 to 10 minutes
Outline	In small groups, students are given a cut up of a table that outlines the form of a grammar structure. They assemble the table and check it against the version in the course book.
Aim	To clarify the form of a tense; to provide students with an opportunity to negotiate form as a group.
Preparation	Word process a grammar table that covers the same points in the grammar table in the course book, so all of the boxes are of a similar size (see example worksheet for *Figure 5.5a* below) and students can focus on the relationships between the different forms and the grammar labels. You will then need to copy and cut up the tables – one copy for each small group of students. If you do this on card, you could re-use the cut ups when you teach this grammar structure again.
Rationale	Most course books include some kind of grammar summary or grammar reference section at the back of the course book, which students are directed to and which expands on the lesson's grammar point. Often the form of the structure is presented in a table format as in *Figure 5.5a*. Asking students to simply read these summaries is a very passive exercise, and it's difficult for teachers to know what information students have understood or processed as a result. This activity involves a problem-solving approach that requires students to think more actively about form relationships.

Procedure

1. After students have completed the grammar tasks in the lesson, ask them to close their books (they do not look at the grammar summary in the back of the course book yet).
2. Hold up a set of cut ups and tell students they need to organise the different pieces to make a table that summarises the form of the grammar structure. In *Figure 5.5a*, students organise the cut ups to summarise the positive, negative and question forms of the past of *be*.
3. Students work in small groups of two to four and organise the cut ups into a table.
4. When most groups have finished, get students to check their tables against the examples in the course book.
5. Ask students what parts of the form were most difficult. If you saw that most students had a problem with one aspect, re-teach this on the board.

Notes and variation

As is the case with many student-centred grammar tasks, students can learn a lot from each other when discussing form. The fact that students can move the cut pieces of paper around and try out different options provides a bit more flexibility than merely filling in a table. It is also possible for this to be a whole class activity. The different elements of the table can be placed on large cards for students to stick on the board while the rest of the class offers guidance. If you have an interactive whiteboard, the table elements can be movable images for students to manipulate. This activity is also useful at higher levels with tenses and verb phrases that are more complex, for example, past modal forms.

Learner reflection questions

1 What was more difficult to remember: the correct order of words or matching subjects to the correct verb form?
2 How was this activity different from writing and filling in a table? What do you prefer to do?

Teacher reflection

Which students were more confident at analysing the form? What did you learn about students' knowledge of grammatical terminology from this activity?

6A Past simple: *be*

My grandparents were at school together, but they weren't friends.

We use *was / were* to talk about the past.
was / were are the past forms of *am / is / are*.
We often use past time expressions with *was / were*, e.g. *yesterday, last year, in 2012*.

2.49

	+		–	
I / he / she / it	*I* ***was***	*at home yesterday.*	*He* ***wasn't***	*at home yesterday.*
you / we / they	*They* ***were***	*at home yesterday.*	*We* ***weren't***	*at home yesterday.*

	***Yes/No* questions**		**Short answers**	
I / he / she / it	***Was*** *she*	*at home yesterday?*	*Yes,* *No,*	*she* ***was****.* *she* ***wasn't****.*
you / we / they	***Were*** *you*	*at home yesterday?*	*Yes,* *No,*	*we* ***were****.* *we* ***weren't****.*

	Wh- **questions**		
I / he / she / it	*Where*	***was*** *he*	*yesterday?*
you / we / they	*Where*	***were*** *you*	*yesterday?*

We can also use *there was / there were*:
There was *a computer on the table.*
There were *some chairs in the garden.*

Figure 5.5a: Doff, A., C. Thaine et al. (2015) *Cambridge English Empower A2*, p. 146.

Worksheet

+	–	yes / no questions	short answers	*Wh-* questions
I / he / she / it	*I was*	*at home yesterday.*	*He wasn't*	*at home yesterday.*
you / we / they	*They were*	*at home yesterday.*	*We weren't*	*at home yesterday.*
I / he / she / it	*Was she*	*at home yesterday?*	*Yes,* *No,*	*she was.* *she wasn't.*
you / we / they	*Were you*	*at home yesterday?*	*Yes,* *No,*	*we were.* *we weren't.*
I / he / she / it	*Where*	*was he*	*yesterday?*	
you / we / they	*Where*	*were you*	*yesterday?*	

If you base your cut up table on a course book grammar point that includes a gap fill exercise like the one in *Figure 5.5b*, it's a good idea to make sure your table only includes completed sentences.

GRAMMAR

have to / don't have to

1 **Complete the sentences from the article on page 67 with *have to* and *don't have to*.**

1 They ________ wash their faces with clean water.
2 To stop trachoma people ________ take expensive medication.

2 **Complete the rule and the table.**

RULE: Use [1] ______ to say 'this is necessary'.
Use [2] ______ to say 'this isn't necessary'.

Positive	Negative
I/you/we/they [0] *have to* help	I/you/we/they don't have to help
he/she/it [1] ______ help	he/she/it [2] ______ help

Questions	Short answers
[3] ______ I/you/we/they have to help?	Yes, I/you/we/they do. No, I/you/we/they don't.
[4] ______ he/she/it have to help?	Yes, he/she/it [5] ______ . No, he/she/it [6] ______ .

Figure 5.5b: Puchta, H., J. Stranks and P. Lewis-Jones (2015) *Think Level 1*, p. 68.

5.6 Form teams

Level	A2 and above
Time	5 to 10 minutes
Outline	Students work in two teams of equal numbers to organise each other into sentences or questions that check correct form of the target grammar.
Aim	To reinforce the form of a grammatical structure; to encourage student-centred, active negotiation of grammatical form.
Preparation	Write out two or more sentences or questions and cut them up so there are only one or two words on each piece of paper (see the questions for *Figure 5.6* below).
Rationale	For some students, the analysis of grammatical form isn't very motivating. This is particularly true where the exercise is heads-down, and it involves filling in sentences or tables. Some students also find the use of grammatical terminology off-putting. This activity makes the analysis of form more active and should appeal to students for whom physical movement aids learning.

Procedure

1 Students complete the grammar analysis task in the course book (exercise 9 in *Figure 5.6* below) and close their books.

2 Put students into teams of about five or six students. If possible, have two teams (but three teams also works).

3 Give Team 1 a cut up sentence or question – each member has a piece of paper with one or two words, which they hold and show to Team 2.

4 Team 2 organises Team 1 into the correct word order. Team 1 doesn't say anything.

5 When Team 2 has finished, Team 1 reads their words aloud and Team 2 gives reasons for the ordering, e.g. *Maria goes first because she is the question word. Pietrek is next because he's the auxiliary* ... etc.

6 You may need to correct the sentence/question order or you could ask a question to check comprehension, e.g. *If Deniz is the subject, why is she after the main verb?*

7 Once Team 2 has successfully presented their ordered sentence or question, reverse the roles and hand out the next sentence or question.

Notes and variation

This activity could also be turned into a competition. The two teams are given the same sentence and members have to organise themselves into the correct order. The winner is the first team to do so correctly. Having the components of form as movable objects helps make the form task more tangible for some students. It also provides practice with language for giving instructions (e.g. imperatives, or *should*) as well as prepositions of place and adverbs of order. Asking students to justify their decisions encourages them to think about the form rather than just guess. Although there is no onus on students to use grammar terminology, it is likely that stronger students will do so, for example by making suggestions about the verb tense, thereby helping students who feel less assured about the correct terminology.

Learner reflection questions

1 How did you decide the correct order – did you think about the individual words or did it just sound correct?

2 Was it easy or difficult to present the correct order to your teacher? Why?

Teacher reflection

Did the students who have good explicit knowledge of grammar lead their team? Or was it the students who have confident personalities? To what extent do you think students drew from their explicit language knowledge as opposed to a more instinctive feel for language?

HELP WITH GRAMMAR Present Simple (1): *Wh-* questions (*I/you/we/they*)

9 **a** Look at the table. Notice the word order in questions.

question word	auxiliary	subject	infinitive	
What time	do	you	get up?	
When	do	you	have	lunch?

b Write questions 1–3 in the table.

1 When do you finish work?

2 What time do you get home?

3 Where do you have dinner?

c Check in **GRAMMAR 3.2** p134.

TIP • Present Simple questions are the same for *I*, *you*, *we* and *they*.

Figure 5.6: Redston, C. and G. Cunningham (2012) *face2face Elementary* (2nd ed.), p.25.

Example questions for ordering – two teams of six

what	time	do	you	start	class
where	do	you	go	for	coffee

5.7 Noughts and crosses grammar review

Level	A2 and above
Time	10 to 15 minutes
Outline	Students play a noughts and crosses quiz as a way of revising previously taught grammar.
Aim	To revise the form of grammar taught in a prior lesson.
Preparation	Think of at least nine language points that can be used to win a square. It's a good idea to think of one or two extra questions in case both teams get an answer wrong.
Rationale	Course books regularly include revision activities at regular intervals. Often these come at the end of a unit. Sometimes these revision activities include gap fill or matching tasks. This means students might do a lot of writing, which, for many, isn't the most motivating way to revise language. It's very easy to turn these revision activities into a game, which students will probably enjoy. This teaching idea uses noughts and crosses (also known as tic-tac-toe).

Procedure

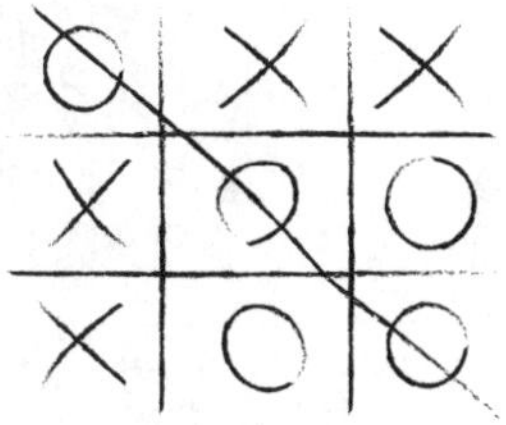

1 Draw an empty noughts and crosses grid on the board and put a number in each square. Check that students know how to play noughts and crosses – do an example on the board if necessary.
2 Put students into two teams and ask each team whether they want to be noughts or crosses and which team will start.
3 Ask Team 1 to choose a square. They will have to give a correct example sentence answer in order to have a nought or a cross (whichever symbol their team is) placed in that square.
4 For *Figure 5.7a* below, put the following categories on the board: *singular, plural, positive, negative, question, short answer* and point to two categories for students to make a sentence using *there*. For example, *singular + negative = There isn't a hotel.* The team members check with each other and then give their answer.
5 If the answer is correct, put that team's symbol in the square they chose. If the answer is incorrect, give the correct answer. It is now the turn of Team 2.
6 The first team to get three noughts or crosses in a row, wins.

Notes and variation

Students usually enjoy the competition (even though it often ends in a draw!) and there is often useful discussion about language when each team agrees on their answer. The noughts and crosses game can be used for a great variety of language items (vocabulary, expressions, pronunciation), not just grammar. As well as asking students to produce examples, you can ask them questions about language. It can also be used as a regular end-of-week revision game.

Learner reflection questions

1 How well did your team remember the grammar? Why do you think that was the case?
2 Did playing the game mean the activity felt less like a grammar lesson?
3 If so, what can you do when you study grammar in your own time?

Teacher reflection

When teams were discussing their answers, what did you learn about their knowledge? Did you find that the game meant some students participated more in the lesson than they normally do?

The course book example in *Figure 5.7a* begins the lesson with a review exercise of the previous lesson's grammar point (see the grammar table below).

7B A new home

Vocabulary roor
Grammar *How n*
some, any, a

QUICK REVIEW *there is/there are* Work in groups. Talk about the good and bad things about the town or city you're in now. Use *there is, there are, there isn't,* and *there aren't.*

HELP WITH GRAMMAR *there is/there are*

6 **a** Fill in the gaps in the tables with *'s, is, are, isn't* or *aren't.*

	singular
POSITIVE (+)	There ______ a nice beach.
NEGATIVE (–)	There ______ a station.
QUESTIONS (?)	______ there a hotel?
SHORT ANSWERS	Yes, there ______ ./No, there ______ .

	plural
POSITIVE (+)	There ______ lots of things to do.
NEGATIVE (–)	There ______ any restaurants.
QUESTIONS (?)	______ there any good pubs?
SHORT ANSWERS	Yes, there ______ ./No, there ______ .

TIP • We use *any* in negatives and questions with *there are.*

b What is the Past Simple of *there is* and *there are*?

c Check in GRAMMAR 7.1 p144.

Figure 5.7a: Redston, C. and G. Cunningham (2012) *face2face Elementary* (2nd ed.), p. 57.

Suggested board prompts to point to for this language

there ...
singular plural
positive (+)
negative (–)
question (?)
short answer

C Practice

5.8 Beep the gap

Level	A1 and above
Time	5 to 10 minutes
Outline	Students mingle with a gapped sentence. They say the sentence using the word 'beep' for the gap and elicit a correct version from their classmates.
Aim	To provide controlled oral practice of a target grammar structure; to encourage students to listen carefully to each other.
Preparation	Copy and cut up the gapped sentences you wish to use. You'll need one sentence for each student so you may need to create extra examples to what is in the course book. Write the correct answer on the back of each individual sentence.
Rationale	Course books are effective in providing controlled written grammar practice activities, but often don't include a lot of controlled speaking practice tasks. Also the controlled writing exercises usually come just after students have analysed some target language. This means a lot of stationary, cognitive effort for students. This activity shows how you can turn controlled writing practice into speaking practice, getting students up and moving around.

Procedure

1 Give each student a sentence with a gap that they fill in with the correct word – in *Figure 5.8a* below, they should choose between *can* and *can't*. Tell students not to check their answers with each other. When all students have completed their sentence, tell them to check the correct answer on the back of their piece of paper.

2 Students then mingle and test their classmates. They should say their sentence and indicate where the gap is, with the word 'beep'. The student listening then repeats the sentence with what they think is the correct word to go in the gap.

3 Tell students not to show their sentence – they have to say it and the other student has to listen carefully.

4 When students have spoken to most of their classmates, in open class, ask who got a lot of correct answers and who got a lot of incorrect answers.

5 If you feel some students need the reinforcement of written practice, they could now open their course books and write answers for all the sentences (or give students a handout of sentences if you have used different ones from those in the course book).

Notes and variation

As the *Aim* above indicates, this activity gives students practice in listening for grammar and processing language items in spoken output. This activity can also be used for sentences where students have to choose the correct word out of two options. When students read out these sentences, they pause, raise their hand to indicate the place where the choice is to be made and then say both options and complete the sentence.

Learner reflection questions

1 To give a correct answer, did you have to understand only the words next to the gap or did you have to understand the complete sentence?
2 Do you prefer practising with written examples or spoken examples or both? Why?

Teacher reflection

Were some students very keen to read the written sentence? What does this tell you about the learning preferences of these students? How good were students at listening to each other? Is this a skill they need more practice in?

11B *can* for ability

Part 1: Positive and negative

a Complete the sentences with *can* or *can't*.

1 I studied Spanish at university for three years. I ____________ speak with Spanish people.
2 Her meals are terrible. She ____________ cook!
3 My brother and I don't like the sea or swimming pools. We ____________ swim.
4 I went to guitar lessons. Now I ____________ play some easy songs.
5 I don't have a bicycle, but I ____________ ride one.
6 I don't like that band. They ____________ sing.

Figure 5.8a: Doff, A., C. Thaine et al. (2015) *Cambridge English Empower A1*, p. 131.

In the example in *Figure 5.8b*, students need to consider not only positive and negative forms but also whether the verb agrees with the subject of the sentence.

4 **Complete the sentences with *have to / has to* or *don't / doesn't have to*.**

1 Our teacher doesn't like mobile phones. We ________ switch them off during lessons.
2 I know that I ________ work hard for this test! You ________ tell me!
3 My sister is ill. She ________ stay in bed.
4 Your room is terrible! You ________ tidy it up.
5 Mario's English is perfect. He ________ study for the tests.
6 I can hear you very well. You ________ shout!

Figure 5.8b: Puchta, H., J. Stranks and P. Lewis-Jones (2015) *Think Level 1*, p. 68.

5.9 Write then speak

Level	A1 and above
Time	10 to 15 minutes
Outline	After completing a written dialogue that practises the target grammar structure, students use prompts to practise a spoken version in pairs.
Aim	To provide controlled spoken practice of a grammar point.
Preparation	Make copies of the dialogue prompts worksheet – see *Figure 5.9* below. If you are using a different course book activity, you will need to write and copy your own dialogue prompts.
Rationale	At lower levels, students often feel they need the structured support that controlled written practice provides them with. However, students need to understand that a lot of the language they study in course books is oral in nature. Therefore, it's important that they are provided with regular opportunities for speaking practice. This activity aims to create a bridge between written and spoken practice that can reassure less confident students.

Procedure

1 Students complete the dialogue by writing in the correct form of the verbs and then read the conversation aloud in pairs – exercise C in *Figure 5.9* below.

2 Students then close their books in order to practise the conversation again using the key words from the dialogue.

3 Write the prompts for the first line of dialogue on the board. For *Figure 5.9* this is: *what / you / do / Saturday?* Elicit and drill the complete question.

4 Give out the worksheet for students to practise the conversation just using the prompt words. They take turns being speaker A and B.

5 Monitor and help where necessary and, if you feel it's appropriate, you can do on-the-spot correction of language errors. Make sure students don't try to write the dialogue again from the prompts on the worksheet.

6 If one pair is confident practising the dialogue, you can invite them to do it for the class.

Notes and variation

While the course book in *Figure 5.9* suggests that students read the conversation aloud in pairs, this is very restricted spoken practice. Getting students to work from prompts is more challenging and requires a greater degree of cognitive effort in order to speak. Another way of managing this activity is to elicit all the lines of the dialogue in open class in order to build the dialogue.

Learner reflection questions

1 Which was more difficult – to write in the gaps to complete the dialogue, or say the dialogue in pairs? Why?

2 Did it help to write it first? Why / Why not?

3 If you have to use English outside the classroom (for example, on holiday or at work) do you need to write or speak?

Teacher reflection

Do you feel that getting students to write the dialogue first helped less confident learners? Was there a difference in students' pronunciation when they used the prompts compared to their reading the dialogue aloud? Why do you think this was the case?

3 GRAMMAR: Present continuous for future plans

A **Circle the correct options to complete the rules. Use the sentences in the grammar box to help you.**

1 You **can** / **can't** use the present continuous for the future.

2 Use the present continuous for **plans or arrangements** / **predictions**.

Present continuous for future plans

Comic Con **is coming** this weekend. **I'm bringing** my camera. **Are** you **going** to Comic Con?

B **Now go to page 132. Look at the grammar chart and do the grammar exercise for 4.1.**

C 1.36 **Complete the sentences with the present continuous form of the verb in parentheses ( ). Listen and check. Then read the conversation in pairs.**

A What [1] *are* you *doing* (do) on Saturday?

B We [2] ________ (go) to the music festival in the afternoon.

A Yeah? I [3] ________ (go), too! My brother's band [4] ________ (play)

B No way! When [5] ________ he ________ (play)?

A At 8:30, on the new music stage.

B Oh, no! We [6] ________ (not stay) that long.

INSIDER ENGLISH

Say *No way!* when you're really surprised to hear something.

D PAIR WORK **Look at the activities. Ask and answer questions about this weekend with your partner.**

go to a concert | go to the movies | see friends | study | visit family | work

Are you going to the movies this weekend?

Yeah. We're seeing the new Star Wars movie.

Figure 5.9: Clandfield, L., B. Goldstein, C. Jones and P. Kerr (2019) *Evolve 2*, p. 35.

Worksheet – dialogue prompts

A: What / you / do / Saturday?

B: We / go / music festival / afternoon.

A: Yeah? I / go too! Brother's band / play.

B: No way! When / he / play?

A: 8.30 / new music stage

B: Oh no! We / not stay / that long.

5.10 Mingle and match

Level	B1+ and above
Time	10 to 15 minutes
Outline	Students memorise sentence clauses and mingle to find their partner to create one complex sentence.
Aim	To provide controlled spoken practice in linking clauses in complex sentences.
Preparation	Copy and cut up the clauses – see the clauses in *Figure 5.10a* below. If you have a large group, you will need to write extra examples. If you focus on a different grammar point, you will need to create the relevant clauses.
Rationale	The examples of grammar exercises in this chapter are typical of most course books. They usually involve students writing and are not especially dynamic in terms of their interaction. This activity makes a typical course book grammar practice exercise for a higher level more animated and engaging. The activity works best with grammar structures that contain more than one clause, e.g. past continuous / past simple; conditional structures; sentences with time linkers *after / before/ as soon as*; sentences with linkers of contrast / concession / reason / result.

Procedure

1 Tell students they are going to move around the classroom to try to make a complete and correct sentence by finding the correct partner.
2 Hand out the clauses, making sure they are mixed up. Ask students to memorise their clause and then collect in the pieces of paper.
3 Students move around the room saying their clause aloud and listening to what others are saying in order to match clauses and make a complete sentence.
4 When all or most students have matched their clauses, check and help those who aren't sure if they've found the correct partner.

Notes

The suggestion for students to memorise the clause puts a bit more cognitive pressure on students. However, at B1+ level and above this should be manageable. If you let students hold on to their piece of paper, they are likely to walk around reading the clause aloud. This activity also works well as a revision or warmer activity at the beginning of a lesson.

Learner reflection questions

1 What grammar clues did you listen for to find the other half of your sentence?
2 What information helped you to understand?
3 Do you agree with this idea: *making sentences means mixing information with grammar to make meanings*. Why / Why not?

Teacher reflection

What are the benefits and drawbacks of getting students to memorise the clauses? Is this similar to or different from memorising irregular verbs? What other kinds of memorisation are useful when learning a language?

a Match the sentence beginnings 1–8 with the most logical endings a–h.

1 If I had more money, [c]
2 I'd be grateful [ ]
3 If I were you, [ ]
4 If you asked her again nicely, [ ]
5 I wouldn't be so relaxed [ ]
6 If he weren't so rude, [ ]
7 I could get a better job [ ]
8 Angela would be really sad [ ]

a she might change her mind.
b more people would like him.
c I could eat in restaurants more often.
d if I spoke better English.
e if we didn't invite her.
f I'd complain to your boss.
g if you didn't tell anybody my secret.
h if I had an exam tomorrow!

Figure 5.10a: Doff, A., C. Thaine et al. (2015) *Cambridge English Empower B1+*, p. 151.

In *Figure 5.10b*, it would be necessary to write out the complete sentence putting the correct word in the gap and then create sentence halves just before the time conjunction in each one.

Time conjunctions

3 **Complete the sentences with the words.**

unless | if | until | when | as soon as

1 I don't know where he is, but I'll tell him ________ I see him.
2 I'm meeting him later, so I'll tell him ________ I see him.
3 It's really important. I'm going to tell him ________ I see him.
4 I won't tell him anything ________ he asks.
5 I'll work ________ he arrives and then I'll stop.

Figure 5.10b: Puchta, H., J. Stranks and P. Lewis-Jones (2015) *Think Level 3*, p. 40.

You can find teacher development activities about grammar on pages 269 to 271.

6 Vocabulary

Introduction

Vocabulary in course books

There are many different approaches in course books to presenting and practising vocabulary – far more so when compared to the presentation of grammar. But we can probably group these different approaches in three main ways:

- as the core learning activity – the main aim is the presentation and practice of some kind of lexical set;
- as a lead in to a reading or audio text – words in the text are pre-taught to aid students' understanding;
- as a post-text activity – words in a reading or audio text are focused on in context.

When there is a focus on vocabulary, a course book will usually aim to deal with meaning and form and also, possibly, the way a word is used. Here are some aspects of meaning, form and use that can be focused on:

Meaning
- the concept we associate with the word
- the meaning of a word in a particular context
- its part of speech, i.e. how it functions grammatically, as verb, noun etc.

Form
- the spelling of the word
- the way it is pronounced
- different parts of the words, such as prefixes and suffixes

Use
- whether the word collocates (goes together) with other words
- whether the word is formal, neutral or informal
- whether the word is used in a specific context (for example, the word *tort* is a legal term), known as the register of a word
- grammar patterns the word is typically used with, for example, the verb *bear (a child)* is typically used in the passive: *I was born in Spain.*

Example approaches

The variation in approaches to presenting vocabulary as well as the different emphases of meaning, form and use mean that it is difficult to pinpoint one representative course book sequence that shows a typical approach. Instead, we will look at some different approaches that course books often use. The range of examples here is not comprehensive, but aims to show frequently used approaches.

Words to pictures

1 VOCABULARY Food 1

a 1.72 Match pictures 1–7 with the words in the box. Then listen and check.

fruit rice meat bread vegetables eggs fish

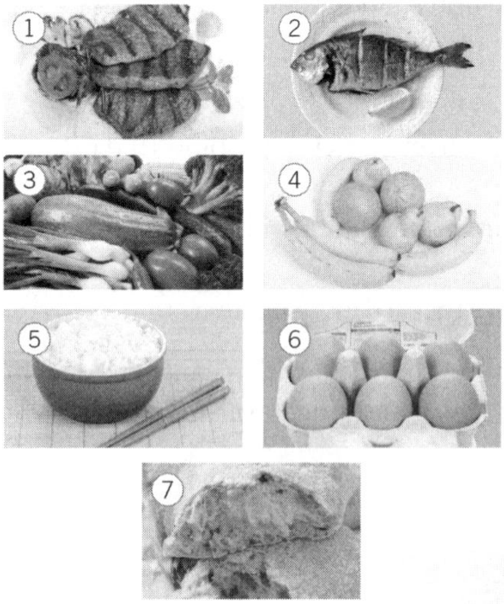

b 1.72 Pronunciation Listen to the words in 1a again. Which word has more than one syllable? Underline the stressed syllable.

c Say two things you like ☺.

I like fruit and I like fish.

d **Sound and spelling** /iː/, /ɪ/ and /aɪ/

1 1.73 Listen and practise these sounds.

1 /iː/ m**ea**t 2 /ɪ/ f**i**sh 3 /aɪ/ **I**'m

2 1.74 What sound do the **marked** letters have in the words in the box? Listen and add the words to the sound groups below.

b**i**g **ea**t n**i**ne s**i**ster **i**t's m**e**
Ch**i**na f**i**ve h**i**s t**ea**cher H**i**

Sound 1 /iː/	Sound 2 /ɪ/	Sound 3 /aɪ/
meat	fish	I'm

3 Practise saying the words.

Figure 6.0a: Doff, A., C. Thaine et al. (2015) *Cambridge English Empower A1*, p. 24.

At lower levels (A1 to B1), using pictures to convey meaning is a commonly found approach because it avoids the need to use explanations or definitions of words (which could end up being more complex than the target vocabulary), and – if the pictures are well chosen – there is little room for ambiguity. In the course book example *Figure 6.0a*, students first match the written forms to the pictures. Oral form is focused on in two ways: students listen for the number of syllables in each word and for the stressed syllable in words that have two or more syllables. There is also a focus on phonemes found in many of the words. The focus on pronunciation is broken up with a simple controlled oral practice activity, where students personalise the vocabulary by telling each other things that they like.

Categories

2 WORD POWER Jobs

A Complete the word map with jobs from the list.

✓ accountant
✓ cashier
chef
✓ dancer
✓ flight attendant
musician
pilot
receptionist
server
singer
tour guide
web designer

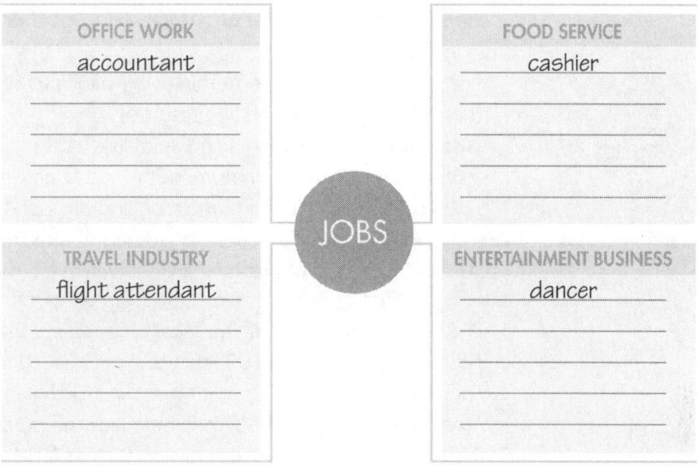

B Add two more jobs to each category. Then compare with a partner.

Figure 6.0b: Richards, J. C. et al. (2017) *Interchange 1* (5th ed.), p. 8.

With this approach, students sort a list of vocabulary items into different categories, usually into some kind of grid or table or spidergram. Generally, this involves copying the word, which means an indirect focus on the written form as students have to check the correct spelling. In the example here, students categorise the words on the basis of meaning. In other course book tasks, students may be asked to categorise vocabulary on the basis of part of speech or correct collocation, for example, matching the verbs *play, go* and *do* to different sporting activities – tennis, sailing, karate. In *Figure 6.0b*, the vocabulary is practised in a subsequent exercise where students have to guess one of the jobs by asking *Yes/No* questions. Then later in the unit, students study the stress of multi-syllable jobs. This indicates that a focus on different aspects of vocabulary does not necessarily occur in adjacent activities. One of the benefits of sequencing activities in this way is that picking up on a different feature of a lexical set (in this case the pronunciation) at a later stage also acts as revision of the target vocabulary.

Sentences and definition

PREPARING TO READ

1 Read the definitions and complete the sentences with the correct form of the words in bold.

chemical (n) a man-made or natural solid, liquid or gas made by changing atoms
destroy (v) to damage something very badly; to cause it to not exist
due to (prep) because of; as a result of
endangered (adj) (of plants and animals) that may disappear soon
natural (adj) as found in nature; not made or caused by people
pollute (v) to make the air, water or land dirty and unhealthy
protect (v) to keep something or someone safe from damage or injury
species (n) a group of plants or animals which are the same in some way

1 The black rhino is one of the most __________ animals in the world. There are only about 5,000 left today.
2 There are three __________ of bears in North America. They are the American black bear, the grizzly bear and the polar bear.
3 Dangerous __________ from factories can kill fish and other animals when they enter lakes and rivers.
4 Smoke from factories can __________ the air and hurt both humans and animals.
5 When new homes are built, it often __________ the areas where animals live.
6 Few people visited the zoo last week __________ the cold weather.
7 I don't like zoos. I prefer to see animals in their __________ environments.
8 Many organizations are working to __________ endangered animals by creating safe places for them to live.

Figure 6.0c: Westbrook, C. and L. Baker et al. (2019) *Unlock Reading, Writing & Critical Thinking 3* (2nd ed.), p. 18.

In the example in *Figure 6.0c*, students are provided with definitions of key words and their understanding of these definitions is checked when they place the words in the sentences. This presentation ensures that students focus on form. They check the spelling of the new words as they copy them into the gaps and also think about which form of some of the words should be used. For example, to answer sentence 3 correctly, students need to realise that *chemical* is a countable noun and therefore should write the plural form. To answer question 5 correctly, they will need to identify *destroy* as a verb and add a third person *-s* when completing the sentence. There is no focus on the pronunciation of these words, and nor is there a subsequent practice activity, but, as we can see from the exercise heading, they are being presented in preparation for reading, so at this stage students only need to be able to recognise the words passively.

An alternative approach is to provide students with example sentences in which new vocabulary items are highlighted. Students then match the highlighted words to definitions.

Using example sentences and definitions is more typical from B1 level and above because the vocabulary focused on begins to become more abstract and meaning cannot be easily represented by visual means.

Dictionaries

VOCABULARY
Verbs about thinking

1 Use a dictionary to make sure you know the meaning of these words.

to concentrate on | to remember | to think | to imagine | to wonder | to believe | to guess | to recognise | to realise | to suppose

2 Choose the correct words.

1 The task was very difficult. I had to *remember / think* for a long time.
2 Come on, don't be silly. I don't *believe / realise* in ghosts!
3 Can you *imagine / concentrate* how great it must be to live at the beach?
4 When the teacher asked the question a different way, I *supposed / realised* that I knew the answer!
5 Did they really say they are moving to New York? I don't *suppose / believe* it!
6 I have not seen her for six years. I don't think I would *realise / recognise* her.
7 I have no idea what the answer is. I'll just have to *imagine / guess*.
8 I was so tired that I found it hard to *think / concentrate on* the test.
9 Have you ever *wondered / supposed* why I haven't phoned you for months?
10 If we want to get there faster, I *wonder / suppose* we should take a taxi.

Pronunciation
Word stress
Go to page 120.

3 SPEAKING Work in pairs. Ask and answer questions.

1 Are there any places where you can think really well or not well at all?
2 Does music help you to concentrate or make it difficult for you to concentrate? Does it matter what kind of music it is?
3 In what situations can you imagine things really well? Do you find it difficult to use your imagination sometimes?
4 Do you find it difficult to remember things sometimes? What sort of things?
5 Do you believe in life on other planets? What do you suppose the people there look like?

Workbook page 20

Figure 6.0d: Puchta, H., J. Stranks and P. Lewis-Jones (2015) *Think Level 2*, p.25.

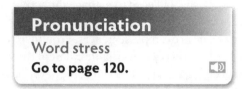

Exercise 1 in *Figure 6.0d* is another way course books focus on definitions for conveying the meaning of new vocabulary, suggesting students use a dictionary to check meaning. Teachers have some discretion as to whether students use bi-lingual or English–English dictionaries. However, given that many learners these days use online dictionaries on their smartphones, there is greater likelihood that students will opt for a bi-lingual dictionary. If a teacher wants her learners to use English–English dictionaries, she will need to manage the activity attentively to make sure this is the case. After students have looked up any new words in the dictionary, exercise 2 checks correct use with a two option choice in example sentences. Pronunciation is focused on in a separate activity at the back of the book, in this case, a syllable count of the verbs and a focus on the main stress. In exercise 3, students do freer oral practice of some of the new words by answering questions that get them to personalise the vocabulary items.

Vocabulary in context

www.newsweb.com/stolenlaptop

WORLDNEWS BUSINESSNEWS SPORTSNEWS

BURGLARS CAUGHT BY STOLEN LAPTOP

On April 27th, two burglars broke into Kait Duplaga's apartment in White Plains, New York, and stole about $5,000 worth of electronic **goods**, including two flat-screen TVs and two laptops. As soon as Kait and her two roommates got home that night, they reported the burglary to the police. Unfortunately the police couldn't find anything to help them catch the burglars.

Nine days later, a friend of Kait's **contacted** her because his computer showed that she was **logged onto** the internet. Kait used another computer to go online and saw that someone was using her laptop to do some shopping.

Then Kait, who works in an Apple computer store, remembered that she could access the camera in her laptop using **remote** technology. At first she could only see an empty room, but then two men came in and started using the computer again. Kait then took photos of the men before they **realised** what was happening. One of her roommates **recognised** the men as friends of friends who were at a party at their apartment a few weeks earlier. Kait immediately contacted the police and gave them the photos and names of the men. The next day the burglars were arrested and the police found nearly all of the stolen **property** in their apartment.

"It clearly makes our job a lot easier when the victim can take a picture of the person using the stolen property," said Daniel Jackson of the White Plains Department of Public Safety. "It was definitely a very **smart** use of the technology."

HELP WITH VOCABULARY
Guessing meaning from context

- Sometimes you can guess the meaning of a word by:

a knowing a similar word in your language or another language you know.
b knowing what type of word it is (noun, verb, adjective, etc.).
c understanding the general meaning of the text and the rest of the sentence.

7 **a** Look at the words in bold in the article. Are they nouns, verbs or adjectives?

b Choose the correct meanings, a or b. What information in the article helped you decide?

1	**goods**	a excellent	b things you can buy or sell
2	**contacted**	a talked to, wrote to or texted	b complained to
3	**logged onto**	a connected to	b downloaded
4	**remote**	a modern	b far away
5	**realised**	a decided	b suddenly understood
6	**recognised**	a forgot a person's name	b knew someone by his/her face
7	**property**	a things you own	b expensive things
8	**smart**	a dangerous	b clever, intelligent

c Check in VOCABULARY 11.4 p149.

Figure 6.0e: Redston, C. and G. Cunningham (2012) *face2face Pre-intermediate* (2nd ed.), p. 91.

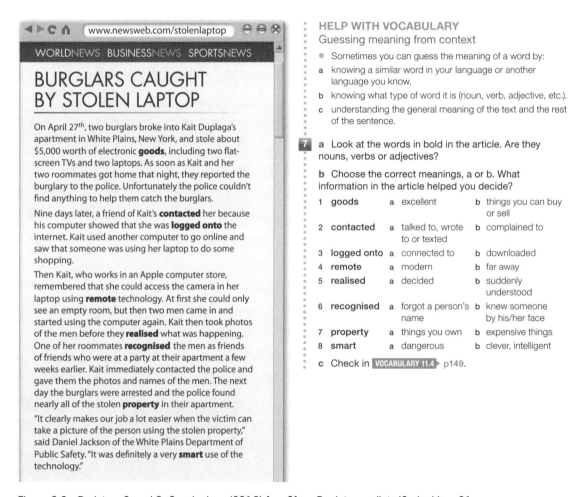

Another common approach in course books from B1 level and above encourages students to try to understand the meaning of new words from the context in which they occur, nearly always a reading text or an audio script. This approach assumes that students will be able to understand most of the information in the text without being familiar with some or all of the target vocabulary. The example in *Figure 6.0e* offers students quite a bit of support. It highlights the target words in the reading text, and after asking students to make a judgement about the part of speech in exercise 7a, they select one of two definitions for each word in 7b. Before students do the exercise, the *Help with vocabulary* section suggests some strategies they could use in order to understand the meaning of new words from context. At higher levels, the words may not be highlighted, in which case students will need to scan read the text in order to find them. In addition, definitions are often not provided and instead, students are encouraged to come up with their own definitions of the words and then, perhaps, eventually check their ideas in a dictionary.

Key word focus

3 WORDPOWER *take*

a Match sentences 1–6 with pictures a–f. What do you think the people are talking about?

1 You can take the number 23.
2 Please take care!
3 It will only take five minutes.
4 Then you take the first left.
5 Let me take your suitcase for you.
6 Take one three times a day before meals.

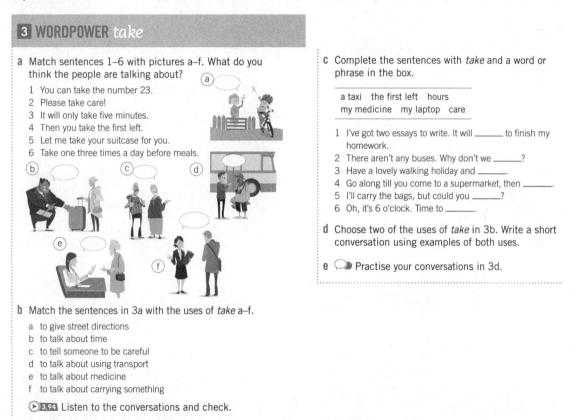

b Match the sentences in 3a with the uses of *take* a–f.

a to give street directions
b to talk about time
c to tell someone to be careful
d to talk about using transport
e to talk about medicine
f to talk about carrying something

3.94 Listen to the conversations and check.

c Complete the sentences with *take* and a word or phrase in the box.

a taxi	the first left	hours
my medicine	my laptop	care

1 I've got two essays to write. It will ______ to finish my homework.
2 There aren't any buses. Why don't we ______?
3 Have a lovely walking holiday and ______.
4 Go along till you come to a supermarket, then ______.
5 I'll carry the bags, but could you ______?
6 Oh, it's 6 o'clock. Time to ______.

d Choose two of the uses of *take* in 3b. Write a short conversation using examples of both uses.

e Practise your conversations in 3d.

Figure 6.0f: Doff, A., C. Thaine et al. (2015) *Cambridge English Empower A2*, p. 128.

A further common approach in many modern course books is a focus on a high frequency word and the different ways it is used and combines with other words to make expressions. The example in *Figure 6.0e* looks at ways this happens with the verb *take*. Exercises a and b focus on the meaning of some expressions with *take* while exercise c encourages students to recognise and use different words that collocate with *take*. This encourages students to consider vocabulary in meaningful blocks or chunks rather than single word meaning. Students then practise two examples by writing conversations and then reading them aloud in pairs. These exercises aim to broaden the range of students' vocabulary and alert them to different meanings of the one word depending on the context and other words it combines with.

Recognition or production?

The examples that we have looked at can be described as *deliberate* vocabulary learning. This is where the teacher and/or the student have a specific aim of learning new lexis. This can be contrasted with what Nation (2013) calls *incidental* vocabulary learning, where students come across new words as they read or listen to a text. The depth of focus on meaning, form and use in targeted vocabulary learning depends on whether the aim of the vocabulary activity is just for recognition of words in a reading or listening text or whether it is for productive use of the new lexis.

Reference

Nation, I. S. P. (2013) *Learning Vocabulary in Another Language* (2nd ed.), Cambridge: Cambridge University Press.

A Focus on meaning and use

6.1 What we know

Level	A1 and above
Time	10 to 15 minutes
Outline	In small groups, students sort a lexical set of picture cards into two piles, those they know and those they don't. They then write and practise the pronunciation of the words before sharing their ideas with other students.
Aim	To present the lexical set in a student-centred way.
Preparation	If you use *Figure 6.1* below, you will need to make enough copies of the set of pictures so that each small group has them. You will need to cut these up, making sure you don't include the word with the picture. If you use different material, the course book you use may provide a similar set of pictures to copy and cut up. If not, you will need to find your own pictures for the lexical set.
Rationale	At low levels, it is very common to focus on lexical sets because students make meaning relationships between the words. Even at very low levels, students often know some words in English. For example, an absolute beginner will probably know the word *hotel* because it's connected with tourism, or because they have a similar word in their first language. This activity acknowledges that students come to their very first English lessons knowing something. This can be a reassuring implicit message for students.

Procedure

1 Put students into small groups of three or four.
2 Hand out the pictures. Students put them into two piles – words that they know and those that they don't.
3 All students in the group write down the words they know and check the pronunciation with each other.
4 Mix students into new groups to share their lists with each other.
5 Check the answers with the whole class and correct any pronunciation problems. Write the words on the board so students can check their spelling.

Notes and variation

In the procedure above, students just see the picture and not the word. With different groups, you can vary this according to the students' level of ability. Students could see the word and the associated picture and sort them in to the 'know' and 'don't know' piles. Alternatively, for higher levels you could do the activity without pictures, with students sorting into 'know' and 'don't know' piles words only, or sentences with the target words highlighted.

Learner reflection questions

1 Did you already know some of the words? Can you remember where you learned them?
2 Do you know any other words in English that you can add to this set?

Teacher reflection

What other lexical sets in your course book are students likely to know? What's the value of using pictures to convey the meaning of new words?

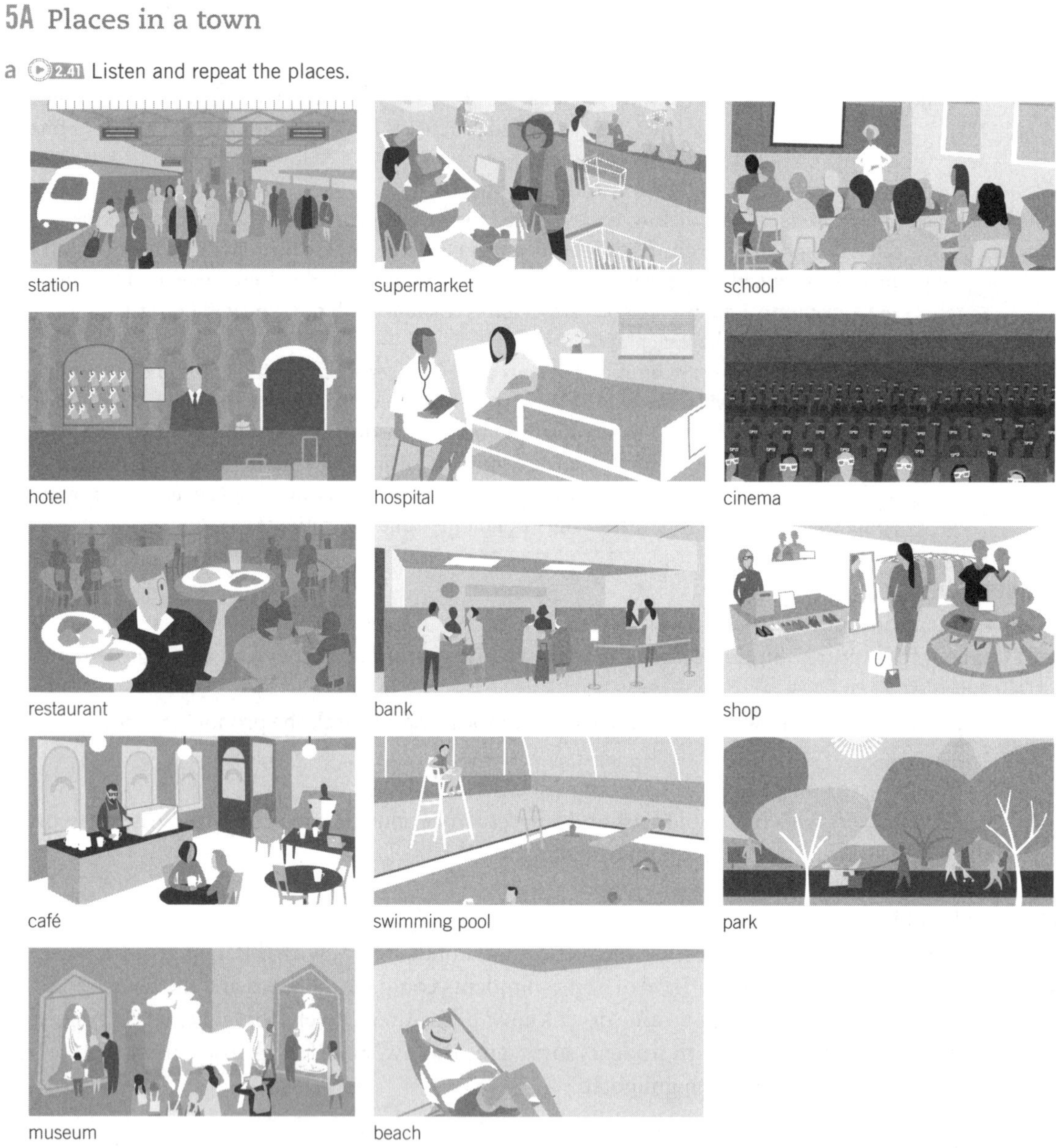

Figure 6.1: Doff, A., C. Thaine et al. (2015) *Cambridge English Empower A1*, p. 148.

6.2 Paired concept questioning

Level	B1 and above
Time	10 to 15 minutes
Outline	Students work in pairs asking and answering concept questions about the target vocabulary before identifying the correct word.
Aim	To check the meaning of new items in a vocabulary set – in *Figure 6.2a* to describe special events – in more detail.
Preparation	If you use the material in *Figure 6.2a*, you will need to copy the Student A and B vocabulary question cards below. If you are using different material, you will need to make your own question cards.
Rationale	As noted in the Introduction to this chapter, from B1 level and above, vocabulary items start to become more abstract in meaning and teachers often use definitions to convey meaning. Concept questions are an effective way of getting students to explore meaning in more depth. Often when a course book presents new vocabulary, a teacher will check understanding by asking concept questions. In this activity, the questioning is more student-centred – you can provide simple concept questions and answers that students use in an information gap activity.

Procedure

1. Students complete a definition matching task – exercise A in *Figure 6.1a* below.
2. Put students in A and B pairs and hand out the concept question cards. Tell students not to look at each other's cards.
3. Students then ask their partner the questions on the card. The partner answers, and the student who asked the question confirms the answer is correct, or provides the correct answer.
4. Do whole class feedback and allow students to ask you any questions about differences of meaning between the words.

Notes and variation

It pays to check the meaning of these words and be clear about differences of meaning. Concept questions are often just one step in a process of students fully grasping meaning, and there are likely to be questions they want to ask you in the feedback stage. At higher levels, students could write their own concept questions.

Learner reflection questions

1. Did the questions help you understand parts of the meaning of some words in more detail?
2. Apart from translation and definitions, how can you get a good understanding of the meaning of new words?

Teacher reflection

What did students find most challenging with this lexical set – understanding the similarities or the differences in meaning? What benefits are there in dealing with concept questions in this student-centred way?

9 WORD POWER Exceptional events

A Match the words in column A with the definitions in column B.

A	B
1. coincidence ____	**a.** an unexpected event that brings good fortune
2. dilemma ____	**b.** a situation that involves a difficult choice
3. disaster ____	**c.** something puzzling or unexplained
4. emergency ____	**d.** an event that causes suffering or destruction
5. lucky break ____	**e.** a great success or achievement
6. mishap ____	**f.** an accident, mistake, or unlucky event
7. mystery ____	**g.** a sudden, dangerous situation that requires quick action
8. triumph ____	**h.** a situation when two similar things happen at the same time for no reason

Figure 6.2a: Richards, J. C. et al. (2017) *Interchange 3* (5th ed.), p. 26.

Student A – Concept questions

1 What is it when you are unable to make a decision about, for example, which event to go to? (dilemma)

2 Which two events might completely change your life in a bad way? (emergency, disaster)

3 Which two events are things that someone might hope for? (lucky break, triumph)

4 What are events that you don't know why or how they happened? (mystery, coincidence)

5 What's a very strange event that you cannot explain? (mystery)

Student B – Concept questions

1 Which two events are surprises, and one of them pleasant? (coincidence, lucky break)

2 Which event is the result of just a little bit of bad luck? (mishap)

3 What are events where you will probably ask for help? (disaster, emergency, mishap)

4 What are events where you feel like a winner? (lucky break, triumph)

5 Which event is often a very good result of hard work? (triumph)

Example *Figure 6.2b* includes multi-word verbs which often have a non-literal meaning, for example, 'run out'. If we look at the literal meaning of 'run' and 'out' we can't understand that it means 'to have no more left'.

WordWise

Phrasal verbs with *out*

1 **Complete each of these sentences from the unit so far with a word from the list.**

come | find | run | went | started | sort

1 Lots of famous musicians ________ **out** playing on the streets of London.
2 His fans ________ **out** and bought all the copies.
3 Their new single has just ________ **out**.
4 Come on, Luke. I'm sure we'll ________ something **out**.
5 I've ________ **out** of money.
6 Listen and ________ **out** how the story ends.

2 **Match the phrases and the definitions.**

1 start out	a discover
2 find out	b begin your working life
3 go out	c leave your house
4 come out	d appear in a shop so people can buy it
5 run out	e find an answer or solution to a problem
6 sort out	f use all of something

Figure 6.2b: Puchta, H., J. Stranks and P. Lewis-Jones (2015) *Think Level 2*, p. 55.

6.3 Collocation dictation

Level	A2 and above
Time	10 to 15 minutes
Outline	In pairs, students write dictated words and phrases into a table alongside the correct verb they collocate with.
Aim	To present key collocations with verbs.
Preparation	If you use *Figure 6.3*, you will need to make copies of the dictation table below for each pair of students. If you use different material, you will need to create your own table.
Rationale	This dictation activity provides students with an opportunity to practise recently acquired vocabulary. The dictation gives useful intensive listening practice and is likely to motivate students to check the answers more carefully than if, for example, they had just completed a multiple choice exercise in a course book. The final checking stage between two sets of pairs encourages students to engage more fully with the vocabulary.

Procedure

1 Students complete any comprehension reading text tasks that might have contextualised the collocations – in *Figure 6.3*, exercise 5 contains vocabulary from an email that students have just read, and the key verbs are *book*, *stay*, *rent* and *get*.

2 Show students how collocation works on the board with two examples from the text: e.g. *stay with you* and *book a hotel room.*

3 Give one table to each pair of students. Tell them you will dictate words and phrases and they should write them below the verb they think they go together with. Students discuss and agree the correct verb collocation.

4 For *Figure 6.3*, dictate the following words and phrases in this order – say them twice, but give students time to confer between each one:

married, with you, a flat, in a hotel, a train ticket, a house, divorced, home, a seat on a train

5 Sets of pairs check their answers together. If students ask you to, say the words and phrases once more. Then check answers in open class.

Notes and variation

It's important that each pair has just one table to encourage co-operative working. This activity could also be turned into a competition between teams of three or more students. Nominate the first team and call out a word or phrase. If they select the correct verb collocation, they win the relevant square in the table. If they get it wrong, it passes to the next team. Another variation would be to create bingo cards. You would need to include more choices and configure the cards differently. At higher levels, you could read out a complete sentence that includes the collocation and students have to listen, isolate and write down the word or phrase in the correct square.

Learner reflection questions

1 How many collocations did you know and how many did you guess?

2 Why is it sometimes a good idea to learn words that go together with other words?

Teacher reflection

To what extent do you think students knew the collocations already and to what extent do you think they guessed from the context? Did students hear small function words (*a, an, on*) with weak forms in the dictation? Do they need more practice in this kind of detailed listening?

HELP WITH VOCABULARY Collocations

5 **a** Read the email again. Find two words or phrases that go with these verbs. Write them in the table.

book	stay	rent	get
	with (you)		

b Choose the correct verbs in these words/phrases.

1 *stay/rent* a flat
2 *book/rent* a train ticket
3 *get/book* married
4 *get/rent* home
5 *book/stay* a seat on a train
6 *rent/book* a house
7 *get/stay* in a hotel
8 *rent/get* divorced
9 *stay/get* at home
10 *book/rent* a table in a restaurant

c Check in VOCABULARY 11.3 p151.

Figure 6.3: Redston, C. and G. Cunningham (2012) *face2face Pre-intermediate* (2nd ed.), p. 95.

Dictation table

rent	book	get ....
stay	book	rent ....
stay	get	stay ....

Answer key

rent **a flat**	book **a train ticket**	get **married**
stay **with you**	book **a seat on a train**	rent **a house**
stay **in a hotel**	get **divorced**	stay **at home**

B Focus on form

6.4 Word snake races

Level	A2 and above
Time	5 to 10 minutes
Outline	Teams compete to decipher a word snake, detecting and correcting errors.
Aim	To highlight separability in simple compound nouns; to focus students on spelling accuracy.
Preparation	If you are using *Figure 6.4a*, you can make copies of the two word snakes to hand out. Make sure the font is large enough for students in teams of four to read. Alternatively, you could just write the word snakes on the board. If you are using different material, you will need to create your own word snakes, and you might also like to come up with a different odd-one-out criterion. Note: there is often variation on how compound words are spelled, for example, *girl friend, girl-friend, girlfriend*. It would pay to double check these in a dictionary so you are ready to deal with students' questions.
Rationale	Focusing on spelling and the separability of compound words are aspects of form that are important for students to know because it helps them recognise words quickly when reading, and means they can write with more accuracy. This activity aims to direct students' attention to these issues of form in a fun way. It's likely to be more motivating than the teacher simply explaining it on the board.

Procedure

1. After presenting and checking the meaning of the new words (after exercise C in *Figure 6.4a*), put students into teams of three or four and ask them to close their books.
2. Show an example word snake on the board, e.g. *gymsoccerbaseballgame*, and indicate how a word snake needs to be broken up into words.
3. Hand out the first word snake face down. Tell students they should find the vocabulary words that they have just practised. One student in each team writes the deciphered word on to a piece of paper. The team then checks that the spelling of the compound word is accurate.
4. To raise the level of challenge, you can introduce other criteria that the teams need to follow. In *Figure 6.4a*, students have to identify one word that is different from the others and correct two spelling mistakes. The first team to finish with the correctly rewritten word list wins.
5. Repeat the procedure with the second word snake.

Notes and variation

In order to determine the winner, you will need to check the accuracy of each team's answers – the first team to finish may not be the most accurate. You can vary the criteria for the odd-word-out, for example, it could be a word that is a different part of speech. A possible extension to this activity is for students in pairs or small groups to create their own word snakes to exchange with another pair/group to decipher.

Learner reflection questions

1 What was interesting about the different parts of the words and phrases? What is important to notice when you learn compound words?
2 If you copy new words into a notebook, do you always check the spelling?

Teacher reflection

What did you learn about the literacy strengths and weaknesses of students in your class? Were some students quicker than others to identify the words? This activity involves students' recognition of words. What activities can help them with writing words accurately?

1 WORD POWER Places and activities

A Match the places and the definitions. Then ask and answer the questions with a partner.

What's a . . . ?	*It's a place where you . . .*
1. clothing store ______	**a.** get food and small items for the home
2. grocery store ______	**b.** can connect to the Internet
3. hair salon ______	**c.** get a haircut
4. laundromat ______	**d.** buy newspapers and magazines
5. newsstand ______	**e.** see a game or a concert
6. stadium ______	**f.** find new fashions
7. Wi-Fi hot spot ______	**g.** wash and dry your clothes

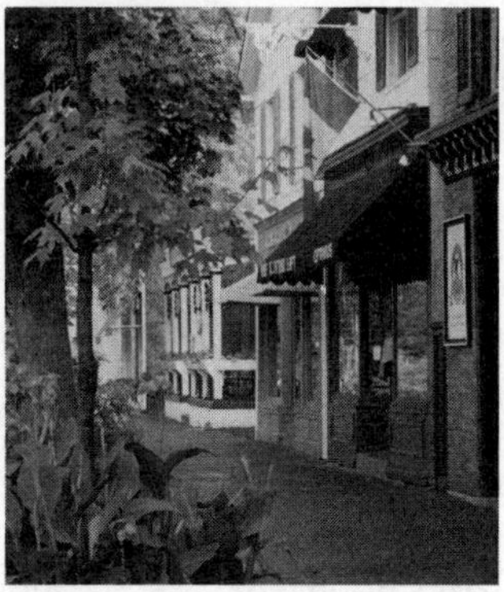

B **PAIR WORK** Write definitions for these places.

coffee shop **drugstore** **gas station** **library** **post office**

It's a place where you drink coffee and tea and eat small meals. (coffee shop)

C **GROUP WORK** Read your definitions. Can your classmates guess the places?

Figure 6.4a: Richards, J. C. et al. (2017) *Interchange 1* (5th ed.), p. 50.

Word snakes

1

2

Answer key
The odd-word-out is the underlined word – it's the only standalone word in the list. But also note that in each word snake, one of the compound nouns isn't separated.

Word snake 1	*Word snake 2*
grocery store	coffee shop (sp)
laundromat	drugstore
hair saloon (sp)	library
gas station (sp)	clothing store
newsstand	post office (sp)

With the lexical set in *Figure 6.4b* an odd word out in the word snake would be 'memory stick'.

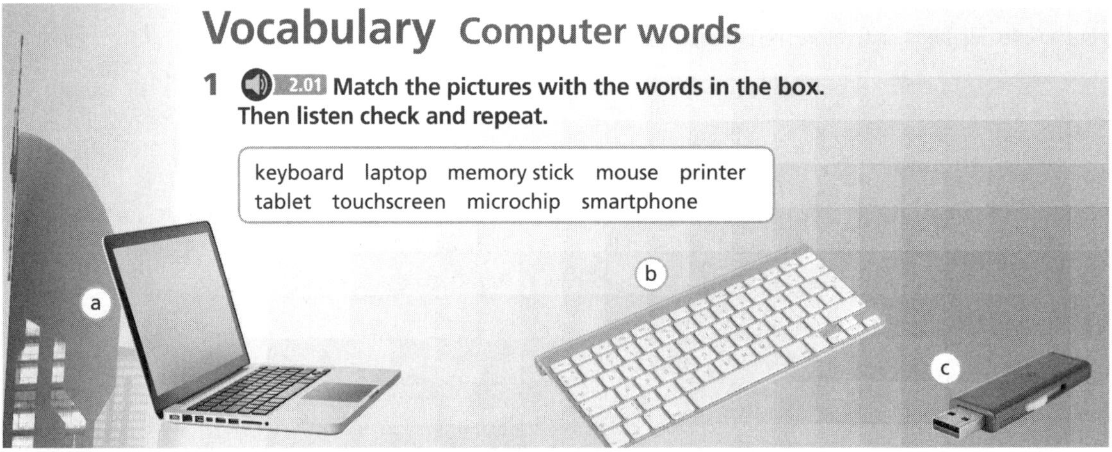

Vocabulary Computer words
1 2.01 Match the pictures with the words in the box.
Then listen check and repeat.
keyboard laptop memory stick mouse printer
tablet touchscreen microchip smartphone
a
b
c

Figure 6.4b: Goldstein, B. and C. Jones (2015) *Eyes Open 3*, p. 53.

6.5 Likely separation

Level B1 and above
Time 10 to 15 minutes
Outline In pairs, students make intuitive predictions about the separability of a number of multi-word verbs.
Aim To highlight the fact there are different categories of multi-word verbs depending on separability of the verb and the particle.
Preparation If you use *Figure 6.5a*, make a copy of the worksheet for all the students. If you use another set of multi-word verbs, you will need to write your own example sentences and make copies.
Rationale While there are clear rules about the separability of multi-word verbs associated with the part of speech of the particle and the transitivity of the verb, these can be complicated for many learners to process. In this activity, students are encouraged to make a guess on the basis of whether separating the verb and the particle sounds 'natural' or not. Clearly, this involves guesswork on the students' part. However, a key, broader aim of this activity is to alert students to the issue of separability, so they know to look for this when they encounter a new multi-word verb. As this might be the first time students deal with separability, the examples in the worksheet focus only on transitive verbs with particles that are either a preposition or an adverb.

Procedure

1 Students do tasks that focus on the meaning of the multi-word verbs – exercise a in *Figure 6.5a*.
2 Use an example on the worksheet (***hang up*** in *Figure 6.5a*) to indicate on the board what is meant by the 'verb' and 'particle' of a multi-word verb.
3 In pairs, students guess which multi-word verbs on the worksheet can be split or not. When they have finished, they can check their guesses with another pair.
4 Then you, the teacher, read aloud the example sentences below with the verb and particle split. Students listen and decide if it sounds natural or not. They can check in pairs or fours together.
5 Write the answers on the board. Depending on your students' knowledge of grammar, you can choose whether you only indicate the separability, or if you give reasons. Also, decide whether or not to use the grammar terminology in the answer key below.

Notes and variation

When setting up this activity, it's important to emphasise to students that they are only guessing and reassure them that it doesn't matter if they give wrong answers. With a strong group, you could also include the intransitive verbs in the *Figure 6.5a* material. At higher levels, the activity could ask students to examine multi-word verbs in a text where they are embedded in a greater density of language. If higher level learners are aware of the rules that determine separability, this could become an analysis task rather than just guesswork.

Learner reflection questions

1 What helped you to guess more – talking to other students or hearing your teacher read the sentences aloud?

2 Is it sometimes a good idea to guess things when studying English? Why / Why not?

Teacher reflection

How much explanation of rules did you give with this activity? Does your current group of students respond well to that? In general, what do you think is a good amount of rule giving? Does it change according to level?

10A Multi-word verbs

a Read the sentences. Which multi-word verb in the box can replace the words in **bold**?

passed on put off carried on came round looked after handed in broke up turned down joined in felt like

1 I asked him to be quiet, but he just **continued** talking. ________
2 It was a really sunny day and he really **wanted** an ice cream. ________
3 She **came to my house** to ask for some advice. ________
4 I **took care of** my friend's cat while he was on holiday. ________
5 They used to go out with each other, but they **ended their relationship**. ________
6 He **said 'no' to** the invitation, because he had too much work. ________
7 The game looked like fun, so I **did it with them**. ________
8 They **delayed** the meeting, because Bob was ill. ________
9 I **took** the keys I found to the receptionist. ________
10 He **told her** the message as soon as he saw her. ________

b Complete the sentences with the correct form of a multi-word verb from **a**.

1 My friend ________ for dinner last night. I cooked her spaghetti.
2 She's ill, so we've ________ the party until she gets better.
3 Can you ________ my new number to Bob? It's 07806 540 234.
4 Mike and I were together for a year but we ________ two months ago.
5 Tom started singing a song and then we all ________. It was pretty noisy!
6 Somebody ________ my wallet at the police station.
7 She ________ the job offer because the pay was too low.
8 "Do you ________ a pizza tonight?" "Yes, that sounds nice."
9 I'm ________ my niece this evening. She's only 7 years old.
10 We were all tired and wanted to stop running but our teacher told us to ________.

Tip

Multi-word verbs have different kinds of grammar. Some transitive multi-word verbs (*hand in, pass on, put off*) can be separated by an object:

*We **put off** the match.* ✓ *We **put** the match **off**.* ✓

If the object of these multi-word verbs is a pronoun, they must be separated:

*I **handed** it **in**.* ✓ ~~*I **handed in** it.*~~ ✗

Other multi-word verbs (*feel like, look after*) can never be separated:

*He **felt like** an ice cream.* ✓ ~~*He **felt** an ice cream **like**.*~~ ✗

c Now go back to p.99

Figure 6.5a: Doff, A., C. Thaine et al. (2015) *Cambridge English Empower B1*, p. 140.

Worksheet

In which sentences can the phrase after the multi-word verb go between the verb (V) and the particle (P)?

 V P V P

Hang up your coat. **Hang** your coat **up** ✓

1 I **passed on** the message. 5 She **put off** the meeting.
2 I **looked after** my friend's dog. 6 We **handed in** the keys.
3 We **turned down** their invitation. 7 I **felt like** an ice cream.
4 They **joined in** the game.

From *Off the Page* © Cambridge University Press 2020 PHOTOCOPIABLE

Examples to read aloud, and answer key

1 I **passed** the message **on**. ✓
2 I **looked** my friend's dog **after**. ✗ *the particle is a preposition*
3 We **turned** their invitation **down**. ✓
4 They **joined** the game **in**. ✗ *the particle is a preposition*
5 She **put** the meeting **off**. ✓
6 We **handed** the keys **in**. ✓
7 I **felt** an ice cream **like**. ✗ *the particle is a preposition*

Phrasal verbs are actually one kind of multi-word verbs, but the terms are often used interchangeably. The young learner's course book example in *Figure 6.5b* would work well with the activity.

VOCABULARY
Phrasal verbs (2)

1 **Find the phrasal verbs in the article on page 111. Match them with the definitions.**

blow out | break down | sort out
carry out | look into | stand out
work out | look forward to

1 be easy to notice
2 be happy or excited about (a future event)
3 do, complete
4 investigate, examine the facts about (a situation)
5 fix (a problem)
6 use air to stop (something) burning
7 stop working
8 understand, find the answer to

2 **Complete the sentences with the correct forms of the phrasal verbs from Exercise 1.**

0 The wind _blew_ the candles _out_ on my birthday cake.
1 The concert is tomorrow. I'm really _____ it!
2 Mum was driving to work when her car _____ .
3 There was a bank robbery last Saturday. The police are _____ it.
4 She's our best player. She really _____ in the team.
5 This question is really difficult. I can't _____ the answer.
6 The doctors are _____ tests to find out what's wrong with him.
7 My best friend and I have a problem, but I'm sure we can _____ it _____!

Workbook page 110

Figure 6.5b: Puchta, H., J. Stranks and P. Lewis-Jones (2015) *Think Level 3*, p. 112.

6.6 Making additions

Level	B1 and above
Time	10 to 15 minutes
Outline	Students work in small groups and decide which prefixes can be placed in front of a set of base words written on the board.
Aim	To show how prefixes build words and change meaning.
Preparation	If you use *Figure 6.6* below, you need to make a copy of the prefix worksheet for each group and cut it up. (You can save time by copying each group's worksheet on different coloured paper.) Students also need some sticky tack to stick prefixes in front of the base words. If you are using different material, you will need to create your own prefix worksheet.
Rationale	As is often the case with grammar, this vocabulary feature blends form and meaning. The prefixes build new word forms and, at the same time, they change the meaning. *Figure 6.6* has a slight testing element to it, but the exercise comes towards the end of a unit, and students have read texts that include some of the words. The selection of base words is taken from the words used in the presentation and practice of the words in the unit.

Procedure

1 Students complete any reading or listening activities that might include vocabulary with prefixes.
2 For *Figure 6.6*, write the following base words on the board:

> *crease, agree, able, vent, build, port, likely, humanise,*
> *organised, large, view, think, atlantic, safe*

3 Put students in groups of three or four and give each group a number. Hand out the cut up prefixes and ask students to put their group number in the corner of each prefix (if the prefixes are on different coloured paper, you don't need to do this).
4 Groups take turns in sending up a representative to the board to place one of their prefixes in front of a base word. Once a prefix has been placed, only the group who has placed it can change it.
5 If students think they can't place a prefix correctly, they can skip a turn.
6 When all the words have a prefix, check the answers and elicit the meaning of each prefix.
7 In *Figure 6.6*, students then fill in the grid in exercise 3 with their own words.

Notes and variation

If you feel it is appropriate for your class, the activity could be framed as a competition between groups. A variation is to give students cut up base words as well as prefixes to match in their groups. At higher levels, where students already have some knowledge of prefixes, you could just invite them to write up what they think is the correct prefix rather than using cut ups.

Learner reflection questions

1 Which words with prefixes did you know and which were easy to guess?
2 How can prefixes help you understand the meaning of new words?

Teacher reflection

How aware were students already of the meaning of the prefixes when they were doing the activity? What can you do during reading and listening lessons to increase awareness of words with prefixes?

PREFIXES

VOCABULARY

A prefix is a group of letters which goes at the start of a word to make a new word with a different meaning. Each prefix has a specific meaning.

sub (prefix meaning 'under') + marine (word related to water) = a kind of boat which goes under the water

Understanding the meaning of prefixes can help you guess the general meaning of difficult academic or technical words.

3 Look at these prefixes, their meanings and the examples. Then, add your own examples to the table. Use a dictionary to help you.

prefix	meaning	example
de-	become less, go down	decrease, ____________, ____________
dis-	opposite	disagree, ____________, ____________
en-	cause	enable, ____________, ____________
pre-	before	prevent, ____________, ____________
re-	again	rebuild, ____________, ____________
trans-	across, through	transport, ____________, ____________
un-	remove, not	unlikely, ____________, ____________

Figure 6.6: Westbrook, C. and L. Baker et al. (2019) *Unlock Reading, Writing & Critical Thinking 3* (2nd ed.), p. 136.

Worksheet – prefixes

de-	de-	dis-	dis-	en-	en-	pre-
pre-	re-	re-	trans-	trans-	un-	un-

Answer key – the first two examples relate to Figure 6.6

de- decrease, dehumanise (deport)
dis- disagree, disorganised (disable)
en- enable, enlarge
re- rebuild, rethink (reorganised, review)
pre- prevent, preview (prebuild)
trans- transport, transatlantic
un- unlikely, unsafe (unable)

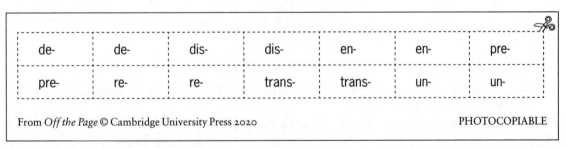

C Practice

6.7 Mime with feeling

Level	A2 and above
Time	10 to 15 minutes
Outline	In pairs, students write an example sentence containing new vocabulary, then they mime and elicit their example sentence from a new partner.
Aim	To provide controlled oral practice of the target vocabulary – in *Figure 6.7a*, adjectives of opinions and feelings.
Preparation	No preparation is needed for this activity unless you want to write the adjectives on pieces of paper to distribute to the first set of pairs.
Rationale	This activity turns written practice into spoken practice. Getting students to produce their own example sentences is a way of personalising the target vocabulary item. Repeating the full sentence in the miming stage provides a kind of student-centred drilling practice and an opportunity to engage with the pronunciation of the new vocabulary.

Procedure

1 Students complete controlled written practice tasks – exercises A and B in *Figure 6.7a*.
2 Demonstrate the miming of a sentence, for example, *I felt tired because last night the baby was crying*.
3 Students work in pairs to write a sentence they can mime (they both need a copy but should try to memorise the sentence). Tell each pair what adjective they should include. Monitor to help and check sentences.
4 Students work in new pairs and mime their example sentence and guess their partner's. Students who are guessing should say the complete sentence.

Notes and variation

If you are using different material from *Figure 6.7a*, you need to be sure that the vocabulary being practised can be mimed successfully. A simpler variation is for students to just mime a word or phrase and not a complete sentence.

Learner reflection questions

1 How quickly did your partner guess the correct adjective? Was it because the word was easy or was it because your mime was clear?
2 Do you think it is useful to practise new vocabulary in a sentence? Why / Why not?

Teacher reflection

How clear was students' pronunciation of the target vocabulary when students elicited the example sentences? You could revise the pronunciation of these words in a subsequent lesson – what would be a secondary aim of doing this?

5.1 DESCRIBING OPINIONS AND FEELINGS (page 45)

A **Replace the emoji in each sentence with the correct adjective.**

1 My first day in college was really ___horrible___ . I felt very alone, and I missed my parents.
2 My 18th birthday was an __________  experience – for the first time, I was an adult!
3 I remember the first day I went skiing. It was really __________ . My friends and I had a great time.
4 The first time that I voted was a very __________  moment for me. It was an important day for my country, and I was part of it.
5 I remember when I traveled by plane for the first time. That was __________ ! Wow!

B **Complete the conversations with the words from the box. Write two more conversations using other words from the box.**

angry cool crazy dangerous loud perfect tired

1 **A** How are you feeling today?
B I'm really __________. I went to bed very late last night.
2 **A** Do you like this music?
B What? I can't hear you. It's really __________!
3 **A** How was your vacation?
B It was __________! The weather was great, and the food was delicious.
4 **A** ____________________
B ____________________
5 **A** ____________________
B ____________________

Figure 6.7a: Clandfield, L., B. Goldstein et al. (2019) *Evolve 2*, p. 145.

The verbs in the course book exercise in *Figure 6.7b* should be easily mimed. The sentences therefore could be slightly extended, for example: *The thief ran away from our car* <u>*when the police came*</u>.

1 Look at the story about a thief. What did the thief steal?

2 1.22 Match the pictures with the words in the box. Then listen, check and repeat.

catch chase climb hide fall over jump run away throw

3 Complete the sentences with the past simple form of the verbs in Exercise 2.

1 The thief ...*ran*... away from our car.
2 I .... the thief.
3 The thief .... into a garden.
4 The thief .... his bag over a wall.
5 The thief .... over a wall.
6 The thief .... the bag.
7 The thief .... .
8 I .... the thief.

Figure 6.7b: Goldstein, B. and C. Jones (2015) *Eyes Open 3*, p. 31.

6.8 Word hunt

Level	A2 to B1+
Time	10 to 15 minutes
Outline	In pairs, students move around the classroom to find words that collocate, then work with a new partner to write a personalised sentence with the collocation.
Aim	To provide both written and spoken practice of new vocabulary items – in *Figure 6.8* below, food-container collocations.
Preparation	If you use *Figure 6.8* below, you will need to copy the food vocabulary cards, cut them up and stick them around the room before the lesson. If you use different material, you will need to make your own vocabulary cards.
Rationale	This kind of collocation matching is often done in a course book by students drawing a line from one word to another. While this helps to reinforce the relationship between the words, it is quite a passive exercise. This activity gets students to note down words and then talk about them, thereby making the practice more active. It is also an opportunity to extend the range of vocabulary focused on. The second part of the activity is a variation of exercises c and d in *Figure 6.8*.

Procedure

1 Students complete any presentation and analysis tasks – exercises a and b in *Figure 6.8*.
2 Put students in pairs and tell each pair which two containers they have (or give them cards).
3 Students move around the room and read the vocabulary cards. They write down all the food that can be put into their two containers.
4 Check the answers with the whole class.
5 Then set a speaking task for students to practise the vocabulary in new pairs – for *Figure 6.8* this could be students saying what they're going to buy at the supermarket.

Notes

This kind of hunting for words activity works best with lower levels where the collocation relationships are very clear. For example, it could be done with *do, play* and *go* to collocate with different sports and physical activities, or *make, do, take* and *have* for everyday activities. If it's difficult for students to move around the room, you could just give each pair a list of the target words.

Learner reflection questions

1 In your first language, can you translate the container words directly into English?
2 Do you write new vocab in a notebook or on your phone? What's the best way for you to write new vocabulary, in a list or a table, or another way?

Teacher reflection

How well did students manage with the extended range of food items in this activity? What do you think is the manageable amount of new words for students to learn in a lesson?

4B Containers

a Match phrases 1–6 with pictures a–f.

1 a **jar** /dʒɑː/ of honey
2 a **bag** /bæg/ of potatoes
3 a **can** /kæn/ (or **tin** /tɪn/) of tomatoes
4 a **bottle** /ˈbɒtl/ of water
5 a **bar** /bɑː/ of chocolate
6 a **packet** /ˈpækɪt/ of biscuits

b 2.12 **Pronunciation** Listen to the phrases in a. Which words are stressed? Listen again and repeat.

1 the nouns 2 the article 'a'
3 the preposition 'of'

c Change the words in italics using phrases in a. Is more than one answer possible?

Yesterday I went shopping and I bought [1]*some oil*, [2]*some jam*, [3]*some spaghetti*, [4]*some chocolate*, [5]*some tuna*, and [6]*some apples.*

1 a bottle of oil 4 ______
2 ______ 5 ______
3 ______ 6 ______

d Write a shopping list. Use the words in 1 to help you. Tell a partner.

Figure 6.8: Doff, A., C. Thaine et al. (2015) *Cambridge English Empower A2*, p. 164.

Vocabulary cards – note that some words can go in two categories

honey	jam	coffee	peanut butter
potatoes	onions	apples	oranges
tomatoes	soup	tuna	beans
mineral water	milk	orange juice	cola
chocolate	granola	biscuits	potato crisps
spaghetti	nuts		

Answer key

Note: some words can go in two categories.

jar: honey, jam, coffee, peanut butter
bag: potatoes, onions, apples, oranges, tomatoes
can: tomatoes, soup, tuna, beans, cola, mineral water
bar: chocolate, granola
packet: granola, soup, coffee, biscuits, potato crisps, spaghetti, nuts
bottle: cola, mineral water, orange juice, milk

6.9 Ranking the problems

Level	B1 and above
Time	15 to 20 minutes
Outline	In small groups, students rank target vocabulary items according to specific criteria, giving reasons for their choices, then compare ideas with the whole class.
Aim	To provide freer oral practice of a lexical set – for *Figure 6.9* below that of urban problems.
Preparation	No preparation is needed for this activity.
Rationale	As is often the case in course books, the exercises in *Figure 6.9* below provide controlled written practice of the lexical set and then have students personalise the language in some way, here by talking about which problems are of most concern in their own city or town. Getting students to also rank the problems adds a problem-solving dimension to the practice that is likely to generate more use of the vocabulary and more speaking overall. It also means that students have an opportunity to use all of the vocabulary and not just the words that relate to their own city.

Procedure

1 Students complete any controlled written or oral practice activities – exercises A and B in *Figure 6.9*.

2 On the board write:

most serious problem ← → *least serious problem*

3 Students work alone to rank the problems accordingly and think carefully about their reasons. If you're using the material in *Figure 6.9*, suggest that they think of issues for cities in general.

4 Students work in small groups of three or four students and negotiate and agree a new ranking.

5 Put two groups together to renegotiate the order before finally presenting their ideas and reasons to the class as a whole.

Notes and variation

Ranking activities can work well with lexical sets where there is a clearly scalable criterion. There are lots of different possibilities for ranking a wide range of vocabulary items. For example, clothing items in the order you would buy them; items that can be taken on holiday from most to least important; crimes according to level of severity, etc. Sometimes the discussion in these activities can get quite heated. If you know your class can get passionate about certain topics, it may pay to remind them of the need to compromise to reach agreement when negotiating ranking.

Learner reflection questions

1 How well do you feel you know the new vocabulary as a result of using it in the discussion?

2 Which words are the most memorable for you? Why do you think so?

Teacher reflection

What differences do you perceive between personalisation and problem-solving as a means to practising vocabulary? Which works better with your students? What different kinds of vocabulary suit one or other approach?

6.1 URBAN PROBLEMS (page 54)

A **Complete the sentences with the correct words.**

air	concrete	graffiti	land	noise	pollution	space	traffic	trash

1 Just outside our office, there's an ugly __________ wall with __________ painted on it.
2 Tall buildings need only a little __________, but they have a lot of __________ inside them.
3 Some people eat as they're walking and throw their __________ right on the sidewalk.
4 My house isn't right next to the highway, but I can hear the __________ from the __________.
5 It's hard to breathe because of all the __________ in the __________ from cars.

B **Use words from exercise A to complete these sentences. Sometimes more than one answer is possible.**

1 The __________ makes a lot of __________.
2 The __________ has __________ on it.
3 There's a lot of __________ in the __________.

Figure 6.9: Hendra, L. A., M. Ibbotson and K. O'Dell (2019) *Evolve 3*, p. 146.

You can find teacher development activities about vocabulary on pages 272 to 276.

7 Pronunciation

Introduction

Pronunciation in course books

There are two ways of considering the teaching of pronunciation in English language teaching. Should lessons have pronunciation as a main lesson aim with a large part of the lesson given over to presenting, analysing and practising a phonological feature? Or should a focus on pronunciation be integrated with other language items such as vocabulary, grammar or functional language?

In the vast majority of course books (and with all the activities included in this chapter), the second approach is taken. Below is a typical sequence of learning from a course book that includes a focus on an aspect of pronunciation.

The example in *Figure 7.0a* is from an A2 level course book, and the pronunciation feature is contrastive stress used to clarify information when responding to a question. This feature is initially exemplified in a short dialogue (8 Conversation), which is followed by presentation and practice of grammar (9 Grammar Focus). In section 10 Pronunciation, the contrastive stress is presented and practised. This lesson follows a typical, generic sequence found in course books:

exemplify the feature of pronunciation in a listening text together with another language item →
present and practise the other language item (vocabulary, grammar, functional expression) →
highlight the pronunciation feature by asking students to listen for it →
students listen for more examples of the feature →
students do oral practice of the feature.

8 CONVERSATION Which one is she?

A Listen and practice.

Brooke: Hi, Diego! Good to see you! Is Cora here, too?
Diego: Oh, she couldn't make it. She went to a concert with Alanna.
Brooke: Oh! Let's go talk to my friend Paula. She doesn't know anyone here.
Diego: Paula? Which one is she? Is she the woman wearing a long skirt over there?
Brooke: No, she's the tall one in jeans and a scarf. She's standing near the window.
Diego: OK. I'd like to meet her.

B Listen to the rest of the conversation. Label Liam, Hina, Sierra, and Matt in the picture.

9 GRAMMAR FOCUS

Modifiers with present participles and prepositions

		Participles
Who's Diego?	He's **the man**	**wearing** a blue shirt.
Which one is Diego?	He's **the one**	**talking** to Brooke.
		Prepositions
Who's Brooke?	She's **the woman**	**with** long black hair.
Which one is Paula?	She's **the tall one**	**in** jeans.
Who are the Harrisons?	They're **the people**	**next to** the window.
Which ones are the Harrisons?	They're **the ones**	**on** the couch.

GRAMMAR PLUS *see page 140*

A Rewrite these statements using modifiers with participles or prepositions.

1. Kyle is the tall guy. He's wearing a yellow shirt and brown pants.
   Kyle is the tall guy wearing a yellow shirt and brown pants.
2. Mark and Eve are the middle-aged couple. They're talking to Michael.
   ______
3. Alexis is the young girl. She's in a white T-shirt and blue jeans.
   ______
4. Britney is the woman in the green dress. She's sitting to the left of Javier.
   ______
5. J.P. is the serious-looking boy. He's playing a video game.
   ______

B **PAIR WORK** Complete these questions using your classmates' names and information. Then take turns asking and answering the questions.

1. Who's the guy (man) sitting next to ______?
2. Who's the girl (woman) wearing ______?
3. Who is ______?
4. Which one is ______?
5. Who are the people ______?
6. Who are the ones ______?

10 PRONUNCIATION Contrastive stress in responses

A Listen and practice. Notice how the stress changes to emphasize a contrast.

A: Is Rob the one wearing the red shirt?
B: No, he's the one wearing the black shirt.

A: Is Rachel the woman on the couch?
B: No, Jen is the woman on the couch.

B Mark the stress changes in these conversations. Listen and check. Then practice the conversations.

A: Is Sophie the one sitting next to Judy?
B: No, she's the one standing next to Judy.

A: Is David the one on the couch?
B: No, he's the one behind the couch.

Figure 7.0a: Richards, J. C. et al. (2017) *Interchange 1* (5th ed.), pp. 61–62.

We can now examine how this works in relation to the example lesson above.

Section 8 Conversation provides the context in the form of a dialogue that students listen to and practise. (Prior to this, students have studied vocabulary and expressions used to describe the physical appearance of people.) The contrastive stress is exemplified when Brooke says 'No, she's the tall one in jeans and a scarf.' The dialogue also acts as a context for a grammar point: the use of present participles and preposition phrases to modify and add meaning to a noun. This is presented and practised in section 9 Grammar Focus.

In section 10 Pronunciation, the target pronunciation feature is isolated and presented in two example exchanges. Students listen and notice the feature and a rule is given in the rubric of 10A: '… the stress changes to emphasize a contrast'. In 10B, students predict the contrastive stress in the replies, and then listen to check their predictions. This is followed by oral practice. The practice might be done as whole class drilling followed by pair work, or a teacher might only drill the whole class and not do pair practice, or she might ask students to practise in pairs without any whole class drilling.

Possible variations to this approach involve the way in which the phonological feature is analysed.

---

3 PRONUNCIATION
Emphasising what we say

a 2.87 Listen to the sentences in 2e. Notice the stress on the underlined words.

1 I'm so sorry I walked into you.
2 I'm really sorry I'm late.
3 I'm sorry I didn't answer.
4 I'm sorry I didn't come.
5 I'm very sorry I broke your cup.

b Why are *so*, *very* and *really* stressed? Choose the best answer.

1 We don't want the other person to hear *sorry* clearly.
2 We want to sound more sorry.
3 We want to speak loudly.

c Practise saying the sentences in 3a.

Figure 7.0b: Doff, A., C. Thaine et al. (2015) *Cambridge English Empower A1*, p. 75.

In the example in *Figure 7.0b*, students are not given the rule, but they are required to work it out for themselves by means of a guided discovery activity in exercise b. The pronunciation feature, namely sentence stress, is focused on together with functional language of excuses and apologies. As a result, and unlike the first course book example, there is an opportunity for students to use the pronunciation feature in a final, freer practice activity (*Figure 7.0c*).

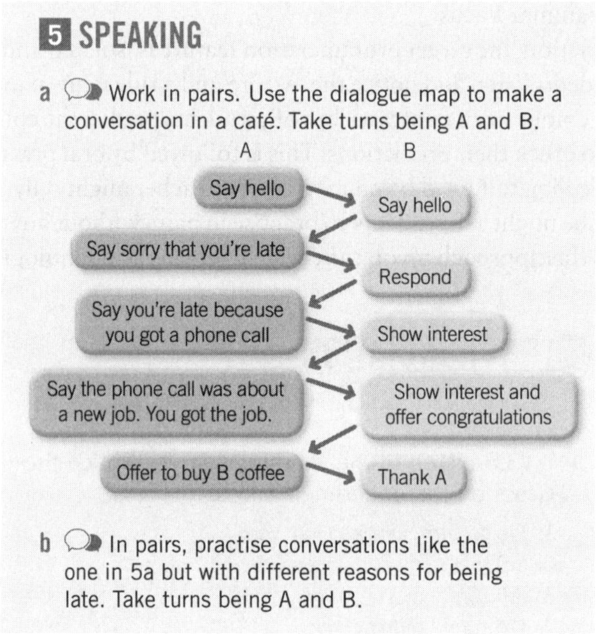

Figure 7.0c: Doff, A., C. Thaine et al. (2015) *Cambridge English Empower A1*, p. 75.

A receptive versus a productive focus

Teachers vary in their opinions about a receptive or productive approach to pronunciation. This will depend on their beliefs and the context that they are teaching in. Regardless of whether a teacher believes oral production of a phonological feature is desirable or not, there is general agreement that ear training is necessary. In effect, students will not be able to produce a sound if, first of all, they cannot hear it. One of the reasons that speakers of many different languages have problems with the 'th' (/θ/, /ð/) sounds in English is that they do not have these sounds in their first language. This means, at an early stage in their English language learning, a student may struggle to perceive a difference, for example, between voiced 'th' /ð/, and /d/. Students need exposure to the sound, and teachers need to point it out. They also need to understand that the difference between the two sounds creates a difference in meaning otherwise there is potential for confusion, for example, between 'brea<u>the</u>' and 'bree<u>d</u>'. This initial receptive focus on pronunciation can more broadly be perceived as awareness raising that gives students an understanding that English phonology is different from their first language.

Beyond this essential 'ear training', the first language of some learners may mean you need to offer students some 'mouth training' that involves productive activities in order to help make them intelligible. This means providing students with opportunities for oral practice of a phonological feature. The activities in this chapter all include some kind of task where students get a chance to produce the phonological feature focused on. This is based on the belief that many students like attempting to produce a pronunciation feature and receiving some kind of feedback on it from their teacher. Furthermore, speaking in a second language often requires you to use muscles in the speech organs that are not normally exercised. For example, one of the reasons why Japanese learners sometimes struggle to make a distinction between /l/ and /r/ when they speak is because they are unaccustomed to pushing their tongue further back on their hard palate. Productive pronunciation practice can be seen as a bit like sending students' mouths to the gym for a work out.

In the two course book examples above, the final exercises have a productive output and get students to practise the phonological feature. Course books nearly always provide some kind of practice exercise, but sometimes the focus on pronunciation may only be on receptive skills, for example, as in *Figure 7.0d*:

3 PRONUNCIATION Tones for continuing or finishing

a 2.71 Listen to two sentences. Does the voice in the underlined parts (1–4) go down then up (↘↗) or down (↘)?

I was going to call you, but my phone was dead.
1 2

I meant to call you, but I had to work a lot.
3 4

b Complete the rule.

When a speaker wants to show that they have something more to say, their voice often goes **down then up / down.**
When a speaker wants to show the information they're giving has finished, their voice often goes **down then up / down.**

c 2.72 Listen to four sentences. Do you think each speaker has finished or has something more to say?

1 I didn't see John
2 I won't have time tomorrow
3 I was going to tell you what happened
4 I didn't call her

Figure 7.0d: Doff, A., C. Thaine et al. (2015) *Cambridge English Empower B1*, p. 83.

Organisation of the chapter

The way that pronunciation is integrated with other language items in course books means that the organisation of this chapter along methodological lines is not helpful. As a result, and for ease of reference, the activities are organised according to the nature of the pronunciation focus, under the headings of A Sounds, B Stress, C Connected speech, and D Intonation.

It is worth bearing in mind that some course books differ in their use of terminology, for example 'emphasis' instead of 'stress', and 'tone' for 'intonation'.

Finally, here is a tip about integrating pronunciation into a teaching programme. Many pronunciation activities are quite short in duration. This means they can make good warmer activities at the beginning of a lesson. Given that many pronunciation features are presented together with other language items, a pronunciation warmer that includes previously taught vocabulary, grammar or functional expressions can be a good way to revise those language items.

A Sounds

7.1 Sound dictation

Level	A2 and above
Time	5 to 10 minutes
Outline	Students listen and note down how many times they hear the target sound in example sentences that you read aloud to them.
Aim	To give students practice in discriminating sounds in context.
Preparation	If you use the activity in *Figure 7.1*, no preparation is required. If you use a different activity with different sounds, then you will need to write your own sentences to read aloud.
Rationale	Many sound discrimination tasks focus only on word-level examples. This activity places the sounds back into a sentence-level context so that students listen for the target sounds amongst others in the sentence. This is not a true dictation because students only need to identify and count or write the words that contain the target sounds, and not the complete sentences.

Procedure

1 Work through any course book exercises focusing on sounds – exercises 1 to 3 in *Figure 7.1*.

2 Tell students that you are going to read aloud some sentences, and they need to listen and count the number of times they hear the target sounds. (See the example sentences below for *Figure 7.1*.)

3 Write an example on the board, e.g.:

I h<u>ear</u>d some b<u>ir</u>ds <u>ear</u>ly this morning. /ɜː/

Students can either simply write down the number 3 in their notebooks, or write the words that contain the sound.

4 Indicate which sound – either /ɔː/ or /ɜː/ for *Figure 7.1* – students should listen for in each sentence.

5 After you have read all the sentences aloud, students check their answers in pairs. Read the sentences a second time if necessary.

6 Write the sentences on the board, underlining the words with the target sounds.

7 In pairs, students can practise saying the sentences, while you monitor and check pronunciation.

Notes and variation

With a strong class, you could alternate between reading aloud sentences with different sounds or for a greater challenge put both sounds in the same sentence. At higher levels, you could get students to dictate sentences to each other that contain the target sounds students have to listen for. Or you could ask all students to write down the words, which could be extended to students coming up with their own sentences that contain examples of the same sound. Apart from getting students to tune into specific sounds, this activity is also very good intensive listening practice that focuses on bottom-up processing skills.

Learner reflection questions

1. Was it more or less difficult to hear the sounds in a sentence than in a single word? Why?
2. Did you think about the spelling of the words as you listened, or did you just try to hear the sound? Which is easier for you to do?

Teacher reflection

Which students wrote down the words they heard, and which only counted the sounds? Is there any relationship between these two groups and your perception of their listening skill ability?

The example sentences in *Figure 7.1* are standard British English. If you speak another variety of English where the sounds are different, you will need to create your own examples.

HELP WITH PRONUNCIATION
/ɔː/ and /ɜː/

1 CD2 ▸ 42 Listen to these sounds and words. Listen again and practise.

/ɔː/ shorts walk four   /ɜː/ shirt work girl

2 **a** Work in pairs. Look at the letters in bold. Write the words in the table.

~~Thursday~~ ~~strawberry~~ tall word August
birthday person bought divorced skirt

/ɔː/ shorts	/ɜː/ shirt
strawberry	*Thursday*

b CD2 ▸ 43 Listen and check. Listen again and practise.

3 **a** Work in pairs. Look at the letters in bold in these words. Are the sounds the same (S) or different (D)?

1 daughter poor *S*
2 boring furniture
3 Turkish German
4 morning always
5 thirty surname
6 sport early
7 dirty water
8 first burger
9 tall floor
10 awful boring

b CD2 ▸ 44 Listen and check. Listen again and practise.

Figure 7.1: Redston, C. and G. Cunningham (2012) *face2face Elementary* (2nd ed.), p. 63.

Sentences for reading aloud

1. My daughter always plays a lot of sport. /ɔː/ x3
2. This morning we walked to the shopping mall. /ɔː/ x3
3. I thought I saw four balls on the floor. /ɔː/ x5
4. I heard that girl worked here last year. /ɜː/ x 3
5. The third word is a verb not a noun. /ɜː/ x3
6. Last Thursday there were thirty people at her birthday party. /ɜː/ x4 (Note the strong form of ‘were’ contains /ɜː/, but in this sentence the weak form /ə/ is used.)

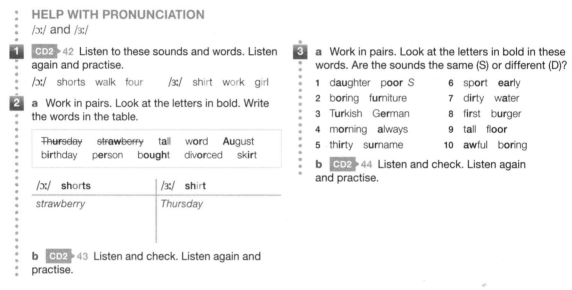

7.2 Long and short mingle

Level	A2 and above
Time	10 minutes
Outline	Students mingle and each reads out a sentence, trying to identify whether the final word of other sentences has the same sound as the one in theirs.
Aim	To give students practice distinguishing between similar long and short sounds; to give practice saying these sounds accurately.
Preparation	If you use the material in *Figure 7.2a*, you will need to copy and cut up the sentences on the worksheets below. If using a different exercise with two different sounds, you will need to create your own example sentences.
Rationale	As indicated above for activity 7.1, tasks that focus on the distinction between two similar sounds often focus on word-level minimal pairs (for example, hearing the difference between 'ship' /ɪ/ and sheep /iː/). This activity extends the task and puts the sounds back into the wider context of a full sentence. It also requires students to produce the sounds, rather than just listen to a recording or a teacher as is often the case with minimal pair exercises.

Procedure

1 Students listen to examples of the two sounds – exercises d and e in *Figure 7.2a*.

2 Give one sentence from the worksheets below to each student. For larger classes, some students can have the same sentence.

3 Explain to students that they will need to move around the classroom saying their sentence and listening to the other sentences to identify the final word sound.

4 If the word has the same sound as their final word, they write it down. Show an example on the board. Here sentences A and B end with the same long sound /uː/, but C ends with a short sound /ʊ/:

> *A That restaurant has very good* ***food.***
> *B At the moment, the sky is* ***blue.***
> *C This coffee is very* ***good.***

5 Tell students not to show their sentences to each other when they mingle.

6 When most have finished, ask them to stop and indicate who they think has the same sentence with the same sound.

7 To check correct answers on the board, write up the final words in the same sound groups.

Notes

You may find as you monitor that you need to help weaker students with their pronunciation of the sentence. Do this by modelling the sound for them, perhaps slightly exaggerating the length or shortness of the sound they are having problems with. At higher levels, this activity can be done with three or four different sounds.

Learner reflection questions

1 Which sound was harder to understand? And which was harder to say?

2 Is it important to say sounds correctly? Why / Why not?

Teacher reflection

Did students who struggled to identify the correct sound in another's words also have problems with their pronunciation? Why do you think this was the case?

The exercise in *Figure 7.2a* comes after the presentation of vocabulary associated with sport.

d 3.5 **Pronunciation** Listen to the marked sounds in these words. Are they long or short?

f**oo**tball j**u**do

e 3.6 Are the marked sounds in these words long or short? Listen and check.

1 f**u**ll	3 p**oo**l	5 f**oo**d
2 g**oo**d	4 p**u**t	6 bl**ue**

Figure 7.2a: Doff, A., C. Thaine et al. (2015) *Cambridge English Empower A1*, p. 166.

In the course book example in *Figure 7.2b*, students have to distinguish between two consonant sounds.

UNIT 9

/tʃ/ and /dʒ/ consonant sounds

1 2.17 **Read and listen to the dialogue.**

CHARLIE If I could be anything, I'd choose to be a journalist. What about you, Jane?

JANE Journalism's a very dangerous job, Charlie. I'm going to be a chess player.

CHARLIE You've changed your mind! You wanted to be a Geography teacher.

JANE Yes. I've just joined a chess club. My coach thinks I've got a good chance of becoming a champion.

2 **Say the words with the /tʃ/ and /dʒ/ sounds.**

Figure 7.2b: Puchta, H., J. Stranks and P. Lewis-Jones (2015) *Think Level 2*, p. 121.

Worksheet 1 /ʊ/

I'm looking for a **book**.
Write other students' words here:

I've got a sore **foot**.
Write other students' words here:

My mother is a very good **cook**.
Write other students' words here:

My glass is very **full**.
Write other students' words here:

Hang your coat on the **hook**.
Write other students' words here:

This chair is made of **wood**.
Write other students' words here:

My pullover is made of **wool**.
Write other students' words here:

To open the door you have to give it a good **push**.
Write other students' words here:

Worksheet 2 /uː/

Her birthday is in **June**.
Write other students' words here:

I think he has the '**flu**.
Write other students' words here:

In winter I like hot **soup**.
Write other students' words here:

She's coming very **soon**.
Write other students' words here:

I think you're in the wrong **group**.
Write other students' words here:

I don't think that's **true**.
Write other students' words here:

I love looking at the **moon**.
Write other students' words here:

The shoes I'm wearing are **new**.
Write other students' words here:

B Stress

7.3 Odd stress out

Level	A2 and above
Time	10 to 15 minutes
Outline	Students listen to detect the one word out of three that is pronounced with incorrect stress, then in pairs check their answers and decide the correct stress.
Aim	To highlight the importance of word stress and to give students practice listening for it.
Preparation	If you use *Figure 7.3a* below, no preparation is necessary unless you choose the optional ending, in which case you will need to photocopy the worksheet. If you use a different set of words, you will need to think of your groups of three words and which one to stress incorrectly.
Rationale	A common word stress activity in course books gets students to sort words into groups with specific stress patterns. This sometimes limits the amount of vocabulary that can be covered by the activity because words that don't fit a pattern are excluded. In *Figure 7.3a*, exercise B, the word 'engineer' isn't included because it doesn't fit one of the three patterns. This activity allows you to focus on a greater range of words.

Procedure

1 Students complete stress pattern sorting tasks – exercises A and B in *Figure 7.3a*.
2 Write on the board: *dancer dentist teacher*
3 Say all three words aloud, but put incorrect stress on the second syllable in 'dentist'. Ask students which word had incorrect stress and explain that this is the word they need to write down.
4 Read aloud the groups of three words with one word stressed incorrectly – see the worksheet for *Figure 7.3a*. Say each group twice.
5 Students identify and write down the incorrectly stressed words.
6 In pairs, students check their answers. You can then read out the words one more time if necessary.
7 Check answers on the board by writing up the words that were stressed incorrectly and eliciting the correct stress. Alternatively, give out copies of the worksheet to each pair to mark the correct stress and practise saying the words.

Notes

Asking students to listen and write down the incorrect word provides more challenge than simply grouping words according to stress pattern, and focuses them on listening carefully. If you feel your class needs more support, you could give them the worksheet before reading out the groups of three words, so they only have to circle the incorrectly stressed one. This activity works well with a specific lexical set. It can be done immediately after the focus on pronunciation in a course book. However, as suggested in the introduction to this chapter, it could also be used as a warmer activity in a subsequent lesson. In this case, a secondary aim is revision of the vocabulary.

Learner reflection questions

1 When your teacher put the wrong stress on a word, was it sometimes difficult to understand what the word was?
2 Why is correct word stress important when you speak?
3 How can you help your classmates to stress words correctly?

Teacher reflection

The principle of this activity is 'correct the teacher'. Did this change the atmosphere in the classroom in any way? How did students react to the idea of helping and correcting each other? How can you encourage this in other areas of language learning?

This pronunciation activity comes after students have studied a larger lexical set of jobs. The words on the worksheet include items focused on earlier in the unit.

8 PRONUNCIATION Syllable stress

A Listen and practice. Notice which syllable has the main stress.

● •	● • •	• ● •
dancer	salesperson	accountant
______	______	______
______	______	______

B Which stress pattern do these words have? Add them to the columns in part A. Then listen and check.

carpenter musician firefighter reporter server tutor

Figure 7.3a: Richards, J. C. et al. (2017) *Interchange 1* (5th ed.), p.11.

Worksheet

firefighter	server	reporter
doctor	front desk clerk	lawyer
mechanic	tutor	police officer
office manager	engineer	accountant
musician	vendor	carpenter

Correct main stress			*Suggested mistake*
<u>fire</u>fighter	<u>ser</u>ver	re<u>por</u>ter	✗ <u>re</u>porter
<u>doc</u>tor	front desk <u>clerk</u>	<u>law</u>yer	✗ doc<u>tor</u>
me<u>cha</u>nic	<u>tu</u>tor	po<u>lice</u> officer	✗ mecha<u>nic</u>
<u>off</u>ice manager	engi<u>neer</u>	ac<u>coun</u>tant	✗ off<u>ice</u> manager
mu<u>si</u>cian	<u>ven</u>dor	<u>car</u>penter	✗ car<u>pen</u>ter

The course book example in *Figure 7.3b* is in two parts. The vocabulary exercise is in the main unit and the word stress exercise is in a special pronunciation section at the back of the book called *Say it right!*. More adjectives of feeling could be included for the three-word dictation.

Vocabulary Adjectives of feeling

4 🔊 **2.34** **Match the pictures a–i with the words in the box. Then listen, check and repeat.**

> angry bored excited tired afraid upset
> interested embarrassed surprised

➡ **Say it right!** • page 97

Unit 8 Word stress

1 **Complete the table with the adjectives of feeling on page 88.**

O	*bored, ...*
oO
Oo
oOo
Ooo

Figure 7.3b: Goldstein, B. and C. Jones (2015) *Eyes Open 2*, pp. 88 and 97.

7.4 Stress match

Level	A2 and above
Time	10 to 15 minutes
Outline	Students are given sentences and questions with the stress marked. They then mingle and say their sentence to other students and try to find a student who has a sentence with the same stress pattern.
Aim	To make students sensitive to phrase stress patterns and provide controlled practice of them.
Preparation	If you use *Figure 7.4* below, you will need to copy and cut up the sentences on the worksheet. If you use a different course book task, you will need to write your own sentences. (Note: in order for stress patterns to match the sentences and questions you write, they need to have the same number of syllables with the same syllables stressed.)
Rationale	Many course book activities that focus on phrase stress are linked to an aspect of grammar (in *Figure 7.4*, for example, stress is linked to a focus on adverbs of frequency). This means that students only have the opportunity of exploring phrase stress with one or two examples and patterns. The activity below is a way of extending students' awareness of phrase stress. It also goes beyond listening to model examples and encourages them to practise saying language examples with a specific rhythm.

Procedure

1 Do any tasks focusing on phrase stress – exercises c and d in *Figure 7.4*.

2 Give each student a sentence or a question with the main stresses marked (see worksheet). They should practise saying their example on their own while you monitor, listen and help, if necessary.

3 Students then mingle saying (and not showing) their sentence or question and try to find another student who has a sentence or question with the same stress pattern.

4 In whole class feedback, students say their sentences and questions, and you confirm if they are correct. Help any students who haven't found a partner.

Notes and variation

As with other activities in this chapter, the emphasis here is getting students to listen to each other. The examples in the worksheet below are made more manageable by the fact that both the stress and grammar pattern match. More challenge can be introduced if they don't match so neatly, for example *Do you <u>work</u> at <u>home</u>?* matches *He can <u>swim</u> quite <u>well</u>.* At higher levels, where students have a greater range of vocabulary that allows for more variation, this activity could be done within the context of one grammar area, for example, different conditional structures.

Learner reflection questions

1 For this activity, did you listen for words or stresses? Why?

2 Are there very clear rules for stress in English or does stress change with different meanings?

Teacher reflection

How many times did students practise their example before getting up to do the mingle? What does this tell you about students' tolerance for repetition? To what extent do you think students were following grammar patterns rather than stress patterns to find their partner?

c 1.62 **Pronunciation** Listen to the question and answer. Notice the stressed words.

MARTIN How often does she go?
KATHERINE Twice a week on Monday and Thursday.

d Which words do we usually stress? Choose the correct answer.

a Important words like time expressions and verbs.
b Less important words.

Figure 7.4: Doff, A., C. Thaine et al. (2015) *Cambridge English Empower A2*, p. 31.

Worksheet

She works in a bank.	I live in a house.
Twice a week on Monday.	Once a year in August.
How often does she go?	How many do you have?
Where are you from?	What do you do?
I never stay out late.	They always go away.
Are you Italian?	Is she Egyptian?
Do you work here?	Does she drink tea?
We don't like chocolate.	They don't hate football.
Where do you want to go?	When does she leave for Rome?
I'm going to meet a friend.	I'd like to drink some tea.

7.5 Contrastive shout out

Level	B1 and above
Time	20 to 30 minutes
Outline	In competing teams, students listen to questions to identify the stressed word and then answer with a correctly stressed reply. Students then practise the questions and replies in pairs.
Aim	To provide students with controlled oral practice of contrastive stress.
Preparation	If you use *Figure 7.5*, and have time, write the example replies to the questions on the board. Alternatively, give the teams printed copies of the replies without the stressed words marked, but in a different order from the questions to be asked. If you write the replies on the board, you will also need to make a copy of the worksheet below for each student. Fold these in half, so students can only see one side or the other.
Rationale	Many course book exercises that practise contrastive stress require students to give a passive response to a prompt. Students often listen to a question or the first part of a sentence and then choose an appropriate response (this is how the course book exercise in *Figure 7.5* works). This activity extends the task and gets students to repeat utterances with contrastive stress, first chorally as a group and then in pairs.

Procedure

1. Students do any highlighting and analysis tasks in the course book – exercises A and B in *Figure 7.5* below.
2. Put students into three or four teams and write the replies to the questions on the board (or give out copies of the replies).
3. Select the first team and ask one of the questions. The team listens for the strongly stressed word and they have 10 seconds to check together and select one of the replies on the board. One of the team members says the answer aloud. If necessary, do an example first.
4. Nominate the teams in turn and work through the questions. Give one point for each correct reply, correctly stressed.
5. Once you have completed all the questions, give each student the folded worksheets. Put students in A and B pairs. Student A looks at the side with the questions and Student B looks at the side with the replies.
6. Student A reads the questions, making sure they stress the marked word. Student B finds the correct reply and answers with the appropriate stress.
7. As pairs finish, students swap roles and repeat the task.

Notes and variation

A possible variation is that students say the question with a different stress than indicated and their partner replies with appropriate stress, for example: A: *Did <u>they</u> get here at eight o'clock?* B: *No, <u>we</u> arrived at eight.* At higher levels, a degree of challenge can be added to this activity by not providing answers and getting students to come up with their own. Students are often amused by the exaggeration of contrastive stress, so they can find activities that focus on this aspect of pronunciation enjoyable.

Learner reflection questions

1 What is easier to say, sentences with normal stress, or sentences where one word is strongly stressed? Why?

2 In your first language, do you use strong stress like this when you correct information? If not, what do you do?

Teacher reflection

What was more challenging for students, deciding on the correct stress or saying it in unison? In the pair work activity, how much correction of stress did you need to do? Do your students find contrastive stress easier or more difficult than neutral stress?

9 PRONUNCIATION Contrastive stress

A Listen and practice. Notice how a change in stress changes the meaning of each question and elicits a different response.

Is the bedroom window cracked? (No, the kitchen window is cracked.)

Is the bedroom window cracked? (No, the bedroom door is cracked.)

Is the bedroom window cracked? (No, it's stuck.)

B Listen to the questions. Check (✓) the correct response.

1. a. Are my jeans torn?
☐ No, they're stained.
☐ No, your shirt is torn.

b. Are my jeans torn?
☐ No, they're stained.
☐ No, your shirt is torn.

2. a. Is the computer screen flickering?
☐ No, it's freezing.
☐ No, the TV screen is flickering.

b. Is the computer screen flickering?
☐ No, it's freezing.
☐ No, the TV screen is flickering.

Figure 7.5: Richards, J. C. et al. (2017) *Interchange 1* (5th ed.), p. 40.

Questions and replies

Write the replies on the board without the stress indicated. Put them in a different order from the questions.

Did they get here at eight o'clock?	No, they arrived at nine.
Have we got grammar homework tonight?	No, we've got vocabulary exercises to do.
Is it going to rain tomorrow?	No, they say it'll be cloudy.
Have you got a German car?	No, we've got a Japanese one.
Is your older sister a lawyer?	No, only my younger one.
Did you go to the cinema last night?	No, we went to a concert.
Do you usually come to school by bus?	No, I normally get here by train.

Are you working full-time at the moment?	No, I'm just part-time this month.
Were you at Emma's party last night?	No, I went to the one at Maggie's place.
Did you find that book interesting?	No, I thought it was really boring.
Do you get up at six in the morning?	No, I get up at seven.
Is that your phone ringing?	No, it's Luca's phone.
Have you got apples on your shopping list?	No, I've only got oranges.
Are you visiting your parents this weekend?	No, I'm going to my grandmother's.
Did you go to a Turkish restaurant last night?	No, we went to a Thai one.

Worksheet

Questions	**Replies**
Did they get here at eight o'clock?	No, I thought it was really boring.
Have we got grammar homework tonight?	No, I'm going to my grandmother's.
Is it going to rain tomorrow?	No, we went to a Thai one.
Have you got a German car?	No, I get up at seven.
Is your older sister a lawyer?	No, I've only got oranges.
Did you go to the cinema last night?	No, they arrived at nine.
Do you usually come to school by bus?	No, we've got vocabulary exercises to do.
Are you working full-time at the moment?	No, they say it'll be cloudy.
Were you at Emma's party last night?	No, it's Luca's phone.
Did you find that book interesting?	No, we went to a concert.
Do you get up at six in the morning?	No, we've got a Japanese one.
Is that your phone ringing?	No, I went to the one at Maggie's place.
Have you got apples on your shopping list?	No, only my younger one.
Are you visiting your parents this weekend?	No, I normally get here by train.
Did you go to a Turkish restaurant last night?	No, I'm just part-time this month.

C Connected speech

7.6 Pass the schwa /ə/

Level A2 and above

Time 10 to 15 minutes

Outline Students first listen and mark weak (schwa) forms on words in short sentences and questions. They then move around the classroom repeating to another student one sentence, before exchanging sentences and repeating this process with a different student.

Aim To give students further practice identifying weak forms in short utterances; to provide controlled practice of saying weak forms in short phrases and questions.

Preparation Copy and cut up the sentences on the worksheet below if you are using the course book lesson in *Figure 7.6a* and give one to each student. You will need to fold each piece of paper along the dotted line so students can't see the sentence or question with the weak forms. If you have a large class, the same sentences can be given to more than one student. If you are using a different course book lesson, you will need to create and copy your own questions and phrases with schwa as per the worksheet.

Rationale The approach that this activity takes is to make the course book task more manageable, but also to broaden the practice. The examples in the worksheet are shorter than those in *Figure 7.6a*, so when it comes to practising utterances with schwa, the language items are of a more manageable length. The initial listening task in this activity adds a sense of challenge, requiring students to listen for their sentence and then identify the schwa sounds.

Procedure

1. Students complete any listening and analysis task – exercise a in *Figure 7.6a* below, and do this *Pass the schwa* activity before moving on to exercise b.
2. Give one sentence or one question to each student and explain that the main stresses are marked. Make sure each paper is folded so students can't see weak forms.
3. Students guess which one syllable words might have a weak form. (Note: only these weak forms are focused on – not those in content words with two or more syllables, e.g. *advice* /əd'vaɪs/ or *later* /'leɪtə/.)
4. You, as teacher, read aloud each question and sentence twice while students listen to identify their sentence/question and the weak form(s) in it. Students unfold their piece of paper to check answers.
5. Ask students to memorise their sentences and put away their piece of paper for later.
6. Students mingle and form different pairs. They practise and memorise each other's examples. They then move on to another student and repeat the process.
7. When you feel students have had sufficient practice, in open class feedback, get each student to say aloud their current memorised sentence. Either show the sentences on the board or get the student who was given the sentence originally to read it aloud.

Notes and variation

At higher levels, it's possible to include more challenging variations. The examples could be given without the main stresses marked, and students could be asked to listen for main stresses and weak forms. You could also add a competitive element to this and set a time limit for the activity. Students count the number of swaps they manage to do. In feedback, you can see who has done the most swaps in the allotted time.

Learner reflection questions

1 Are the words with the weak forms important to understanding the meaning of the sentences you heard and practised? If not, what helps you understand the meaning?
2 When you said the sentences, was it easier to concentrate on the words with the weak forms or the words with the main stress?

Teacher reflection

When you read out all the examples and students had to listen for theirs, which listening subskill did students practise? What problem can occur if students focus too much on the words with schwa?

The example sentences and questions included in the worksheet are based on language items that were taught in the lesson prior to the pronunciation task. It's not necessary to do this, but it helps students if the sentences are drawn from the same broader context.

PRONUNCIATION
The schwa sound 1

5 a 2.27 **You usually say grammar words like and, the, of, etc. without stress and with a schwa /ə/. These are *weak forms*. Listen and notice the words with /ə/.**

CARLA Hi, Dean. This is Carla. Listen, can you talk now? I'm planning my seminar and I want your advice.
DEAN Sorry, Carla, but I'm in the middle of dinner. Can I call you later?
CARLA Yes, no problem. Talk to you later.

b Practise the conversation with the weak forms. P

Figure 7.6a: Tilbury, A., T. Clementson et al. (2010) *English Unlimited A2*, p. 60.

Worksheet
The main stresses are underlined.

Can you <u>talk</u> now?	I'm at <u>home</u> and I want your ad<u>vice</u>.
..	..
/ə/ Can you <u>talk</u> now?	/ə/ /ə/ I'm at <u>home</u> and I want your ad<u>vice</u>.
<u>Talk</u> to you <u>later</u>.	<u>Sorry</u>, but I'm in the <u>middle</u> of <u>dinner</u>.
..	..
/ə/ <u>Talk</u> to you <u>later</u>.	/ə/ /ə/ /ə/ <u>Sorry</u>, but I'm in the <u>middle</u> of <u>dinner</u>.
I'm in a <u>meeting</u> now.	I'm <u>working</u> on a re<u>port</u>.
..	..
/ə/ I'm in a <u>meeting</u> now.	/ə/ I'm <u>working</u> on a re<u>port</u>.
I'm <u>not</u> on the <u>internet</u> at the <u>moment</u>.	<u>Sorry</u>, but I'm <u>busy</u> right now.
/ə/ /ə/ /ə/ I'm <u>not</u> on the <u>internet</u> at the <u>moment</u>.	/ə/ <u>Sorry</u>, but I'm <u>busy</u> right now.
Can I <u>call</u> you <u>later</u>?	<u>Sorry</u>, but I'm <u>not</u> interested.
..	..
/ə/ Can I <u>call</u> you <u>later</u>?	/ə/ <u>Sorry</u>, but I'm <u>not</u> interested.

From *Off the Page* © Cambridge University Press 2020 PHOTOCOPIABLE

In the course book example in *Figure 7.6b*, the focus on weak forms is related to a specific grammar point: comparative adjectives. Extra sentences to be used in the activity could all be comparative sentences.

Unit 4 *schwa*

1 🔊 **1.31** **Listen to the sentences. How do we pronounce the letters in bold?**
1 France is smaller than Brazil.
2 I'm better at Maths than at History.
3 This classroom is bigger than our classroom last year.

2 🔊 **1.31** **Listen again and repeat the sentences.**

3 **Underline the** *schwa* **sounds in the following sentences.**
1 Mark is older than Julia, but Peter is the oldest in the class.
2 The River Nile is longer than the River Danube.
3 The weather is warmer in Spain than in England.

4 🔊 **1.32** **Listen and check your answers.**

Figure 7.6b: Goldstein, B. and C. Jones (2015) *Eyes Open 2*, p. 96.

7.7 Writing down the links

Level	A2 and above
Time	10 to 15 minutes
Outline	Students listen to and write down dictated sentences and, where they think linking occurs, they write the two words as one word.
Aim	To make students sensitive to consonant–vowel linking; to provide controlled oral practice of this linking.
Preparation	For the course book exercise in *Figure* 7.7 below, if you want to give a copy of the example sentences and questions to students, you will need to make a copy of the dictation worksheet. If you use different material, you will need to create your own linking examples to dictate. Make sure they are on the same topic area as the material you're using.
Rationale	One drawback of connected speech exercises on a printed page is that they can only provide visual representation of the feature. While the visual representation is useful for many learners, in order to be able to understand how words are often pushed together in natural speech, it helps if students get practice hearing this before writing down a visual representation.

Procedure

1 Students study consonant–vowel linking (exercises a and b in *Figure* 7.7 below), then close their books.
2 If necessary, dictate some sentence and/or question examples of linking – for the material in *Figure* 7.7, about buying clothes.
3 Tell students that when they hear linking between words, they should write the words together as one word. Do an example on the board, e.g. say: '*Men's clothes are over there*' and write on the board: *Men's clothesareover there.*
4 Read each sentence twice, or a third time if you feel students need more help.
5 Students check answers in pairs and you can then read the sentences one more time.
6 Write the answers on the board and show the linking.
7 Students can then work in pairs to practise these examples while you monitor.

Notes and variation

This is quite a challenging activity for some students, so if you want to make it easier, you could put one key content word for each example on the board; for *Figure* 7.7, these could be: 1 *credit*, 2 *size*, 3 *try*, etc. This activity could be adapted for other features of connected speech such as intrusion and assimilation, with students writing the intrusive or altered sound above the sentence in the relevant place.

Learner reflection questions

1 When you listened for the linking in the sentences and questions, did you think about the spelling or just listen to the sounds?
2 When you listen to English, is it possible to hear every individual word? What kinds of words might it be better to listen for?

Teacher reflection

Did students have trouble hearing linking or did they mark linking where it didn't exist? Do you think they were working more from sound or were they working from spelling? How does this activity help listening skills?

6 PRONUNCIATION Joining words

a 3.35 Listen to the sentences. Notice the marked words. Is there a pause between them?

1 **Can I** help you?
2 What **size are** you?
3 Can I try **them on**?
4 How **much are** they?
5 The fitting rooms **are over** there.

b Notice how the marked words in 6a are joined.

In 1–4, the consonant sound moves to the start of the next word:

1 Can I → Ca ni
2 size are → si zare
3 them on → the mon
4 much are → mu chare

In 5, we add the sound /r/ to join the words:

5 are over → are **r**over

c In pairs, take turns saying the sentences in 6a and giving a reply. Try to link the marked words.

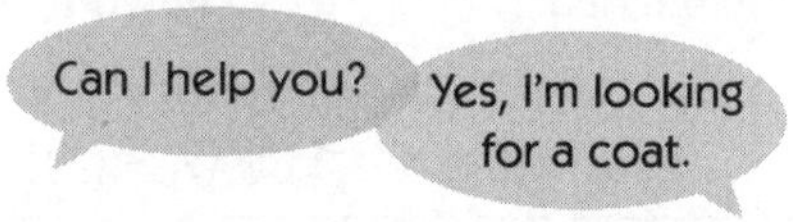

Can I help you?
Yes, I'm looking for a coat.

Figure 7.7: Doff, A., C. Thaine et al. (2015) *Cambridge English Empower A2*, p. 95.

Sentences and questions for dictation

1 Can‿I pay by credit card?
2 What size‿is he?
3 Can‿I try it‿on?
4 I'm looking for‿a shirt.
5 These‿are nice jeans.
6 Have you got them‿in blue?
7 I'm size‿eight and‿a half.
8 The checkout‿is‿over there.

Note: in question 3 there is also an intrusive /j/ between *try* and *it*, but don't focus on this unless students ask about it.

D Intonation

7.8 The surprise competition

Level A2 and above

Time 10 to 15 minutes

Outline A mingle activity where some students say personal statements and other students react with surprise and ask a question with the appropriate intonation.

Aim To give students practice in producing an expressive intonation range.

Preparation If you use *Figure 7.8* below, you will need to copy and cut up the worksheet. If you use a different course book exercise, you will need to create your own questions and answers to copy and cut up.

Rationale Drilling students in new language that sounds more natural with varied intonation, such as functional language with requests and suggestions, can sometimes be problematic. Students can feel uncomfortable and sound unnatural when trying to vary their tone to reach a higher pitch. This activity moves away from traditional drilling and makes the practice more student-centred and interactive. It also introduces a slightly competitive but light-hearted element that gives students the freedom to exaggerate and explore their range.

Procedure

1 Students first listen to and analyse examples of surprise reactions – exercises a to d in *Figure 7.8* below.

2 Give some students sentences and other students questions that are surprise reactions.

3 Explain that students with the sentences must find the two students that have the correct question in response. Demonstrate this on the board:

A: I'm getting married! → B: Are you? ✓
Did you? ×
Have you? ×
→ C: Are you? ✓

4 Tell students to memorise their sentences or questions and not show them to each other. Students with the reactions should try to be as enthusiastic and surprised as possible. They begin mingling, speaking and reacting.

5 Each student with a sentence finds and listens to the two students with the correct reaction and chooses the one who shows the most surprise as their partner.

6 Students who weren't selected, work together to practise saying their reactions more enthusiastically in preparation for a challenge in open class.

7 In open class feedback, there will be a group of pairs and a group of students who weren't selected. Pairs perform their exchange. The student who wasn't selected can challenge and try to sound more enthusiastic. The student with the sentence can change partner at this final stage.

8 When you finish feedback, the students whose responses didn't 'win' a partner are given the sentences and the activity is repeated.

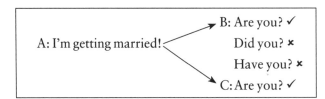

Notes and variation

For this activity to work well, it helps to emphasise the light-hearted and exaggerated nature of the reactions in the game. While some students may exaggerate to the point of sounding unnatural, it still means they explore the pitch range of their voice. For students who are usually shy about doing this, the game element may make them more relaxed. At higher levels, you could provide just the sentences and students could then come up with their own expressions in reaction.

Learner reflection questions

1 What did you need to do to show a lot of surprise?
2 Sometimes showing surprise by making your voice go high feels uncomfortable. How do you think it sounds to other people?

Teacher reflection

By encouraging students to exaggerate, did their intonation sound more or less natural? What do you think makes some students feel uncomfortable about varying their intonation – the influence of their first language or culture or do you think it's more personal?

In the example in *Figure 7.8*, the surprise reaction is conveyed by short questions that have a dramatic rise.

2 CONVERSATION SKILLS Showing surprise

a Look at the conversation. Underline the two ways that Dan shows surprise.

MARTINA I've won a competition.
DAN Have you? Fantastic. What's the prize?
MARTINA A weekend for two in Bath …
DAN Really? That's great.

b Which question in 2a can you use to reply to any news?

c 3.85 Match 1–4 with a–d. Listen and check your answers.

1 I'm getting married.	a Do you?
2 I really like grammar.	b Have you?
3 I went to New York for the weekend.	c Are you?
4 I've eaten an insect.	d Did you?

d 3.85 **Pronunciation** Listen again. Does the tone in a–d in 2c go up ↗ a little or a lot?

e Think of two surprising things. They don't have to be true! Make notes.

f In pairs, take turns telling each other your surprising things and showing surprise. Use expressions from 2a and 2c.

Figure 7.8: Doff, A., C. Thaine et al. (2015) *Cambridge English Empower A2*, p.124.

Worksheet

I'm going to live in Australia!	Are you?	Are you?
I've tried surfing in Hawaii.	Have you?	Have you?
I love studying maths as a hobby!	Do you?	Do you?
I bought a new car yesterday!	Did you?	Did you?
I can play the violin very well.	Can you?	Can you?
I don't like chocolate.	Don't you?	Don't you?

7.9 Have you finished?

Level	B1 and above
Time	10 to 15 minutes
Outline	In groups, students practise rising and falling intonation, by orally preparing supermarket shopping lists.
Aim	To provide freer practice of rising and falling intonation to indicate continuing or finishing; to encourage students to listen carefully to each other's intonation.
Preparation	There is no preparation for this activity unless you would like to think of a list of topics that would work well with your students.
Rationale	It is useful for students to understand and practise rising and falling tones to help recognise whether someone has finished speaking or not. The activity below uses students' own ideas, and it encourages them to work co-operatively and listen closely to each other. Developing this kind of practical awareness is particularly useful for students who might need to give a presentation of some kind. It signals the need for pitch variation in longer stretches of speaking.

Procedure

1 Students complete analysis and practice activities – the Pronunciation box and exercises 8 and 9 in *Figure 7.9* below.
2 Students first work alone and make a list of things to buy at the supermarket (it doesn't just have to be food) – 10 or more items. Then put students into groups of three to five.
3 Write on the board:
We're going to the supermarket, let's buy ...
And that's all!
4 Tell students that in their groups they are going to make some spoken shopping lists (no writing), with these beginning and ending phrases.
5 The first student begins by saying *We're going to the supermarket, let's buy ...* and adds one item using rising intonation. The next student repeats the sentence and the first item and adds something to the list. Students continue, in turn, in this way until a student adds an item with falling intonation. When this happens, the next student says, *And that's all!* Demonstrate if necessary.
6 The group then starts a new list with another student starting.
7 Monitor and check students' intonation and be available as a referee if necessary.
8 If time allows, you can finish off this activity by doing a whole class list with the turn passing from one group to the next (students take it in turns to add items).

Notes

The vocabulary focused on in this activity is different from the vocabulary in course book *Figure 7.9*. In order to keep students focused on intonation, it pays to choose a lexical area that is known to students. The environmental context in the example material might be quite challenging. Another typical context for listing is items to take away on holiday.

Learner reflection questions

1 If you are having a discussion, what can you signal to other people in the group with your intonation?
2 Is intonation used in this way in your first language? Is the intonation different at all?

Teacher reflection

If students don't vary their intonation when speaking, how do they sound? What other phonological feature is closely linked to intonation?

PRONUNCIATION FOR LISTENING

SKILLS

Intonation of lists

Speakers often list examples of what they are talking about. Giving a list of examples can help persuade the audience. These lists have their own intonation patterns. Speakers pause between each example in the list and stress each word.

If the list is complete, the last example in the list has falling intonation, like this:
1.4 ... beautiful ↗, powerful ↗, majestic ↘

If the list is not complete, the last example has rising intonation, like this:
1.5 ... warmer temperatures ↗, floods ↗, droughts ↗, huge storms ... ↗

When you are taking notes, it is important to listen for this intonation so you know that the list isn't complete yet.

8 1.6 Listen to the lists. Is each list complete or not complete? Tick the correct answer.

	complete	not complete
1 large, white, strong		
2 pandas, sea turtles, chimpanzees, tigers		
3 human contact, climate change, industrial development		
4 more lights, electric fences, warning plans		

9 1.6 Listen to the lists again. Practise saying each list with rising and falling intonation.

Figure 7.9: Ostrowska, S., N. Jordan et al. (2019) *Unlock Listening, Speaking & Critical Thinking 3*, pp. 27–28.

You can find teacher development activities about pronunciation on pages 277 to 280.

8 Discourse

Introduction

What do we mean by discourse?

The three easily identifiable language systems are grammar, vocabulary and phonology. The fourth language system is known as *discourse*. Identifying discourse as a fourth system arose out of a way of studying language that gained currency in the 1960s and 1970s. Known as *discourse analysis*, this approach involves the study of language use in both spoken and written contexts (McCarthy 1991). It takes into account language items that might not be complete sentences, and it also looks at the way longer stretches of language made up of two or more sentences fit together.

Consider this example of spoken language:

A: *Looking forward to the game.*
B: *Yeah, can't wait.*

Neither speaker uses a full sentence to communicate. This is not wrong and, in fact, the absence of the pronoun 'I' in this exchange makes it sound more natural. Although this exchange is grammatically incomplete, a fluent English speaker knows this is a perfectly appropriate exchange. Discourse analysis looks at the reasons why this is the case. It also acknowledges that, in much spoken language, there are many omissions, in particular pronouns and auxiliary verbs. This is known as *ellipsis*.

Now look at this example of written language:

Throughout the country, dairy farmers have been asked to change their farming practices so they are more environmentally friendly. This is one step towards ensuring cleaner waterways in the future.

The pronoun *this* at the beginning of the second sentence refers back to the idea in the previous sentence. In order to understand this linking of ideas, we need to look at the two sentences together. They form an extended and cohesive stretch of language. While we can label *this* as a pronoun, in discourse analysis terms it is an example of *reference*. In other words, the pronoun *refers* back to the change in dairy farming practices. Discourse analysts also note that the use of *this* makes the two sentences fit together well . This is known as *cohesion*.

Discourse analysis was initially a theoretical study of how language worked. However, over time, insights from that study have trickled down into English language teaching and course books. For the sake of clarity, we are using two terms to outline how discourse is represented in course books: *functional/situational language* and *extended text*. *Functional/situational language* is largely associated with spoken language and *extended text* is associated with stretches of both written and spoken language. While discourse does not usually appear as a clearly defined syllabus strand in a course book in the way that grammar, vocabulary and phonology do, it is an important language system to focus on.

Functional/Situational language in course books

Most course books include lessons that focus on language that occurs in a range of social contexts that is called *functional* and/or *situational language*. It involves the study of particular expressions and phrases used in a variety of situations. *Functional language* comprises expressions such as requests, invitations, suggestions and advice. If we are planning an evening out, we will perhaps *invite* friends to join us and then *make suggestions* about what we can do.

Different expressions can be grouped together as serving the same function even if they contain quite different grammatical forms. For example, in order to give someone advice we can use a second conditional (*If I were you, I'd see a doctor*), or we could use the modal verb *should* (*You should see a doctor*), or we could be very direct about the advice we give and use an imperative (*Please, see a doctor*). All of these expressions are 'correct', and as speakers, we can choose which one to use. What expression we use depends on how well we know the person we are talking to and it might also depend on whether we perceive the nature of the medical problem as being urgent or not. We would probably use the second conditional with someone we do not know well and the imperative with a good friend or family member who looks very ill. Course books usually provide clear contexts for functional language to illustrate which expressions are appropriate in different social settings.

Situational language refers to the kind of language that is used in specific situations or settings. For example, when we go to a restaurant, there is specific language that a waiter will use towards a customer, and that a customer will use to order a meal. Other typical situations that are covered in course books are: shopping for clothes, asking for tourist information, going to the doctor and giving directions. In effect, situational language is similar to the kind of expressions you can find in a tourist phrase book. Sometimes there is overlap between functional and situational language. For example, when someone orders a coffee in a café (*Can I have an espresso?*) they are also making a request.

Functional and situational language is often conflated as one syllabus strand in course books and can be labelled in a variety of ways. Here are some example headings from course books:

2 USEFUL LANGUAGE
Asking for things and replying

Doff, A., C. Thaine et al. (2015) *Cambridge English Empower A2*, p. 24.

Speaking Shopping

Goldstein, B. and C. Jones (2015) *Eyes Open 2*, p. 16.

Real World apologies, reasons and promises

Redston, C. and G. Cunningham (2012) *face2face Pre-intermediate* (2nd ed.), p. 28.

8 CONVERSATION What time does it start?

Richards, J. C. et al. (2017) *Interchange 1* (5th ed.), p. 25.

FUNCTIONS
Giving warnings and stating prohibition

Puchta, H., J. Stranks and P. Lewis-Jones (2015) *Think Level 1*, p. 19.

In most cases, functional and/or situational language is embedded in a conversation that students listen to (audio or video) because it is language we use when speaking.

6 a Read Paul and Clare's conversations with the waitress. Fill in the gaps with the questions from **4b**.

WAITRESS Would you like to order now?
CLARE Yes, I'd like the chicken salad, please.
PAUL Can I have the cheeseburger and chips, please?
WAITRESS 1 ______________________?
CLARE We'd like a bottle of mineral water, please.
WAITRESS Still or sparkling?
CLARE Sparkling, please.
WAITRESS 2 ______________________?
PAUL No, that's all, thanks.

WAITRESS 3 ______________________?
CLARE Yes, I'd like the fruit salad, please.
PAUL And can I have the apple pie with cream?
WAITRESS Certainly.

WAITRESS 4 ______________________?
CLARE Not for me, thank you.
PAUL No, thank you. Can we have the bill, please?
WAITRESS Yes, of course.

b VIDEO 4 CD1 77 Watch or listen again. Check your answers.

REAL WORLD
Requests and offers

7 a Look at sentences 1–3. Which sentences are requests (we want something)? Which sentence is an offer (we want to give something or help someone)?

1 **Would you like** to order now?
2 **I'd/We'd like** a bottle of mineral water, please.
3 **Can I/we have** the bill, please?

b Complete the rules with the phrases in bold in **7a**.

- We use ______________ and ______________ for requests.
- We use ______________ for offers.

c Look at the conversation in **6a** again. Find four more requests.

REAL WORLD 4.1 p137

8 a CD1 78 Listen to the sentences in **7a**. Notice the stress and polite intonation.

Would you like to order now?

b CD1 79 PRONUNCIATION Listen and practise the offers and requests in the conversation in **6a**. Copy the stress and polite intonation.

9 a Work in groups of three. Decide who is the waiter/waitress and who are the customers. Practise the conversation in **6a** until you remember it.

b Close your book. Practise the conversation again.

10 a Work in the same groups. Look at the menu. Write a new conversation between a waiter/waitress and two customers.

b Swap conversations with another group. Correct any mistakes.

c Practise the new conversation with your partner. Then role-play it for the other group.

Figure 8.0a: Redston, C. and G. Cunningham (2012) *face2face Pre-intermediate* (2nd ed.), p. 37.

Figure 8.0a is an example where functional/situational language are presented together: the situation of ordering food in a restaurant, and the functional expressions focused on of requests and offers. Prior to exercise 6, students have listened to the conversation and completed a comprehension task. They have also looked at some example questions containing *Would you like ...?* without focusing on the functional meaning (an offer) of this question stem. Students use these examples to complete the conversation in exercise 6a.

Exercises 7 to 10 follow a typical course book sequence for presenting functional and/or situational expressions:

identify the expressions → present the forms and the way they are used →
focus on relevant pronunciation → do controlled oral practice → do freer spoken practice.

In exercise 7a, the target expressions are listed, and the part of the expression that is fixed is highlighted in bold. This highlighting also indicates that the expressions can be used with both *I* and *we*. Students identify which of the expressions are requests and which are offers. In exercise 7b, students isolate the specific words or phrases that are used to make a request and an offer. The aim here is to generalise so students understand we can use these language items to make different requests and offers. Exercise 7c consolidates the focus on the target language by getting students to identify more examples in the dialogue.

Exercise 8 focuses on the pronunciation of the target language with a focus on the stress and intonation, and how this can help make requests and offers sound more polite. In exercise 8b, students practise the pronunciation.

Exercise 9 asks students to practise the conversation in 6a until they are familiar with it. Many course books practise functional or situational dialogue in this way, but not all take the next step, as this exercise does, and suggest that students try to replicate the dialogue with their books closed. A common variation to this approach is that students complete a gapped dialogue that is similar to the one they have listened to, which they then practise in pairs.

Before the freer oral practice of a role play in exercise 10c, students write their own conversation in groups based on the example they have heard. Again, not all course books include this writing stage, but often suggest students just improvise and do the role play without writing the conversation.

Some teachers think that getting students to read a dialogue aloud is useful while others have doubts about its effectiveness because it involves little by way of cognitive effort. See activity 8.3 for an alternative to reading aloud.

Extended text in course books

In the *Extended text* sections of this chapter, the focus is on continuous stretches of written and spoken language. There is a slight emphasis on written language because discourse features are often focused on in course book writing lessons. There are three main areas that we can focus on in these stretches of language:

- how the information in an extended spoken or written text is organised;
- what the connections are between sentences and/or longer stretches of language in extended text;
- what the connections are between different turns in a conversation.

The way information is organised in a text contributes to its *coherence*. A text is more likely to be coherent when it conforms to the reader's or listener's expectations. For example, does it adhere to a recognisable genre? Is all the information relevant? Is it organised in a way that is easy to follow?

The way that the elements of a text – its words, sentences or paragraphs – are connected is known as *cohesion*. As we saw above, we can use pronouns to refer back and forward to ideas, people and things mentioned in a text. Another very common feature of cohesion is the use of linking words and expressions such as *however, another point, as a consequence, in summary*. These help a text to hang together and guide a reader's or listener's attention. When they occur in spoken language, they are sometimes referred to as *signposting language*.

A focus on these extended texts is almost never labelled as 'discourse' in course books. More often than not, the heading is the discourse feature being focused on, for example 'linking', 'paragraphing', 'essay structure', 'referring words', 'signposting language' etc. Often these are found in lessons that focus on writing skills, but they can also be found in lessons that focus on extended spoken language which include conversational dialogues as well as monologues and presentations.

Figure 8.0b is an example of how a feature of extended written text is focused on in a course book.

3 WRITING SKILLS Paragraphing

a Match the descriptions with paragraphs a–d in Anita's email.

1 ☐ closing the email
2 ☐ the introduction
3 ☐ how the team raised money
4 ☐ information about the National Trust

b What information does Anita include in the introduction? What does she mention in the closing paragraph?

c Put the paragraphs below in the correct order to make an email.

☐ Oxfam will use the money on projects around the world to help people have happier and healthier lives. Last year, they helped 13.5 million people. A small amount of money can make a big change. For example, just £15 can give free health care to a mother and her baby.

☐ Many of you have bought tickets to our 'Quiz and Pizza' nights. Others gave their unwanted clothes to the very successful 'Clothes Market' in March. We really hope you enjoyed these events. Your money and time will help Oxfam to continue their important work.

☐ Would you like to help us raise more money for Oxfam? Just email me and I'll tell you what we're planning next. Thanks again for all your help.

☐ This email is to say a big 'Thank you!' to everyone who has helped us to raise money for Oxfam over the last few months. We have now raised £750.

4 WRITING

a Choose one of these emails to write.

1 Write about a real experience of raising money for charity. Write to the people who gave you money to thank them. Tell them about how much money you raised, how you raised the money and about the charity.
2 You and some friends have raised £1,000 for a charity at work/school. Write to everyone who helped you to say thank you. Tell them about how much money you raised, how you raised the money and about the charity.

b Plan the email. Use four paragraphs. What information will you put in each paragraph?

c Write the email.

d Swap emails with a partner. Read your partner's email. Are there four paragraphs in the email? What information is in each paragraph?

Figure 8.0b: Doff, A., C. Thaine et al. (2015) *Cambridge English Empower B1*, p. 35.

The sequence of exercises here is as follows:

identify the extended text feature → analyse key aspects → do controlled written practice → do freer written practice.

Before students begin this series of tasks, they have read a model email and done comprehension exercises. The model contains clear paragraph divisions. In exercise 3a, students identify the key purpose of each paragraph and the most appropriate order. Exercise 3b analyses in more detail the kind of information included in the opening and closing paragraphs. Apart from determining what is included in paragraphs, this activity also provides students with a model of how to structure an email that is acting as a kind of report.

Exercise 3c provides controlled practice of the discourse feature. Students have four paragraphs that they need to order appropriately. All of exercise 4 provides freer written practice of this feature of extended text – students are reminded to use paragraphs in the email that they write. Exercise 4d encourages peer feedback on this language feature.

As has been noted in Chapter 5 Grammar, an alternative Task-Teach-Task (TTT) approach to focusing on discourse features involves getting students to perform a task first and then focusing on the feature. With the example in *Figure 8.0b*, a teacher would do exercise 4 first. She would then monitor and note students' ability to use paragraphs well (or collect in students' writing to check). If it is clear they need further work, she would then do exercise 3 and get students to revise the emails they wrote in exercise 4, or give them an alternative writing task that is similar.

Chapter organisation

In this chapter, we group the page activities under the headings most commonly used in course books. Firstly, there are activities exploiting functional/situational language course book exercises, divided into presentation and practice sections. These are followed by activities to exploit features of written and spoken extended text (often presented in course books under writing or speaking skills) again divided into activities focusing more on presentation and those with more of a focus on student practice.

Reference

McCarthy, M. (1991) *Discourse Analysis for Language Teachers*. Cambridge: Cambridge University Press.

A Functional/Situational language: presentation

8.1 Unscramble and match

Level	A1 and above
Time	5 to 10 minutes
Outline	Half the students unscramble questions asking for directions, and the other half unscramble answers, then mingle and match questions and answers.
Aim	To present core expressions used to ask for and give directions in a student-centred way.
Preparation	If you use *Figure 8.1a* below, you will need to copy and cut up the individual words on the worksheet. If you use a different course book exercise, you will need to create your own cut up worksheets. Note: the first time you do this activity, there is a bit of preparation involved in cutting up the expressions. However, once you have done this, you can use the material again.
Rationale	The target language items in *Figure 8.1a* below (and in much situational language) are set phrases that relate to a specific context. The ordering task is a kind of word puzzle. Students are likely to find the tactile nature of the activity more motivating than completing a gap fill. The mingle and match part of the activity encourages students to make connections between questions and answers and it indirectly focuses on *there is/are* as well as a cohesive device – the indefinite pronoun *one*.

Procedure

1. Divide the class in half and put students into groups of three (two or three groups of four are also fine with two students working together). Give out the cut up words to each group.
2. The groups in one half of the class unscramble the words to make questions; the other half unscramble the words to make answers.
3. Monitor and check groups are ordering words correctly.
4. When all groups have finished, each student takes one question or answer. Students then mingle to find someone from the opposite half of the class to correctly match question and answer. Tell students not to show their question or answer, but to read it aloud.
5. Elicit the correct question–answer examples on to the board.
6. Students can then do any course book exercises that present the language – exercises 4a and b for *Figure 8.1a* below.

Notes and variation

At higher levels, with longer expressions, you could give out cut up phrases rather than individual words to unscramble. You could also ask students to memorise their question or answer for the mingle. Aside from the language presentation aim of this activity, it can also work well in terms of group dynamics, encouraging students to work together and ensuring they interact with a number of students.

Learner reflection questions

1 What helped you put the questions or answers in the correct order – the vocabulary or grammar?
2 What words helped you match question and answer?

Teacher reflection

What did you learn about students' ability to use the language point? Does the language point need to be revised? What did you notice about the way students worked together in the word ordering activity? Does this tell you anything about the way you will pair or group students in future classes?

4 USEFUL LANGUAGE Asking and saying where places are

a 2.60 Complete the questions with words in the box. Listen and check.

near where there

1 ______'s your flat?
2 Is ______ a supermarket near here?
3 Are there any shops ______ here?

b 2.61 Match the two possible answers in a–c with questions 1–3 in 4a. Listen and check.

a Yes, there are. There's one in this street. / No, sorry, there aren't.
b Yes, there's one near my flat. / No, sorry, there isn't.
c It's in the next street. / It's in this street.

c 2.62 Put the conversation in the correct order. Listen and check.

A ☐ Great, thank you. And is there a good restaurant in this part of town?
A 1 Excuse me, can you help me?
A ☐ OK, thanks for your help.
A ☐ Are there any good cafés near here?

B ☐ Yes, there's one in the next street – Café Milano.
B ☐ No, I'm sorry, there aren't any restaurants near here. But there's one near the station.
B ☐ Yes, of course.
B ☐ No problem.

Figure 8.1a: Doff, A., C. Thaine et al. (2015) *Cambridge English Empower A1*, p. 45.

Worksheet – questions

where's	your	flat
is	there	a
supermarket	near	here
are	there	any
shops	near	here

Worksheet – answers

it's	in	the	next	street
yes	there's	one	near	my
flat	no	sorry	there	aren't

Answer key

Q1: Where's your flat?
Q2: Is there a supermarket near here?
Q3: Are there any shops near here?

A1: It's in the next street.
A2: Yes, there's one near my flat
A3: No, sorry, there aren't.

The course book example in *Figure 8.1b* focuses on language to order food in a restaurant. Three or four waiter–customer exchanges can be selected for the activity.

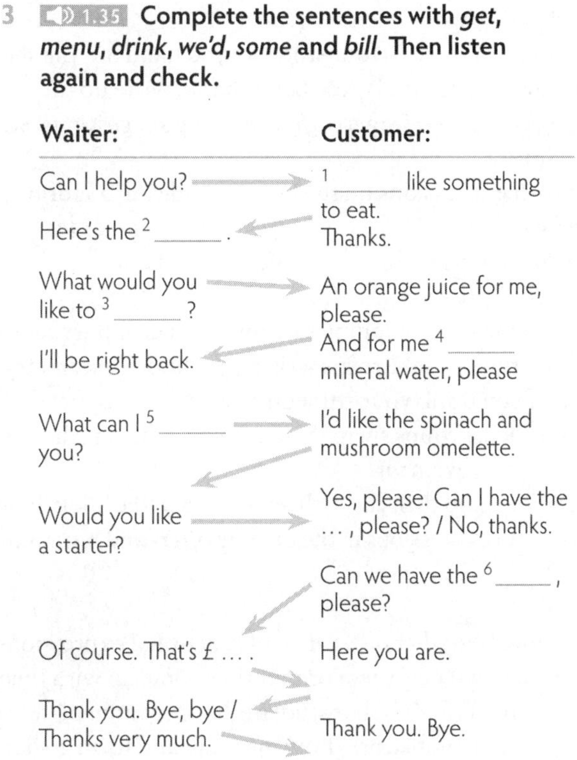

3 1.35 Complete the sentences with *get*, *menu*, *drink*, *we'd*, *some* and *bill*. Then listen again and check.

Waiter:	**Customer:**
Can I help you?	[1] ______ like something to eat.
Here's the [2] ______ .	Thanks.
What would you like to [3] ______ ?	An orange juice for me, please.
I'll be right back.	And for me [4] ______ mineral water, please
What can I [5] ______ you?	I'd like the spinach and mushroom omelette.
Would you like a starter?	Yes, please. Can I have the … , please? / No, thanks.
	Can we have the [6] ______ , please?
Of course. That's £ … .	Here you are.
Thank you. Bye, bye / Thanks very much.	Thank you. Bye.

Figure 8.1b: Puchta, H., J. Stranks and P. Lewis-Jones (2015) *Think Level 1*, p. 33.

8.2 Functional dictation

Level	B1 and above
Time	15 to 20 minutes
Outline	In small groups, students work together to write down dictated functional expressions and categorise them.
Aim	To present and contrast functional expressions associated with offers, suggestions and requests; to provide practice in listening for detail; to provide practice in written accuracy.
Preparation	Each group will need a blank piece of paper to draw and label a quadrant (see example for *Figure 8.2* below). Alternatively, to save time, you could prepare the quadrants before the class.
Rationale	The context for the functional expressions in *Figure 8.2* in the course book was a listening text (a conversation about planning a charity event). The written sorting task in the course book works well, but framing this as a dictation activity gets students more actively focused on the forms and differences between them. It also provides students with further detailed listening practice.

Procedure

1 Students complete any listening or reading tasks associated with providing a context for the functional expressions (for *Figure 8.2* below, students do listening activities that precede exercises 3 to 5), and then close their books.

2 Put students in small groups of three to four students and hand out the sheets of paper they need in the dictation. If you haven't prepared these beforehand, write up the quadrant and category headings (e.g. *making offers, responding to offers, making suggestions, making requests*) on the board for students to copy.

3 Write up some of the target expressions on the board beside the quadrant, for example:

I'll do that if you like.	*Yes, that's a good idea.*
Let's decide who does what.	*Can you do that?*

4 Elicit which category each expression goes in.

5 Dictate eight more expressions – see examples below. Each group writes the expression and puts it in the correct category. Students take turns writing or choose a secretary. Say each expression at least twice – three times if you think your students need more support.

6 When the dictation is finished, groups swap their answers with another, check each other's work and make suggestions for improvement.

7 Students return the dictations, and then check their answers in the book. Note: in exercise 3a in *Figure 8.2* there are two extra expressions in the *making offers* and *responding to offers* categories.

Notes and variation

An alternative approach would be to dictate a range of functional expressions, and then ask students to sort them into categories that you give them or that they come up with themselves. One feature of the approach suggested in the activity is that students have to immediately map the form (as they hear it) to a meaning category. It demonstrates how meaning and form go hand-in-hand.

Learner reflection questions

1 When you heard the expressions, what did you think of first – the spelling of words or the correct category?
2 Do you think it is important to know different ways of saying the same thing? Why / Why not?

Teacher reflection

Could you perceive any differences in students' reactions during the dictation, for example, those who seemed more focused on the spelling and those who were more focused on the correct categorisation? What did students give feedback to each other about when checking another group's sentences? What is the benefit of this kind of peer feedback?

REAL WORLD
Offers, suggestions and requests

3 **a** Write these headings in the correct places a–d in the table.

making suggestions   making requests
making offers   responding to offers

a	b
I'll do that, if you like. **Shall I** make some posters? Do you want me to do that? **Can I** give you a hand?	Yes, that'd be great. Yes, (that's a) good idea. Yes, if you don't mind. No, don't worry. Thanks anyway.
c	**d**
Shall we start? **Let's** decide who does what. **Why don't we** ask Jason?	**Could you** give me a hand? **Will you** organise that? **Can you** do that?

b Which verb form comes after the phrases in bold? Which verb form comes after *Do you want me ... ?*

c Check in REAL WORLD 5.1 ▸ **p137.**

4 Look at Audio and Video Script VIDEO ▸ **5** CD2 ▸ 13 **p158.** Read the conversation and find all the offers, suggestions, requests and responses.

5 CD2 ▸ 14 PRONUNCIATION Listen and practise the sentences in **3a**. Copy the stress and intonation.
I'll do that, if you like.

Figure 8.2: Redston, C. and G. Cunningham (2012) *face2face Pre-intermediate* (2nd ed.), p. 44.

Quadrant and expressions for dictation with function category in brackets

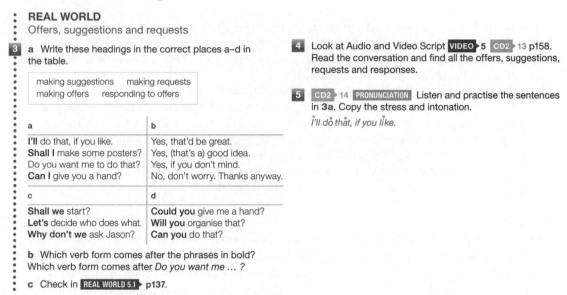

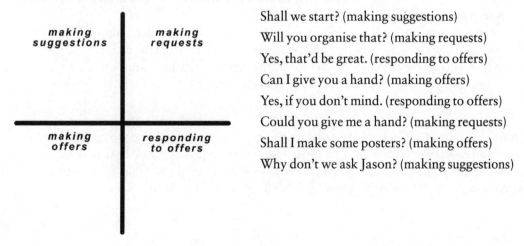

Shall we start? (making suggestions)
Will you organise that? (making requests)
Yes, that'd be great. (responding to offers)
Can I give you a hand? (making offers)
Yes, if you don't mind. (responding to offers)
Could you give me a hand? (making requests)
Shall I make some posters? (making offers)
Why don't we ask Jason? (making suggestions)

B Functional/Situational language: practice

8.3 Rebuilding the dialogue

Level A1 to B1
Time 10 to 15 minutes
Outline You, the teacher, elicit a functional dialogue line-by-line, choral and individual drilling and ending with closed pair practice.
Aim To provide controlled oral practice of functional expressions (in *Figure 8.3* below, expressions for travel information); to highlight natural pronunciation of the target language.
Preparation If you use *Figure 8.3*, no preparation is necessary. You may wish to write up all the prompts on the board before the lesson, but you can also write them up as you go. If you use different material, you will need to plan the prompts to put on the board and decide where main stresses in each expression are.
Rationale Many course books include exercises such as gap filling or ordering for situational or functional dialogues, and then suggest students read the dialogues aloud for oral practice. The activity below slightly ups the ante in terms of students' cognitive effort. The use of prompts means they have to think carefully about language around the key words. The elicitation and drilling also places a greater emphasis on their pronunciation of the target language, in particular, achieving natural stress and rhythm. The activity blends whole class choral drilling and closed pair work to vary the interaction.

Procedure

1 Students complete any controlled written practice tasks – exercise 4d in *Figure 8.3* below.
2 Point to the first two prompt exchanges on the board and elicit the complete expression. Don't write up the full version and don't let students write anything for the duration of the activity. Give a clear oral model with a natural rhythm and stress and do choral and individual drilling of the two examples. You can also do open pairs – nominate Student A and Student B to say the exchange in open class.
3 Do the same with the next two exchanges, then students practise the dialogue so far elicited in pairs, practising both parts.
4 Continue in this vein (elicit – model – drill – pairs practise) for the remainder of the dialogue. Whenever students practise in pairs, they always start at the beginning of the dialogue.
5 When you have elicited the complete dialogue, students work in new pairs and practise it a final time. You can then write it on the board for students to copy.

Notes

The success of this activity depends on clear planning – you need to work out the prompts and be clear about the stress of the expressions. You also need to maintain good pace in the delivery of the activity to keep it lively. The dialogue in *Figure 8.3* is at the outer limit of a suitable length – it's not recommended that you aim for anything longer. This activity works best with lower levels.

Learner reflection questions

1 Is it more difficult to write or say the dialogue using the key words? Why?
2 How does saying the dialogue help your speaking?

Teacher reflection

What difference did you notice with students working from the prompts rather than complete expressions? What did you have to keep in mind during the activity? How did you try to maintain a good pace when managing this activity?

4 USEFUL LANGUAGE Asking for travel information

a Who says these expressions – a passenger (P) or the station official (SO)?

1 The next train is at 4:35.
2 Which platform is it?
3 Excuse me.
4 The train leaves in three minutes.
5 No, you change at Reading.
6 Yes? How can I help?
7 What time's the next train to London?
8 Is it a direct train?
9 It's Platform 3.

b 4.24 Listen and check your answers in 4a. Then listen again and repeat.

c 4.25 Complete the sentences with *at* or *in*. Listen and check.

1 The next train leaves ______ half an hour.
2 The next train leaves ______ five o'clock.

d 4.26 Put the conversation in the correct order. Then listen and check.

A
- [ ] So, at 5:15. And is it a direct bus?
- [ ] Great! Thanks for your help.
- [ ] What time's the next bus to Cambridge?
- [1] Excuse me.
- [ ] OK, and which bus stop is it?

B
- [ ] The next bus leaves in 20 minutes.
- [ ] It's stop 7, near the ticket office.
- [ ] No problem.
- [ ] Yes? How can I help?
- [ ] No, you change at Birmingham.

e Practise the conversation in 4d with a partner. Take turns to be the station official and the passenger. Change the times, kind of transport and the platforms / bus stops.

Figure 8.3: Doff, A., C. Thaine et al. (2015) *Cambridge English Empower A1*, p. 85.

Board prompts and correctly ordered dialogue for Figure 8.3 with main stresses underlined

A: Excuse /	A: Excuse me.
B: Yes? How / help?	B: Yes? How can I help?
A: / time / next bus / Cambridge?	A: What time's the next bus to Cambridge?
B: The next / leaves / 20 /.	B: The next bus leaves in 20 minutes.
A: / 5.15. And / direct /?	A: So, at 5.15. And is it a direct bus?
B: No / change / Birmingham.	B: No, you change at Birmingham.
A: OK / bus stop /?	A: OK, and which bus stop is it?
B: / 7 / ticket office.	B: It's stop 7, near the ticket office.
A: Great! Thanks / help.	A: Great! Thanks for your help.
B: / problem.	B: No problem.

8.4 Onion ring plans

Level	A2 and above
Time	5 to 10 minutes
Outline	Students do an onion ring activity with controlled oral prompts and have short conversations planning social activities with different students.
Aim	To provide semi-controlled oral practice of expressions used to invite people to do things.
Preparation	If you use *Figure 8.4a* below, you will need to copy the worksheet so that both A and B students have one copy each of their half of the worksheet. Note: one extra prompt has been added to each student's worksheet relative to the course book task.
Rationale	As is the case in *Figure 8.4a*, course books often provide solid semi-controlled practice of the target language. However, with this type of exercise students can obviously see how their partner is going to reply in pair work speaking practice, so there is complete predictability – an information gap is missing. This activity introduces more creativity into the task because students are free to choose their own answer and then continue the conversation.

Procedure

1 This activity comes after the course book presentation stage – in *Figure 8.4a* it is an adaptation of exercise 6.

2 Set up an onion ring – Student As form an inner circle facing outwards and Student Bs form an outer circle facing inwards. They can be sitting or standing depending on your class and room size.

3 Student As begin by asking Student Bs something from their list. Student Bs reply using something from their list. Students can choose anything from their lists and shouldn't ask them in order, but they should try and use all the ideas by the end of the activity. They then continue the conversation.

4 You could give an example on the board, e.g.:

> *A: Would you like to go to the cinema?*
> *B: Not really, I'd rather go out for a coffee.*
> *A: OK, where would you like to go?*
> *B: How about going to Rosa's Café?*
> *A: Great. Let's do that.*

5 Explain to students that when you call 'move!' the conversation ends and everyone should move one place to their right, so they are facing a new student. Student Bs now invite and Student As reply.

6 Continue until all students have had plenty of practice inviting and replying.

Notes

The onion ring interaction means students work with different partners which adds variety to the activity. It also means that you need to monitor attentively to see when most students have finished and it's time to say 'move'. At higher levels, where the practice activity might be freer in nature and last longer, you can give students a time warning letting them know they will need to finish their conversation.

Learner reflection questions

1 How were the expressions different for asking and replying? Is there one expression you need to practise more?

2 Why, in this speaking activity, is it better <u>not</u> knowing how your partner will reply?

Teacher reflection

How did the onion ring formation work with your students? What did you learn about how to manage this kind of interaction? What other activities could be adapted to an onion ring formation?

REAL WORLD Deciding what to do

4 **a** Look at these questions and answers. We use them when we're deciding what to do.

asking people what they want to do	saying what you want to do
What **would you like** to do?	**I'd like** (to go to the beach).
Where **do you want** to go?	**I want** (to go to Longleat).
Would you like (to go to London)?	Yes, that's a good idea.
Do you want (to go to Regent's Park)?	Not really. **I'd rather** (stay at home).

TIPS • *Would like* is more polite than *want*.
• We use *I'd rather* to say *I want to do this more than something else.*

b Complete the rules with *would/'d like*, *want* and *would/'d rather.*

- After ____________ we use the infinitive (*go*, *do*, etc.).
- After ____________ and ____________ we use the infinitive with *to* (*to go*, *to do*, etc.).

REAL WORLD 9.1 ▸ p148

5 CD3 ▸ 8 PRONUNCIATION Listen and practise the sentences in **4a**. Copy the stress.

What would you /wʊdʒə/ *like to do?*

I'd /aɪd/ *like to go to the beach.*

6 **a** Work in pairs, A and B. Take turns to ask your partner what he/she would like to do.

Would you like to go to the cinema?

I'd rather watch a DVD.

1 **A** go to the cinema? **B** watch a DVD
2 **B** go for a walk? **A** ✓
3 **A** play tennis? **B** go swimming
4 **B** watch TV? **A** go out
5 **A** go shopping? **B** ✓
6 **B** go out for a meal? **A** go out for a drink

b Take turns to make and respond to three more suggestions.

Figure 8.4a: Redston, C. and G. Cunningham (2012) *face2face Elementary* (2nd ed.), p. 77.

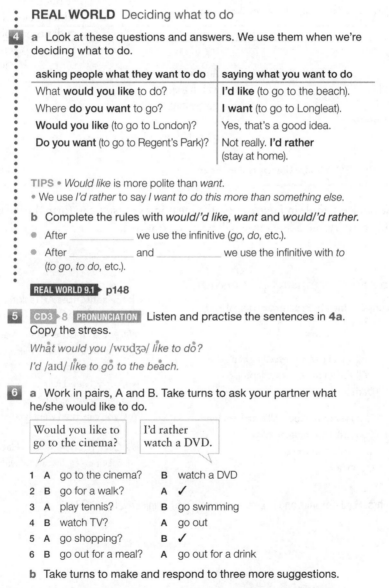

Worksheet

Student A

Ask	*Answer*
go to the cinema?	✓
play tennis?	go out
go shopping?	go out for a drink
go to a pop concert?	play a video game

Student B

Ask	*Answer*
go for a walk?	watch a video
watch TV?	go swimming
go out for a meal?	✓
play cards?	go out for a coffee

In the course book example in *Figure 8.4b*, the ideas in exercise 2 can form the basis of the prompts for an onion ring activity, but a few more will need to be added.

FUNCTIONS
Asking and giving / refusing permission

1 Put the dialogues into the correct order. Write the numbers 1–4.

☐ DAD Yes?
☐ DAD I'm afraid I need it myself right now.
☐ NICK Will you let me use your laptop?
☐ NICK Dad?

☐ ANNIE Can I watch the football match tonight?
☐ ANNIE Can I ask you something, Mum?
☐ MUM Yes, of course you can.
☐ MUM Go ahead.

2 Mark the sentences *AP* (asking permission), *GP* (giving permission) or *RP* (refusing permission).

1 Will you let me use your camera? ______
Yeah, sure. Of course I will. ______
2 Can I borrow your bike? ______
No, sorry. I need it. ______
3 Can I use your laptop? ______
Yes, you can, but I want it back tomorrow.
______
4 Is it OK if I borrow this necklace? ______
Yeah, but be really careful with it, OK?
______

Figure 8.4b: Puchta, H., J. Stranks and P. Lewis-Jones (2015) *Think Level 2*, p. 23.

8.5 Rehearse the role play

Level	A1 and above
Time	10 to 15 minutes
Outline	Students work in separate groups to prepare and practise one side of a role play. They think about what they are going to say, then practise example expressions with each other, then work with a student from the other group to do the role play.
Aim	To provide freer oral practice of requests and suggestions (for *Figure 8.5a* below, in the context of health problems); to build students' confidence for a role play.
Preparation	There is no preparation for this activity. Note: the material in *Figure 8.5a* is aimed at A2 level students.
Rationale	Role plays are an effective way of giving freer oral practice of target language. However, they put particular demands on students because not only do they have to think about what they're going to say, but also how they will say it. (See the introduction to Chapter 2 Speaking.) This activity takes the idea a step further and gets students to think about and practise what they will say before doing the actual role play. This involves students speaking and not writing down questions or expressions – in effect, solely spoken preparation and practice for what is a speaking activity. An indirect aim of this activity is peer co-operation with the opportunity for students to give feedback to each other on their spoken language.

Procedure

1 Divide the class into two halves: Student As and Bs, then put them in small groups of three or four students – either all As or all Bs.
2 Students read the instructions for their role – for *Figure 8.5a*, exercise 1, Student As are customers and Student Bs are pharmacists.
3 In their groups, students brainstorm the different things they could say in their role and practise saying them. Don't let them write anything down, it should only be oral preparation.
4 When students have practised enough, put them in A and B pairs to do the role play.
5 Students can then change roles. Having heard each other in the opposite role, they probably won't need to rehearse.

Notes and variation

Ensuring that there is no writing adds a level of challenge. If students wonder about this, point out that when they need to speak English outside the classroom, they don't have the opportunity to write down what they want to say. You can add a further step in the preparation with mumble drilling. This means students say expressions quietly to themselves a few times before they say them aloud to each other. A variation for stronger students is that when they re-do the role play, the customer asking for help could be given an attitude role play card (see example below for *Figure 8.5a*).

Learner reflection questions

1 What things did you help each other with when you worked in small groups – the expressions, the pronunciation, something else?
2 How ready were you to respond to what your partner said when you worked in pairs?

Teacher reflection

How varied were the request and advice structures when students did the role play? To what extent did students help each other and give feedback to each other when they worked in groups? Do you feel you need to do more to foster this kind of peer co-operation with your students?

In *Figure 8.5a* there are two excerpts from the course book: the example that students analyse and practise in a controlled way in exercise 8, and the role play for freer practice of the target language.

8 CONVERSATION Can you suggest anything?

A Listen and practice.

Pharmacist Hi. May I help you?

Mr. Peters Yes, please. Could I have something for a backache? My muscles are really sore.

Pharmacist Well, it's a good idea to use a heating pad. And why don't you try this cream? It works really well.

Mr. Peters OK, I'll take one tube. Also, my wife has a bad cough. Can you suggest anything?

Pharmacist She should try these cough drops.

Mr. Peters Thanks! May I have a large bag? And what do you suggest for insomnia?

Pharmacist Well, you could get a box of chamomile tea. Is it for you?

Mr. Peters Yes, I can't sleep.

Pharmacist A sore back and your wife's bad cough? I think I know why you can't sleep!

B Listen to the pharmacist talk to the next customer. What does the customer want?

11 ROLE PLAY Can I help you?

Student A: You are a customer in a drugstore. You need:

something for a backache
something for dry skin
something for the flu
something for low energy
something for sore feet
something for an upset stomach

Ask for some suggestions.

Student B: You are a pharmacist in a drugstore.
A customer needs some things.
Make some suggestions.

Change roles and try the role play again.

Figure 8.5a: Richards, J. C. et al. (2017) *Interchange 1* (5th ed.), pp. 81–82.

Attitude role play cards

1	Your mother/father/brother/sister told you that you had to visit the pharmacy and ask for help. You really don't want to be there.
2	You have just won $500,000 in Lotto. You have a health problem, but you are feeling great.
3	You aren't sure if the pharmacist's ideas are very good.
4	You have to cook dinner for 20 people this evening. You are thinking about how you will do this.
5	You can't hear what the pharmacist is saying very well.
6	You think the pharmacist is very nice and kind. You wish more people in shops were like this.
7	Your bus is leaving in just two minutes. You are in a hurry.
8	Yesterday you joined a movie streaming service. There are lots of great films and you're thinking about the one you'll watch when you get home.
9	You think the pharmacist is a secret policeman. You are trying to understand why they are working in the pharmacy.
10	Pharmacists always try to sell you things and make lots of money. This one is probably doing it too.

In *Figure 8.5b* the target expressions (invitations and suggestions) are given for the role play.

4 Complete the conversation with the useful language.

Useful language

What time shall we meet (then)?	That's a great idea!
Yeah, why not?	Let's go together.
Do you fancy *-ing* … ?	How about *-ing* … ?
Sounds good!	Shall I (ask my dad to get us)?

Fran: Nicky, do you [1] *fancy going* to a concert tomorrow?
Nicky: Yeah, [2]…. ? Who's playing?
Fran: A **pop rock** band called **The Sweets**. They're a new band. I've got free tickets.
Nicky: [3]…. good! Where are they playing?
Fran: The **Apollo Club**, in **Market Street**.
Nicky: OK. What time [4]…. meet then?
Fran: It starts at **8.30**, I think. [5]…. together. [6]…. coming to my house at **half seven**?
Nick: OK. [7]…. ask **my dad** to come and get us at the end?
Frank: Yes, that's a [8]…. !
Nick: OK. See you tomorrow, then.

7 Change the words in bold in the conversation. Use the ideas below. Take turns to ask and answer the questions.

Concert 1
The Black Roots
The Hacienda Club
Station Road

Doors open: 9pm **Band starts:** 9.30

Concert 2
Live concert with
Don't be Shy
The Black Bee Club,
Miller Street

Doors open: 7.30pm **Band:** 8pm

Figure 8.5b: Goldstein, B. and C. Jones (2015) *Eyes Open 3*, p. 38.

C Extended text: presentation

8.6 Eliciting the text type

Level	A2 and above
Time	15 to 20 minutes
Outline	Students brainstorm reader expectations of a particular text type, and use these as criteria for the analysis of example texts before putting the criteria in a logical order.
Aim	To present a typical structure of a particular text genre (in *Figure 8.6a* below, a film review); to relate this structure to reader expectations.
Preparation	There is no preparation for this activity. In *Figure 8.6a*, there is a task that focuses on text structure, but if you are doing a writing lesson, and there isn't such a task, it's a good idea to think about a typical structure for the text type you are focusing on in the lesson.
Rationale	This activity is an alternative approach to analysing text structure (in *Figure 8.6a*, exercise 3a, students analyse the structure of a film review). It assumes that students have some prior knowledge from texts in their first language, and of what information they would expect to find in a review. By tapping into this knowledge, the activity makes a connection between students' own experience and the analysis. Students also get useful speaking practice when they discuss and order their own criteria.

Procedure

1. This activity could be done before or after students read example texts (note: the course book reading comprehension tasks are not included in *Figure 8.6a*). If done before, it could act as a lead in to reading activities.
2. Write on the board a relevant question for students to brainstorm ideas, e.g.:

   When a friend talks about a film they've seen, what do you want to know?
3. Elicit ideas and a possible logical order – accept variations.
4. Students read any example texts and check if all their points are included and if the order is similar. (If they've already read the texts, this time they read to check the order of information only.)
5. For *Figure 8.6a*, students now do exercise 3a. In feedback indicate that this is a useful way to organise a review. Point out that the order can be flexible for the middle sections, but it is typical to begin by indicating where you saw the film and to end with a recommendation.

Notes

A benefit of this approach to the analysis of the text structure is that it allows you to negotiate a degree of variation. The structure suggested by the course book acts as a useful template and point of reference, but there is the flexibility to look at alternatives. It helps to personalise the analysis question, for example: *If you read a social media posting about a friend's holiday, what do you hope to find out? If you receive a text invitation to a party, what information do you need to know?*

Learner reflection questions

1 What differences were there between your ideas for the structure of a film review and the example in the course book?
2 When you write something, why is it a good idea to think about the way you organise the information?

Teacher reflection

Did students come up with any ideas that you felt were inappropriate for a film review or unnecessary? To what extent does the structure of different text types differ in your students' first language? Do you think this is a linguistic issue or a cultural one?

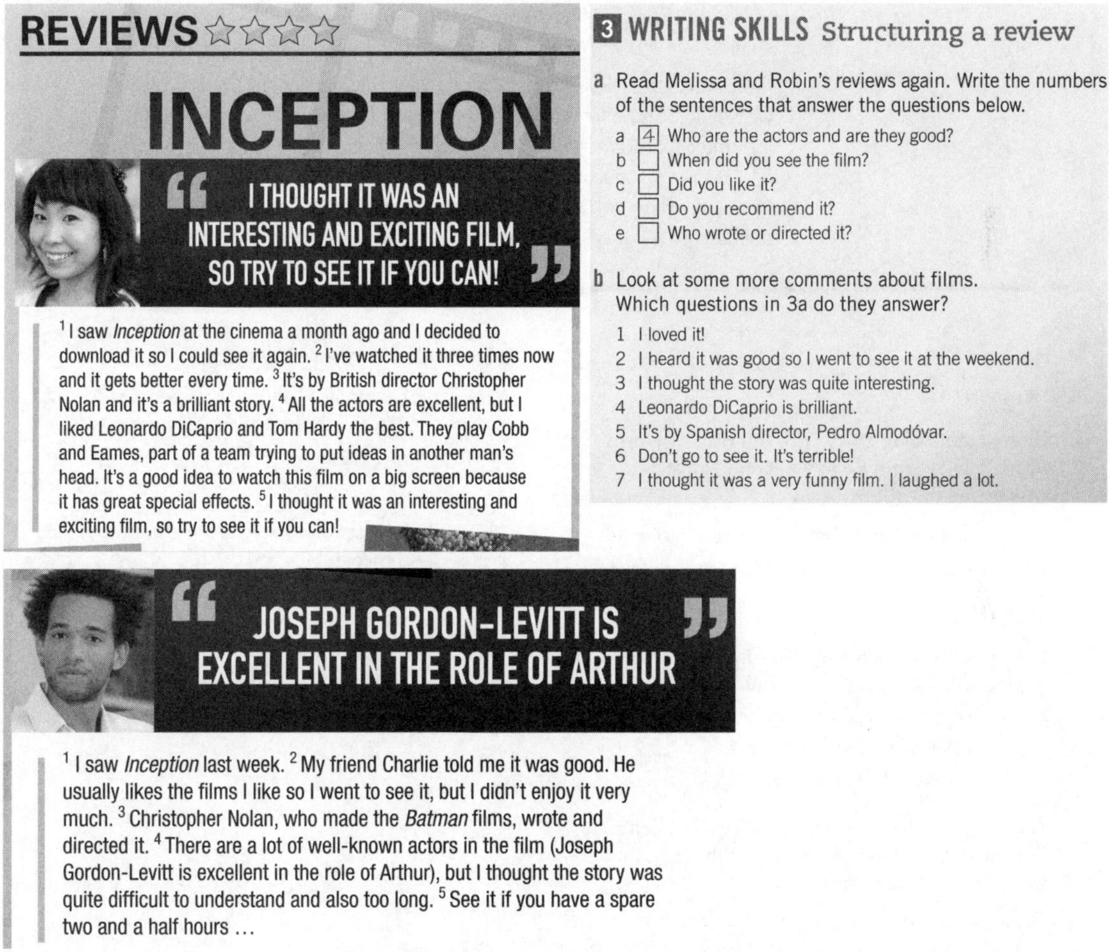

REVIEWS ☆☆☆☆

INCEPTION

“ I THOUGHT IT WAS AN INTERESTING AND EXCITING FILM, SO TRY TO SEE IT IF YOU CAN! ”

[1] I saw *Inception* at the cinema a month ago and I decided to download it so I could see it again. [2] I've watched it three times now and it gets better every time. [3] It's by British director Christopher Nolan and it's a brilliant story. [4] All the actors are excellent, but I liked Leonardo DiCaprio and Tom Hardy the best. They play Cobb and Eames, part of a team trying to put ideas in another man's head. It's a good idea to watch this film on a big screen because it has great special effects. [5] I thought it was an interesting and exciting film, so try to see it if you can!

“ JOSEPH GORDON-LEVITT IS EXCELLENT IN THE ROLE OF ARTHUR ”

[1] I saw *Inception* last week. [2] My friend Charlie told me it was good. He usually likes the films I like so I went to see it, but I didn't enjoy it very much. [3] Christopher Nolan, who made the *Batman* films, wrote and directed it. [4] There are a lot of well-known actors in the film (Joseph Gordon-Levitt is excellent in the role of Arthur), but I thought the story was quite difficult to understand and also too long. [5] See it if you have a spare two and a half hours …

3 WRITING SKILLS Structuring a review

a Read Melissa and Robin's reviews again. Write the numbers of the sentences that answer the questions below.

a [4] Who are the actors and are they good?
b [ ] When did you see the film?
c [ ] Did you like it?
d [ ] Do you recommend it?
e [ ] Who wrote or directed it?

b Look at some more comments about films. Which questions in 3a do they answer?

1 I loved it!
2 I heard it was good so I went to see it at the weekend.
3 I thought the story was quite interesting.
4 Leonardo DiCaprio is brilliant.
5 It's by Spanish director, Pedro Almodóvar.
6 Don't go to see it. It's terrible!
7 I thought it was a very funny film. I laughed a lot.

Figure 8.6a: Doff, A., C. Thaine et al. (2015) *Cambridge English Empower A2*, pp. 116–117.

In *Figure 8.6b*, analysis of the text structure could be done after exercise 2 and students' ideas could be contrasted with the suggested structure in exercise 5.

Ellen's blog

A world without television

[1] It isn't easy to imagine life without television, but people only started to have television at home about sixty years ago. So a lot of people who are alive today lived without it in the past. Before television, people used to read in the evening, or listen to the radio. I read once that families used to get together and sing songs or tell each other stories. I think it was probably a bit boring but perhaps people enjoyed it.

[2] If we didn't have television these days, I think things would be OK. I mean, we would still have films and the Internet, wouldn't we? We would get all the information and entertainment we need there, and in fact many people already do. I know a lot of people who don't watch television at all, they watch sport and things by streaming them. But of course, they're using TV programmes when they do that – so maybe a world without TV wouldn't be such a good idea!

WRITING
A blog entry

1 Ellen wrote a blog entry with the title, 'A world without television'. Read what she wrote and answer the questions.

a What did people do before they had television?
b What does Ellen think life would be like without TV?

2 Look at Ellen's blog entry again.

1 In which paragraph does Ellen use *used to*? In which does she use the second conditional?
2 Match the paragraphs with these headings:
A Imagine life without television
B Life before television

3 You are going to write a blog entry like Ellen's. Choose one of these pieces of technology, or another one if you prefer:

- mobile phones
- the Internet
- tablets
- calculators

4 Make notes for your blog entry.

Paragraph 1: what life was like / what people did before the piece of technology was invented

Paragraph 2: what life would be like now without the piece of technology

5 Write your blog entry. Write 120–180 words altogether.

Figure 8.6b: Puchta, H., J. Stranks and P. Lewis-Jones (2015) *Think Level 2*, p. 81.

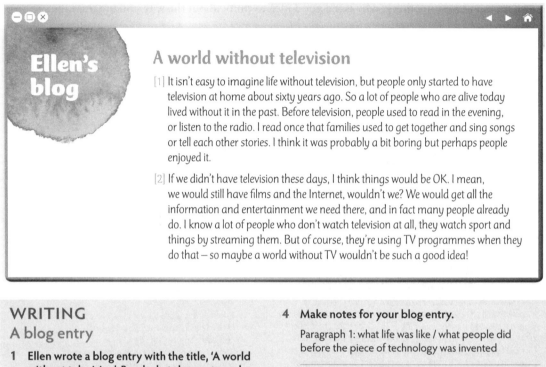

8.7 The right response

Level A2 and above
Time 10 to 15 minutes
Outline In pairs, one student has a role card with interesting or surprising news about themselves and the other student has the same role card that tells them how to respond, e.g. with little interest.
Aim To highlight the importance of interaction in a conversation; to present expressions that can be used.
Preparation If you use *Figure 8.7a*, you need to copy enough role cards so that each pair has an A and a B. (If you have an uneven number in a group, give more news cards than reaction cards.) The role cards can work with a range of course book material that focuses on this context, but you may want to adapt them.
Rationale Stretches of language don't only involve spoken language produced by one speaker, they also include language that is produced by two or more speakers who interact together. Often responses and reactions involve small words or phrases that don't translate easily from one language to another. The approach in this activity highlights for students what it feels like to try and communicate with someone who doesn't react, thereby underlining the importance of this language.

Procedure

1 Do the activity before any analysis exercises in the course book – e.g. before exercise 2 in *Figure 8.7a*.
2 Put students in A and B pairs. Hand out the role cards and give students a minute to think about what they want to say and how to say it.
3 Student As announce their news to Student Bs who react according to the instructions on the role card.
4 Do whole class feedback and ask Student As if it was easy to talk to Student Bs. Establish that the problem was the lack of reaction.
5 Elicit some example reaction phrases on to the board (e.g. *Really? Did you? Have you? That's amazing! Fantastic!*), then students can do any analysis exercises in the course book – in *Figure 8.7a*, exercises 2a–c.
6 You can then get students to repeat the role play with students changing roles and/or news stories, but this time reacting correctly with interest, using the expressions and phrases on the board.

Notes and variation

When you are eliciting the words and phrases students could use, it's a good idea to also point out that it helps to use a wide intonation range. (Also see activity 7.8 in Chapter 7 for more practice of this.) At higher levels, the Student As can be encouraged to invent their own news stories, or given freedom to enlarge on the prompts you give them.

Learner reflection questions

1 What kind of words or expressions do people use in your first language to show they are listening and interested?
2 Why is it important to use these words and expressions?

Teacher reflection

How wide a range of reaction expressions did students have when you elicited examples? Which of the responses need to be grammatically cohesive? In general, do you think students are more or less likely to use these expressions? Why?

2 CONVERSATION SKILLS Showing surprise

a Look at the conversation. Underline the two ways that Dan shows surprise.

MARTINA I've won a competition.
DAN Have you? Fantastic. What's the prize?
MARTINA A weekend for two in Bath …
DAN Really? That's great.

b Which question in 2a can you use to reply to any news?

c 3.85 Match 1–4 with a–d. Listen and check your answers.

1 I'm getting married.	a Do you?
2 I really like grammar.	b Have you?
3 I went to New York for the weekend.	c Are you?
4 I've eaten an insect.	d Did you?

d 3.85 **Pronunciation** Listen again. Does the tone in a–d in 2c go up ↗ a little or a lot?

e Think of two surprising things. They don't have to be true! Make notes.

f In pairs, take turns telling each other your surprising things and showing surprise. Use expressions from 2a and 2c.

Figure 8.7a: Doff, A., C. Thaine et al. (2015) *Cambridge English Empower A2*, p. 124.

Student A – News role cards

1 You have just won an English language competition. You had to answer a quiz and give a short speech. Your prize is a two-week study holiday in London. You're really excited about going.
Tell one of the B students your news. Don't tell them everything at once – wait for them to react before saying the next thing. You can add your own ideas and information.

2 You've just got back from a holiday in Tahiti. You were there for 10 days. The flight was long, but it was the most beautiful place you've ever been to and the people were so friendly.
Tell one of the B students your news. Don't tell them everything at once – wait for them to react before saying the next thing. You can add your own ideas and information.

3 You've just done your first bungee jump. It was from a bridge and you dropped into a river. You were very nervous before the jump. But the feeling was amazing and you feel so happy that you have done this.
Tell one of the B students your news. Don't tell them everything at once – wait for them to react before saying the next thing. You can add your own ideas and information.

Student B – Response cards

Listen to the news that one of the Student As tells you. Each time they say something respond by using only one of these two words:

OK. *Right.*

Don't say anything else or ask any questions.

Listen to the news that one of the Student As tells you. Each time they say something respond by using only one of these two words:

OK. *Right.*

Don't say anything else or ask any questions.

Listen to the news that one of the Student As tells you. Each time they say something respond by using only one of these two words:

OK. *Right.*

Don't say anything else or ask any questions.

With the example in *Figure 8.7b*, you could establish a broader context – a conversation about Mike who is a very good swimmer. Student As could then be given sentences that contain the interesting information in the dialogue (for example *Mike's afraid of open water. Mike's scared when he can't see the bottom of the sea. Being afraid of deep water is very common.*) Student Bs are given similar non-reactive role cards like the ones in *Figure 8.7a*. After the activity, students compare their conversations with the dialogue in the course book.

4 Complete the conversation with the useful language.

Useful language

What?	I don't believe you/it!
That can't be true!	Are you serious?
You're joking!	No way!
That's impossible!	

Rosa: Is Mike going to come sailing with us?
Jack: No [1] *way* ! He's terrified of deep water.
Rosa: [2] .... ? That's [3] .... ! He's a really good swimmer!
Jack: No, it's true. He's got a phobia.
Rosa: That [4] .... true! He's competing in the 50 metre freestyle at the swimming club next week.
Jack: I know, but he's scared of swimming in open water. I think it's because you can't see the bottom.
Rosa: [5] .... serious? I didn't think Mike was scared of anything.
Jack: Well, he's afraid of deep water. It's quite a common phobia, actually.
Rosa: You're [6] .... ! I've never heard of it.
Jack: Mike told me himself.
Rosa: I don't [7] .... you! I'm going to call Mike and ask him.

Figure 8.7b: Goldstein, B. and C. Jones (2015) *Eyes Open 3*, p. 70.

D Extended text: practice

8.8 Reference mingle

Level	A2 and above
Time	15 to 20 minutes
Outline	Students mingle and say sentences that contain nouns that could be replaced by reference words. As they listen to each other's sentences, they suggest a referencing word to replace the unnecessary repeat of the noun.
Aim	To provide controlled practice of referencing words.
Preparation	If you use *Figure 8.8*, you will need to copy and cut up the sentences on the worksheet. If you use different material, you will need to create your own example sentences.
Rationale	While the context for these referencing words is a written one in *Figure 8.8*, the language of the email is close to spoken language. Providing oral practice of this language increases the level of challenge, but it makes the activity more interactive.

Procedure

1 Students complete any presentation and analysis tasks – exercises 1 to 3 in *Figure 8.8* below.
2 Each student has one sentence from the worksheet. In the worksheet below, the two nouns are in bold and a replacement referring word for the second noun in bold is given in brackets.
3 Students mingle and read their sentences to each other without saying the referencing word in brackets. When a student hears a sentence, they listen for the repeated noun and try to say the sentence back using a suitable referencing word. Students will need to say their sentence more than once.
4 Students can do a written activity to consolidate the oral practice – exercise 4 in *Figure 8.8* below.

Notes and variation

The fact that students have to say the sentence back to the other students means they have to listen carefully and the activity works as a kind of student-centred drilling task. A variation is to give students a mix of sentences – some need to be changed by using a referencing word while others are correct. At higher levels, you can increase the challenge by including two nouns that need to be replaced with a referencing word, or by giving students two sentences. If it's difficult to do a mingle activity, students can work in pairs and have seven sentences each that they say to each other.

Learner reflection questions

1 If you always repeat the noun in a sentence, how does it sound?
2 Do we use referencing words only in writing?

Teacher reflection

Which of the referencing words did students have most problems with? How often did the first student need to repeat the sentence with two nouns before the other student could say it back? What does this suggest to you about modelling and drilling new language items with students?

1 Look at the photo and read Sara's email. What is she planning to do?

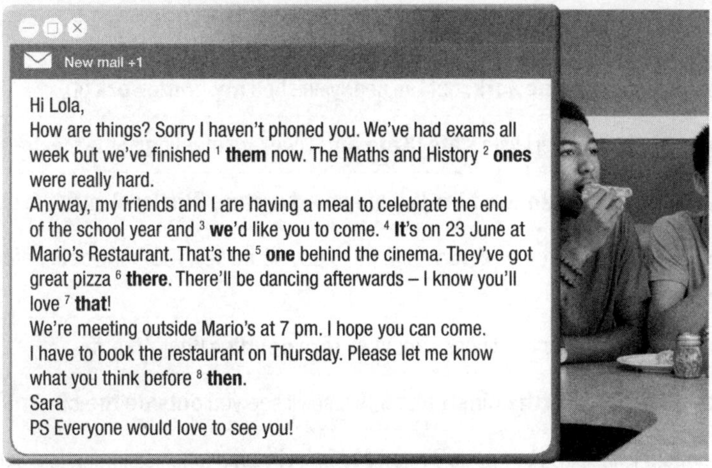

New mail +1

Hi Lola,
How are things? Sorry I haven't phoned you. We've had exams all week but we've finished [1] **them** now. The Maths and History [2] **ones** were really hard.
Anyway, my friends and I are having a meal to celebrate the end of the school year and [3] **we**'d like you to come. [4] **It**'s on 23 June at Mario's Restaurant. That's the [5] **one** behind the cinema. They've got great pizza [6] **there**. There'll be dancing afterwards – I know you'll love [7] **that**!
We're meeting outside Mario's at 7 pm. I hope you can come.
I have to book the restaurant on Thursday. Please let me know what you think before [8] **then**.
Sara
PS Everyone would love to see you!

2 Read Sara's email again and answer the questions.

1 What are Sara and her friends celebrating?
2 How are they going to celebrate? Where?
3 Are they going to do anything afterwards?
4 What time are they meeting for the celebration?
5 When does Lola need to tell Sara if she can go to the celebration?

Useful language

Referencing words

We often use referencing words so we don't repeat the noun:

- *I took* ***my new bag*** *to the party, but I left* ***it*** (my new bag) ***there*** (at the party).
- *I can't find* ***my red pen****. Have you got* ***one*** (a red pen)*?*
- *There's* ***pizza*** *for dinner. I know you like* ***that*** (pizza).
- *I'm having a party on* ***Saturday****. I have to buy some food before* ***then*** (Saturday).

3 Find examples of referencing words in bold in the email. What does each one mean?

1 *the exams*

4 Look at the useful language and write a referencing word for the words in bold.

1 I'm still doing **my homework** but I've nearly finished *it*.
2 I'm going to the concert with **Kate**. .... 're meeting at the theatre.
3 I'd like to see **an adventure film**. Is there .... on at the cinema?
4 'Shall we **play cards** after dinner?' 'Yes, I'd love .... .'
5 'Let's meet outside **the cinema** at 8.30.' 'OK. See you .... .'
6 I've got a football match on **Friday**. I need to buy some new football boots before .... .

Figure 8.8: Goldstein, B. and C. Jones (2015) *Eyes Open 2*, p. 93.

Worksheet – the first four examples are taken from exercise 4 of the course book in Figure 8.8.

1	I'm still doing **my homework**, but I've nearly finished **my homework** (it).
2	I'm going to the concert with **Kate**. **Kate and I** (we) are meeting at the theatre.
3	I'd like to see **an adventure film**. Is there **an adventure film** (one) on at the cinema?
4	I've got a football match on **Friday**. I need to buy some new football boots before **Friday** (then).
5	We're having **noodles** for dinner. I know you like **noodles** (that / them).
6	We can meet **outside the cinema** at 8.30, so I'll see you **outside the cinema** (there) then.
7	**My cousin Lisa** is a really good singer. **My cousin Lisa** (she) is singing in a concert tomorrow.
8	I've saved **the video** on my tablet. We can watch **the video** (it) now.
9	**My smartphone** is getting old. I'd like to buy a new **smartphone** (one).
10	There's a **café** opposite my house. They make great coffee **at the café** (there).
11	I'm seeing Leo **on Thursday**. I'll ask him **on Thursday** (then).
12	Do you know **Paolo**? I'm playing tennis with **Paolo** (him) on Saturday.
13	**All her friends** are in the volleyball team. **All her friends** (they) are playing a game this afternoon.
14	**Susanna and I** are going to the party now. Why don't you come with **Susanna and me** (us)?

8.9 Disorganisation sorted

Level	A2 and above
Time	10 to 15 minutes
Outline	In pairs, students unjumble an email message, deciding on paragraphs and locating an incorrectly placed sentence and an irrelevant sentence. Once corrected, students present their work to another pair with a different email.
Aim	To provide practice in paragraphing an email message and establishing its coherence.
Preparation	If you use *Figure 8.9* below, you will need to make a photocopy of the worksheet for each student. This should be folded in half, so students only work on one of the two emails in the first stages of the activity.
Rationale	This activity extends the practice in the course book and adds another dimension. As well as thinking about paragraphing, students also focus on the overall coherence of the message in terms of a logical order of information and the exclusion of irrelevant information. The student-centred feedback when students form new pairs and explain their answers to each other means students get some extra speaking practice during a writing lesson.

Procedure

1 Students complete presentation and practice tasks – exercises 3a to 3d in *Figure 8.9*.
2 Divide the class in half – Student As and Student Bs – and give out the folded worksheet. Students work on only their email, A or B, and don't look at the other one.
3 In pairs (As together and Bs together), students decide which sentence is in the wrong place and which sentence isn't necessary. They then divide the message into paragraphs. They discuss reasons for their decisions.
4 Students work in new pairs (one Student A and one Student B). They unfold the worksheet and students explain to each other how they have corrected their email, giving reasons.
5 Check the answers with the whole class.

Notes and variation

The 'disorganisation' of the texts for this activity is reasonably straightforward given the language level that it is aimed at. At higher levels, you can introduce more complexity into the way that you 'disorganise' the text, for example, more jumbling of sentences, removing a topic sentence and more digressions. You don't always need to include a whole text – you could focus on two or three paragraphs from a longer text.

Learner reflection questions

1 Why do we use paragraphs? How do they help the reader?
2 What was the problem with the unnecessary information in each email?

Teacher reflection

Why is it useful to focus on text coherence and organisation at a low level? How do these activities also help develop students' reading skills?

3 WRITING SKILLS Paragraph writing

a Read Karin's email on page 126 again. Make four paragraphs.

Paragraph 1 talks about Elliot's email: sentences 1 to ___
Paragraph 2 talks about things to do: sentences ___ to 12
Paragraph 3 talks about the weather: sentences 13 to ___
Paragraph 4 finishes the message: sentences ___ to ___

b Look at Paragraph 2. Underline three linking words that order the information.

c Read the email from Alice to you and answer the questions.

1 What is she going to do?
2 What does she want to know?

Hi!

Hi there

[1]My name is Alice and I'm going to visit your home town soon. [2]A friend told me that you can give me useful information, so I have some questions if that's OK. [3]I would like to do some sightseeing. [4]What are some interesting things to see? [5]I'd also like to do some kind of sports activity. [6]What are some interesting things to do? [7]I hope you can help me!

Kind regards

Alice

d Make three paragraphs in Alice's email in 3c.

Figure 8.9: Doff, A., C. Thaine et al. (2015) *Cambridge English Empower A2*, p. 127.

Worksheet

Email A

Hi Sam

[1]My name's Joe and I'm planning to visit your country next month. [2]I don't like cities very much and enjoy skiing. [3]There are quite a few mountains in your country. [4]Is there one that's good for skiing? [5]Last week I bought a new pair of skis, they were quite expensive. [6]I'd also like to go kayaking on a lake or river. [7]Where's a good place to go? [8]My cousin Kelly told me she met you last year and that maybe you can help me plan my trip. [9]Looking forward to hearing your suggestions.

Kind regards

Joe

Email B

Hi Ava

[1]My name's Rachel and I'm coming to your city next week. [2]My friend Danny Richards, who you know well, gave me your email address and said you can perhaps give me ideas for my visit. [3]Maybe you would like to join me for a meal. [4]I've just found out I can't eat anything with milk in it – I feel better now I've stopped eating that kind of food. [5]I'm only going to stay for one day and would like to visit an art gallery or a museum and have a nice meal. [6]Which is better to visit – the National Museum or the Modern Art Gallery? [7]And can you suggest a good restaurant? [8]I hope we can meet when I visit.

Kind regards

Rachel

Answer key

Email A: 1, 8, 2, 3, 4, 6, 7, 9 (sentence 5 is unnecessary)
Email B: 1, 2, 5, 6, 7, 3, 8 (sentence 4 is unnecessary)

8.10 Expression count

Level B1 and above
Time 20 to 25 minutes
Outline In pairs, students practise saying part of a short presentation using signposting expressions. They do this by using notes that you give out based on an audio text that they have already heard.
Aim To provide students with semi-controlled oral practice of signposting expressions used in a mini presentation.
Preparation If you use *Figure 8.10* below, make a copy of the notes worksheet and fold in half. If you use different material, you will need to create your own notes based on a model listening.
Rationale In order to practise signposting expressions in the context of an extended turn of speaking, such as a presentation, students need to speak continuously for a period of time. It is often difficult for students to do this without actually preparing a presentation, which can be very time-consuming. The model presentation in *Figure 8.10* for this activity is of a manageable length and students have heard the model two or three times during the listening stage of the lesson. The notes provided give students support.

Procedure

1 Students complete the listening comprehension tasks as well as any analysis and written practice tasks – exercises 1 to 4 in *Figure 8.10* below.
2 In pairs, students then read the audio script and underline the target language – signposting language in the presentation in *Figure 8.10*.
3 Check answers with the whole class.
4 Give out the notes and allow students five minutes to study them and practise saying the presentation to themselves, without referring to the audio script.
5 Students then take turns giving the presentation to their partner using the notes. The student listening has the audio script open and ticks any signposting language their partner uses and also writes down any extra examples used but not in the audio script.
6 When both students have given the presentation, they compare the number of expressions they each used and whether they used the same expressions in the same places.
7 Do feedback and find the pair that used the most expressions.

Notes and variation

This activity requires attentive monitoring as students will want to turn the notes into written sentences, but the aim is to get them to speak from notes. With a higher-level class, you could ask them to use their own notes made from listening. If the listening model you are working from is much longer, you can get students to do excerpts from it.

Learner reflection questions

1 Did your version of the presentation need to be exactly the same as the original? Why / Why not?
2 What is the difference between speaking from notes and reading something aloud? In a presentation like this, which is better? Why?

Teacher reflection

Apart from the use of signposting expressions, did you notice if students had any other needs in their presentation delivery? What was their pronunciation like? Did they use pausing well? Did students give any kind of feedback to each other during either pair work phase? Is this something you could encourage more next time?

SIGNPOSTING A PRESENTATION

1 1.7 Listen to a presentation about using animals for entertainment. Answer the questions.

1 What is the speaker's opinion about using animals for entertainment?

____

2 What points does the speaker make?

____

____

____

3 What examples does the speaker give to support each point?

____

____

____

4 What advice does the speaker give at the end of the presentation?

____

____

SKILLS

Using signposting language

Use signposting phrases to help your audience follow your presentation.

To introduce the first point

First,
First of all,

To add another idea

Furthermore,
Second,
Another point is that ...
Finally,

To introduce a conclusion

To sum up,
In conclusion,
To summarize,
In short,

PLUS

2 Choose the correct signposting phrase for each sentence.

1 __________, I'd like to remind you that you can make a difference. Thank you so much for coming today. You've been a great audience!
a Another point is that b First of all c To conclude

2 There are several issues with producing oil in the Arctic. First, it's expensive. __________, it's bad for the environment.
a In short b Furthermore c To summarize

3 Today I'm going to talk about endangered species and what we can do to help them. __________, we can give money to environmental organizations.
a First b To sum up c Second

PLUS

SKILLS

Introducing examples

Speakers also use signposting phrases (*for instance, for example, such as*) to introduce examples.

Another point is that zoos have an important educational role. **For instance**, children can see animals up close.
Keeping animals in zoos helps protect them. **For example**, many species, **such as** the giant panda and the snow leopard, are endangered.

3 Work with a partner. Add your own examples to these points.

1 I think that zoos are sometimes good for animals. For example, ______ ______.

2 You can see many exotic animals in zoos, such as ______ ______.

3 Animals are sometimes unhappy in zoos. For instance, ______ ______.

SKILLS

Expressing general beliefs

In a presentation, use phrases like *It's believed that* ... to talk about what most people think or believe. This shows that the idea is not only your idea.

It's often said that it's cruel to use animals for entertainment.
It's believed that most of the polar bears will be gone by 2050 if nothing changes.
It's widely known that climate change is a threat to polar bears.

4 Work with a partner. Complete the sentences with your own ideas.

1 It's often said that ______.
2 It's believed that ______.
3 It's widely known that ______.

1.7

It's often said that it's cruel to use animals for entertainment. However, I would like to argue against this idea. I know that many animal lovers would disagree with me, but let me explain my point of view.

First of all, keeping animals in zoos helps protect them. For example, many species, such as the giant panda and the snow leopard, are endangered in the wild, so they are safer in zoos. Another point is that zoos have an important educational role. For instance, children can see animals up close. When I was a child, my father took me to the zoo. I learned about exotic animals and I also learned to care about animals.

Modern zoos have improved their conditions. Animals are no longer kept in small cages and zoos have large areas where animals can feel as if they are in their natural habitat.

To summarize, zoos help protect animals and educate us. In short, modern zoos are comfortable, safe places for wild animals. In conclusion, I believe that we should help zoos by visiting them and donating money.

Figure 8.10: Ostrowska, S., N. Jordan et al. (2019) *Unlock Listening, Speaking & Critical Thinking 3*, pp. 32–33 and 203.

Notes worksheet

- cruel – use animals for entertainment
- argue against – many animal lovers disagree – explain my point of view
- keeping animals in zoos – helps protect
- many species – giant panda & snow leopard – endangered in wild – safer in zoo
- zoos have important educational role
- children see animals up close
- when child – father took me to zoo
- learned – exotic animals & caring for animals
- modern zoos – improved conditions – animals not in small cages – larger areas
- zoos – comfortable & safe – protect animals – educate

You can find teacher development activities about discourse on pages 281 to 284.

9 Teacher development

Introduction

The activities in *Off the Page* are intended to have a strong practical focus to help teachers extend and develop their repertoire of teaching skills. However, learning-by-doing is only one way for teachers to engage in professional development. Exploring some of the theoretical concepts behind methodology, reflecting on them and engaging in some kind of professional enquiry helps teachers broaden and deepen their knowledge of language and learning.

In this chapter, there are a range of activities that aim to help teachers engage in this kind of professional development. Most of the activities can be done by a teacher working on her own, but some are better done working together with colleagues. Each section of this chapter links to an earlier chapter in the book. So, for example, once you have tried out some of the activities that focus on vocabulary teaching in Chapter 6, you might then work through the teacher development activities in section 6 of this chapter.

Each section comprises:

- an excerpt from a text that provides a theoretical insight into an aspect of the relevant language skill or system;
- some kind of practical professional development activity;
- a set of reflection questions.

The insight text provides some relevant background theory with pre, while and after reading reflection questions. The aim here is to begin linking theory to practice, and thereby extend a teacher's knowledge base. All the ideas for the practical classroom activities in this book have a basis in background theory. For example, the activities that aim to get students producing oral language are informed by skill acquisition theories that suggest we learn by doing, i.e. we learn to speak a second language by actually speaking it.

The practical experiments in this chapter sometimes involve creating materials, doing some form of small scale classroom-based research, or trying something new with your learners. Some of these activities might mean working with your students in a slightly different way from usual while others involve working with colleagues and sharing insights.

The general reflection questions at the end of each section refer to activities in the preceding chapters of *Off the Page* as well as ideas referred to in the reading text and the practical experiments. They aim to help you think about ideas you may have explored and consider how they can inform your teaching in the future. These questions might also be used as the basis of some kind of teacher development log or journal.

As indicated above, the material in this chapter can mostly be used by teachers working alone. However, a teacher educator might also use the ideas here as part of an institution's teacher development programme. For example, they could focus on a particular language skill or system and suggest teachers try two or three different activities from the book. At the same time, the teacher educator could suggest teachers read the relevant background theory text, and in a follow up workshop, share their impressions of the activities and discuss the reading. If teachers have tried the practical activity, they could report back on that and the general reflection questions might also be discussed.

There are no right or wrong answers to the tasks and activities in this chapter. They are there as prompts and suggestions for teachers' ongoing enquiry into their professional activity, and they aim to serve as a starting point for the formation of each teacher's individual beliefs about language and language learning.

1 Listening

An insight into teaching listening

Before reading

1 The text below discusses the ways in which classroom-based listening can have an isolating effect on some students. Why do you think this might happen?
2 The author makes the point that 'listening takes place in real time'. What pressure might this put on students?

While reading

3 Check what the writer has to say about questions 1 and 2 above.
4 What is the third aspect of the comprehension approach that has an effect on students in listening lessons?

Note: CA = comprehension approach: traditional course book listening exercises in the classroom in which learners listen and answer comprehension questions in order to check understanding.

3.1 The individual and the group

A major theme of the chapter is the tension between the nature of the listening skill, which is personal and internalised, and the whole-class teaching situation, where the teacher is obliged to consider the needs of a whole group and to pace the lesson accordingly.

In some respects, listening is a very individual activity. A speaker does not implant a message in the listener's mind. The listener has to remake the message: trying to gauge what the speaker's intentions are and extracting from the message whatever seems relevant to the listener's own goals. The message is a product of the individual listener, not something which a group of listeners hold identically in common. Second language listeners also vary in how they approach the challenge of making sense of input that has only been partly understood. Some are prepared to form hypotheses as to what the speaker said; others are more reluctant to do so and depend upon recognising as many words as possible. There is thus a tension between the personal nature of the skill and the pedagogical tradition of practising it in groups – a tension that is heightened by the fact that individual copies of the text to be studied are not available as they are in reading; there is one recording, which is played to the group as a whole.

Three specific aspects of classroom listening deserve mention because of their impact upon the learner. One derives directly from the tradition of the comprehension approach, the other two from the very nature of listening.

(a) *The listening class is teacher-centred.* The comprehension approach does not fit comfortably into a teaching culture which favours communicative methodology, in that its procedures are very much under the control of the teacher. It is the teacher who operates the button on the CD or cassette player, predicts where problems are likely to occur, asks relevant questions, replays certain passages and decides how much time is spent on each breakdown of understanding.

(b) *Playing a recording to a group of learners has an isolating effect.* Most teachers have at some time had the experience of a lively, interactive class becoming withdrawn and non-committal after a period of listening. It may be that the learners are reluctant to contribute because they are uncertain about whether they have fully understood the recording; here, the CA can partly be blamed for fostering the notion that listening is about achieving a right answer rather than discussing what has been heard. A second explanation is a social-psychological one: the experience of silent listening fragments an established group into a set of individuals and they find it difficult to revert to the normal dynamics of the communicative classroom.

It could be said that classroom listening is, of its very nature, isolating. Of the four skills, it is the most internalised. At least with reading, we can see the reader's eyes moving down the page. But we cannot force learners to listen if they do not want to, and we cannot be sure whether they are listening at all or whether their minds are elsewhere. Here is a problem that current practice rarely addresses: how can we ensure that the weaker listeners do not simply give up and daydream instead of attempting to impose meaning on what they hear?

(c) *Listening takes place in **real time**.* The cassette moves on, and the learner's mind has to keep up with it. There are really two issues here. Firstly, listening is not under the control of the listener: the speaker decides how much to say, how fast to speak and so on. It is even less under the control of the listener if the speaker's voice is on a CD and cannot be interrupted with a request for an explanation. The second point is that listening is not recursive like reading. The learner cannot look back to check a word or words that they have only partially recognised or to resolve ambiguities in their understanding. Returning to the earlier point about teacher control, in a whole-class situation it is the teacher who identifies actual or potential problems of understanding and rewinds the cassette to enable learners to listen again. An individual listener may need more time to listen and re-listen than the group as a whole is allowed.

The three factors identified contribute to learner anxiety and provide a reason for learners citing listening as a difficult skill to acquire. There is a clear need to revise the current approach in ways that increase the level of interaction and give learners greater control over the listening processes.

Field, J. (2008) *Listening in the Language Classroom*, Cambridge: Cambridge University Press, pp. 37–39.

After reading

5 Have you noticed the kind of anxiety that the author describes with your students? What have you done to try and help?
6 Think about the activities in Chapter 1 Listening. Which of them try to help reduce some of the listening anxiety described in the text?
7 How can you give your learners 'greater control over the listening process'? Consider how technology can help with this.

Creating your own listening material

You may sometimes feel that there isn't enough listening material in a course book you are using, or that the listening texts aren't always interesting to your learners. Most smartphones have a recording function that allows you to create your own audio material.

How to do it

1 Decide on your topic and write the script and/or notes. Make sure you choose a topic that your students will find interesting. Don't make the script too long – particularly for lower level students.
2 Find colleagues or friends who don't mind being recorded (teachers are usually better at controlling their language to some degree, which might be preferable, particularly if you have a low-level class). You may need to do the recording two or three times. Try to get the speakers to improvise as the end result will probably sound more natural.
3 Write an audio script of the final recording. You may find interesting language that you can get your students to notice. Make sure you include redundancies such as *um* and *ah* in the audio script – it's representative of natural speech, and students often find this interesting.
4 Create the following tasks for your listening text:
   - A speaking lead in task that gets students interested in the topic. You might want to pre-teach one or two difficult words before students listen.
   - A first listening task. This will probably focus on a gist understanding of the text. Make sure it's not too difficult so students feel confident that they can understand the listening.
   - A task that requires students to understand the listening in detail. Typical tasks are *True/False* or comprehension questions, but you can try other ways to do this. For example, students could complete a table, make notes or give a personal response to questions about the listening.
   - For any interesting language features in the listening, create a task that gets students to notice them. You may get students to listen for the pronunciation of certain words or phrases, or to listen for certain vocabulary or grammar points.
5 After the listening, give students some kind of speaking activity such as a discussion or a role play.
6 After the listening, get feedback from learners on the text. Did they find it interesting? How difficult was the recording to understand? How easy or difficult were the listening tasks you created?

Evaluation

Use the following criteria to evaluate the listening material you created:

- Quality of the audio: clear, too fast, natural enough?
- Lead in: was it interesting, motivating, enough vocabulary pre-taught?

- Listening tasks: were they easy, difficult, unclear, boring?
- Follow on speaking: did it link well to the listening, and was it manageable / motivating for students?
- What would I do differently next time?

Reflection on teaching listening

- Did you try any of the activities in Chapter 1 Listening? How did your learners react? What did you learn about developing learners' listening skills as a result?
- How do you balance listening tasks that are manageable with those that are more challenging and potentially extend students' listening skills more?
- In what ways do you think listening tasks should differ? For example, do the same kind of tasks work for both airport announcements and personal narratives?
- If your students are preparing for an English language exam, which listening subskills do you think you need to emphasise in your lessons?

2 Speaking

An insight into teaching speaking

Before reading

1 The text below outlines some of the characteristics of a competent speaker of a second or additional language. Before you read, note down what you think these characteristics are.

2 In discussing spoken communication, the text also makes a distinction between *knowledge about language* and *specific skills in using the language.* What is your understanding of this distinction?

While reading

3 Read the excerpt and compare your predictions in questions 1 and 2 above with the information given in the text.

Introduction

To teach speaking effectively, as teachers, you need to understand what speaking competence entails. You also need to know how different aspects of speaking competence relate to one another. This understanding will help you plan and deliver lessons that develop your learners' speaking ability in a balanced and comprehensive way. It will also help you approach teaching materials you work with every day in an informed and critical manner. If your concept of speaking competence is too narrow, the activities you plan will be skewed towards developing only certain features of speaking, and other important features of speaking competence will be neglected. On the other hand, if your concept of speaking competence is too vague, you will not be able to identify specific objectives that your lessons hope to achieve. For example, if you think that good speaking competence simply means speaking fluently, your activities will aim to give learners lots of practice in talking, in the hope that, through cumulative practice, they will become increasingly fluent in expressing their ideas. Practice without a specific focus on relevant speaking skills or linguistic knowledge, however, will not be maximally beneficial to learners in the long run. If you are using prescribed materials in your school or institution, knowledge of what constitutes speaking competence will help you adapt existing activities so as to meet your students' needs more effectively.

Here are the combined views of several language teachers. Which of the points below do you agree with?

A competent second language speaker is someone who . . .

- Has good pronunciation.
- Speaks standard English.
- Can speak fluently and with few or no grammatical mistakes.
- Speaks in a manner indistinguishable from a native speaker.
- Is confident when speaking to a large audience.

- Knows when to say the right things and says them in the most effective way possible.
- Can communicate well with native speakers.
- Can be understood easily by others.
- Can speak effectively and clearly in various situations.
- In bilingual settings, knows how to code-switch from the first to the second language, according to circumstances.
- Can speak fluently and clearly on a wide range of topics.

The statements above show diverse perspectives on speaking a second language. Your view of what a good second language speaker can do will influence the way you conceptualize your teaching objectives. If you think it is important for students to speak with good pronunciation, it is likely that you will spend a great deal of time focusing on their pronunciation. If, on the other hand, your view of what is important is oriented towards grammatical accuracy, you may spend a great deal of time correcting ungrammatical utterances that your learners produce. One consequence of a narrow view of speaking competence is that we lose sight of the larger context where speaking is a social act and the fact that the way we speak will be influenced by many factors related to the social nature of speech.

Communicative competence and speaking

One way in which we can examine the notion of speaking competence is to refer to the concept of communicative competence put forward by Dell Hymes (1979) and expanded on by many researchers who have followed. According to Hymes (1979), an individual's communicative competence is his or her ability to use language effectively in actual communication. This ability consists of both *knowledge* about the language and specific *skills* in using the language. Hymes contrasted an idealized notion of linguistic competence with speakers' actual performance in social situations. Individuals with a high level of communicative competence produce utterances that are grammatically accurate, easy for listeners to process, and contextually appropriate and acceptable. The concept of communicative competence was further developed by Canale and Swain (1980) in order to explain it within second language acquisition contexts (see also Canale 1983). They identified four components that made up communicative competence: grammatical competence, discourse competence, sociolinguistic competence, and strategic competence. Grammatical competence referred to knowledge about grammar, vocabulary, and phonology, while discourse competence was seen as the ability to connect utterances to produce a coherent whole. Sociolinguistic competence consisted of the ability to use language that is accurate and appropriate to sociocultural norms and consistent with the type of discourse produced in specific sociocultural contexts. Finally, strategic competence referred to verbal and non-verbal actions taken to prevent and address breakdowns in communication.

Goh, C. C. M. & A. Burns (2012) *Teaching Speaking – A Holistic View*, Cambridge: Cambridge University Press, pp. 49–51.

After reading

4 Which comments in the list *A competent second language speaker is someone who ...* did you agree with?
5 What do the authors mean when they say that 'speaking is a social act'?
6 The authors refer to Canale and Swain's outline of the four competencies associated with spoken communication: grammatical, discourse, sociolinguistic and strategic. In your current teaching programme, which of these competencies do you tend to emphasise? Which do you think you need to give greater prominence to, if any?

Evaluating students' speaking

Teachers are often asked to evaluate students' speaking. This can be for different reasons:

- your institution requires you to do this as part of formal assessment;
- your institution may ask you to do this informally for individual students to determine whether they should go up to the next level;
- students may request it because they want systematic feedback on their speaking;
- you may decide it's necessary in order to determine students' strengths and weaknesses and help them set specific learning goals associated with speaking.

Evaluating students' spoken language can be done by means of some kind of speaking test. Students may be given two or three speaking tasks (some done alone, some done with other students) while you listen and evaluate their speaking. Alternatively, you may carry out evaluation informally over a period of three or four classes just by tuning into students' speaking and noting strengths and weaknesses. The following mini research project suggests an alternative way of conducting the evaluation of students' spoken language.

How to do it

1 Decide how many students you will include – the whole class or just a sample group?
2 For each student involved in the project, note down what you perceive to be their strengths and weaknesses in terms of their speaking. Consider fluency, accuracy, pronunciation, interaction, organisation of what they say etc. Don't worry too much about the categories you use – just make sure you note key points.
3 Ask students if you can record them speaking. Aim to get students doing a monologue as well as some kind of conversation in pairs. If necessary, to motivate them to agree to the recording, explain to them they will get extra, detailed written feedback on their speaking.
4 Find suitable material – the first place to look is in the course book you are using with students because there is likely to be material that you can use or easily adapt. The monologue should allow students to speak on their own for about a minute. The pair activity can be a discussion or some kind of role play.
5 Record the students doing the activities (or they record themselves on their phone and email you the audio file). Either do this in class time or set aside a special time after class when you can supervise them. If you let students do it on their own, they will probably script what they want to say and read it aloud. This won't give you a good idea of their speaking ability.

6 Listen carefully to the recordings and make notes on the strengths and weaknesses you hear.
7 For each student, decide on a balance of about three key strengths and weaknesses and write them a feedback summary. Give students a specific indication of what they can focus on in terms of developing their speaking skills.

What did you find out?

- Compare your original notes about the students with the strengths and weaknesses you have heard in the recording. Are there any differences?
- What are the benefits of recording a student's spoken language to evaluate it? And what are the drawbacks?
- In what ways, if any, is evaluating a recording of spoken language different from marking a piece of writing?

Reflection on teaching speaking

- The activities in Chapter 2 Speaking focus on fluency and interaction in students' speaking. If you focus systematically on these two aspects of spoken language, what broader outcome might you achieve with your students?
- To what extent do you think a student's personality has a bearing on their ability to speak confidently in a second language? How can you help students who lack confidence?
- The reading text above referred to sociocultural norms in spoken language. What are some social rules that you can think of when people speak in their first language?
- Do you only evaluate your students' speaking when there's some kind of test? Or do you evaluate it all the time during lessons? Find out what other teachers do.
- When a teacher evaluates students' spoken language (either formally or informally) should the outcome only ever be a grade? In what ways is consistent evaluation of students' spoken language useful in your day-to-day teaching?

3 Reading

An insight into first and second language reading

Before reading

1 The text below makes reference to top-down and bottom-up processing of information when we read. Thinking about different reading subskills referred to in Chapter 3 Reading, which do you think are associated with top-down processing and which with bottom-up processing?

2 How do you think these two ways of processing information work? Are they independent of each other or do they work together? Why do you think so?

3 Do you think reading is more of a passive or an (inter)active skill? Why?

While reading

4 Read the text and compare your ideas in questions 1–3.

How we understand text

Just as with the skills of listening, speaking and writing, there is a tendency to think of reading as a single skill. However, reading is complex, made up of a whole range of different processes happening very quickly and often simultaneously. When we read, we decode the combinations of letters quickly. In order to do this, we may need to 'sound out', at least in our heads, the sounds the letters represent (*th* can represent a /θ/ or a /ð/ sound, for example). We match the pattern that emerges from the decoding to our lexical knowledge. So, when we see the combination of letters *t-h-i-r-d* we recognize it as a word and that links to what we understand *third* to mean. Perhaps the biggest single difference between L1 and L2 reading is that the L1 reader has a much wider lexical store to draw on and the knowledge held on each item is likely to be richer and more detailed. We will discuss L1 and L2 reading differences more fully a little later.

As well as lexical knowledge, when reading we also use our knowledge of grammar to group words into phrases (*the third man*) and we make connections from one part of the text to another using our understanding of discourse. In addition, we infer anything that is not explicitly stated from what we have already understood, or our general background knowledge of the topic and text type. All of these knowledge bases are constantly being used as we process text and the deeper our lexical, phonological, grammatical and discourse awareness is, the easier the reading task becomes. These complex processes happen very quickly. When reading for understanding (that is constructing a mental summary version of the text), readers in their L1 process text at somewhere between 250 and 300 words per minute (Carrell and Grabe, 2010, p. 216). In order to be able to operate at such speeds, readers must be able to recognize the vast majority of words instantly and automatically, emphasizing the importance of lexical knowledge to reading.

The recognizing of letter–sound combinations, words and grammar patterns is often referred to as 'bottom-up processing'. This is usually contrasted with 'top-down processing' (Grabe and Stoller, 2011, pp. 285 and 295), which is characterized as sampling the text in order to confirm our expectations of content. Those expectations may be based on our background knowledge, awareness of the context, and also what we know of the discourse structure (or text type). As we read, we make use of both top-down and bottom-up processes, with failures in one potentially being compensated by the other. For example, a reader working in their L2 may increasingly rely on what they know about the context to try to make sense of a text if they fail to recognize a significant proportion of the words on the page.

The balance between bottom-up and top-down processing will vary in any given situation. This variation will depend on a whole host of factors, not least the type of text being read and the purpose for reading it (see below), along with the difficulty of the text, the reader's familiarity with the topic and the presence or absence of relevant contextual information. In addition, in L2 reading situations, the kind of task that has been set is also likely to influence the distribution of bottom-up and top-down processing.

These two types of processing work together and contribute to comprehension, which, Grabe (2009) argues, can also be seen as consisting of two parts. The first part is a 'text model of comprehension' and involves the reader processing words and grammar from the text and building them into a mental representation of meaning. This representation of meaning needs to be held in working memory so that new information from the text can be fitted into the developing picture. The text model, as the name suggests, deals very much with meaning derived from the text and therefore draws on bottom-up processing. Grabe's explanation of understanding texts also has a 'situation model of comprehension', which is much more reader-based. Here, the reader combines their own background knowledge with information derived from the text to arrive at a richer interpretation of what has been read. This layer of understanding will include our attitudes to the text, writer and situation. It explains how two readers can read the same text, agree on its content, but interpret it differently. Potentially the two layers of comprehension develop simultaneously as we read and they combine to produce a coherent message. We can see that we do not just decode information from the text, but also build that information into what we already know, or believe, about the topic, and in this sense, each reader constructs meaning as they read, rather than simply 'receiving' meaning.

While in the past reading has been characterised as a passive skill (Nunan, 2015), the situation model of comprehension implies that reading is much more than the passive decoding of the writer's message. It is 'an active – even interactive – process' (Thornbury, 2017, p. 238).

Much of the two-fold comprehension process described above happens without conscious thought in proficient readers. However, there will be times when we need to manage our mental resources and take deliberate actions to help when we find understanding difficult. This happens in both L1 and L2 and may take the form of such things as rereading sections of text, finding, or guessing, the meaning of unknown words, or consciously summarizing parts of a text. These are examples of reading strategies and successful readers not only use a range of strategies but also use strategies in combination (Anderson, 1991). These types of reading strategy are deployed to help us process texts, or parts of texts, that are otherwise difficult to understand.

Watkins, P. (2017) *Teaching and Developing Reading Skills*, Cambridge: Cambridge University Press, pp. 1–3.

After reading

5 This excerpt indicates that there is a connection between language knowledge and the ability of a student to decode information in a text. What evidence of this have you seen in your students?
6 To what extent do you think your students 'receive meaning' and to what extent do they process and interpret information? In what ways can you help learners to 'construct meaning' as they read?
7 What is an example of a reading strategy you have used recently in order to help you understand the meaning of a text? Was this a conscious or an unconscious process?

Establishing a culture of reading

Teachers often say they encourage their students to read in English not only for the practice but also to expose them to a greater range of language items. One way to do this is to emphasise reading with your learners over a period of time, such as a month, in an effort to develop a culture of reading with the learner group.

How to do it

1 Discuss with your students what things they read in English already, and the benefits of reading in a language that you are learning.
2 Explain that as a class you are going to do a set of activities to encourage more reading. Agree with your students on a time period. Do some or all of the following activities.
   - Set reading as a homework task frequently.
   - Ask students to maintain a reading record (see activity 3.9). Get students to compare their records in pairs while you monitor and check.
   - Encourage your students to read online in English. Find websites that contain topics that you think will be of interest and mostly manageable for your students. It may help to provide a guideline on how to read online texts including how much they should read, how much time they should spend, and how to deal with new vocabulary. The advice you give will depend on the level of your students.
   - Help your students select and use a graded reader if they are available at your institution. Students could all read the same reader (if there is a class set) or each student could select their own. Allow some class time for students to do speaking activities associated with the reader, for example, re-telling the story, predicting what will happen next, role plays based on the characters in the story, or spoken reviews of the reader.
   - Provide opportunities for students to tell each other about different texts they have read and make suggestions or recommendations to each other. This will encourage students to read something so that they have something to talk about. It also gives them useful speaking fluency practice.
   - Devote some class time to silent reading of something you or your students have chosen. At low levels, you could read aloud to students. Students could take turns in suggesting a text for you to read aloud, and tell their peers their reasons for the choice (at very low levels in a monolingual setting this could be done in the students' first language).

- Get students to evaluate their own reading ability in line with the CEFR descriptors of reading competence and help them identify aspects of reading they need to improve. They can do this using the self-assessment grids here:

  https://www.coe.int/en/web/common-european-framework-reference-languages/table-2-cefr-3.3-common-reference-levels-self-assessment-grid
- Talk to students about your own reading. Tell them the kind of things you read, how often you read and if you have read something interesting.

3 Once the agreed period of time has finished, review its impact with your students. Think about how your students' reading in English may have changed (or not):
- reading fluency
- range of genres
- self-motivation
- reading speed
- awareness of reading subskills
- new language items acquired
- ability to decode information accurately
- ability to infer information and read critically
- ability to determine own reading needs

Reflection on teaching reading skills

- Think of a learner group that you have taught with the same first language. What do you think is the culture of reading in these students' first language environment? What impact does this have on their ability to read in English?
- While reading is often paired with writing as a language skill, many of the activities in Chapter 3 Reading are linked with speaking. Why do these two skills often go together? What are the learning benefits of linking reading to speaking?
- Often there is a tension between reading tasks that *check understanding* and those that *test comprehension*. Which tasks do you think are better at checking comprehension rather than testing? In which teaching and learning contexts is it a good idea to also test comprehension?
- If your students are preparing for an English language exam or are studying English for Academic Purposes (EAP), why is practising and developing reading skills critical? Which reading subskills are you likely to emphasise with these learners?

4 Writing

An insight into teaching writing

Before reading

1 Think about the following writing activities and rank them from 1 = *I do this a lot with my students* to 6 = *I (almost) never do this with my students.*

- analysis of genres
- imitating parallel texts
- collaborative writing
- gap fill writing
- journal/diary writing
- research projects

2 In the introduction to Chapter 4 Writing, a distinction is made between process and language-focused writing skills associated with different genres. What do you think are the advantages and disadvantages of focusing on these two different skill approaches?

3 Complete the sentence stem below with three different ideas. If working with colleagues, compare your lists.

Good writers are able to ....

While reading

4 Read the text and compare your ideas in questions 1–3 with the ideas in the text.

Toward a synthesis: Process, purpose, and context

The different perspectives outlined above provide teachers with curriculum options, or complementary alternatives for designing courses that have implications for teaching and learning. These orientations are summarized in Table 1.3.

Table 1.3: *Summary of the principal orientations to L2 writing teaching*

Orientation	Emphasis	Goals	Main pedagogic techniques
Structure	Language form	• Grammatical accuracy • Vocabulary building • L2 proficiency	Controlled composition, gap-fill, substitution, error avoidance, indirect assessment, practice of rhetorical patterns
Function	Language use	Paragraph and text organization patterns	Free writing, reordering, gap-fill, imitation of parallel texts, writing from tables and graphs
Expressivist	Writer	• Individual creativity • Self-discovery	Reading, pre-writing, journal writing, multiple drafting, and peer critiques
Process	Writer	Control of technique	Brain-storming, planning, multiple drafting, peer collaboration, delayed editing, portfolio assessment
Content	Subject matter	Writing through relevant content and reading	Extensive and intensive reading, group research projects, process or structure emphasis
Genre	Text and context	Control of rhetorical structure of specific text-types	Modeling-negotiation-construction cycle • Rhetorical consciousness-raising

I have stressed that L2 writing classrooms are typically a mixture of more than one approach and that teachers frequently combine these orientations in imaginative and effective ways. Most commonly, however, these favor either a process or genre orientation and we should not gloss over the protracted – and often bitterly argued – debate on these two positions. This debate boils down to the relative merits of predominantly text-focused pedagogies, which emphasize the social nature of writing, and more writer-centered process methods, which stress its more cognitive aspects. By laying out the main attributes of these two orientations side-by-side, however, it can be seen how the strengths of one might complement the weaknesses of the other (Table 1.4).

Although this stark opposition of the two orientations oversimplifies far more complex classroom situations, it also helps to show how one might complement the other. The conflict between process and product can only be damaging to classroom practice, and the two are more usefully seen as supplementing and rounding each other out. Writing is a sociocognitive activity which involves skills in planning and drafting as well as knowledge of language, contexts, and audiences. An effective methodology for L2 writing teaching should therefore incorporate and extend the insights of the main orientations in the following ways:

- Broaden formal and functional orientations to include the social purposes behind forms
- Locate the process concepts of strategy, schema, and metacognition in social contexts
- Respect students' needs for relevant content through stimulating readings and source materials
- Support genre pedagogies with strategies for planning, drafting, and revising texts
- Situate writing in a conception of audience and link it to broader social structures

Table 1.4: *A comparison of genre and process orientations*

Attribute	Process	Genre
Main Idea	Writing is a thinking process	Writing is a social activity
	Concerned with the act of writing	Concerned with the final product
Teaching Focus	Emphasis on creative writer	Emphasis on reader expectations and product
	How to produce and link ideas	How to express social purposes effectively
Advantages	Makes processes of writing transparent	Makes textual conventions transparent
	Provides basis for teaching	Contextualizes writing for audience and purpose
Disadvantages	Assumes L1 and L2 writing similar	Requires rhetorical understanding of texts
	Overlooks L2 language difficulties	Can result in prescriptive teaching of texts
	Insufficient attention to product	Can lead to overattention to written products
	Assumes all writing uses same processes	Undervalue skills needed to produce texts

In practice this means a synthesis to ensure that learners have an adequate understanding of the *processes* of text creation; the *purposes* of writing and how to express these in effective ways through formal and rhetorical text choices; and the *contexts* within which texts are composed and read and which give them meaning. While I have discussed processes and purposes already, it is worth considering context in a little more detail as it is central to understanding and teaching writing.

The notion of context echoes the belief in genre that writing does not take place outside particular communities and that the genres we teach should be seen as responses to the purposes of those communities, whether professional, academic, or social (Bruffee, 1986). Skilled writers are able to create successful texts by accurately predicting readers' background knowledge and anticipating what they are likely to expect from a particular piece of writing. In our own domains – our homes, workplaces, or classrooms – we are comfortable with the genres we write because we are familiar with them and have a good idea how to create texts that will connect with our readers. We are able to draw on a shared community schema to structure our writing so that our audience can process it easily. But this knowledge of readers and their needs may be lacking when we try to communicate in an unfamiliar situation, such as a new profession, a new discipline, or a foreign language.

Hyland, K. (1996) *Second Language Writing*, New York: Cambridge University Press, pp. 22–25.

After reading

5 In your writing lessons, do you tend to prioritise activities more associated with process writing or more associated with a language focus? Why is this the case? Is it something you need to rethink?

6 The author emphasises the importance of context in writing activities. To what degree do you make this explicit to your students?

7 What experience as a writer do you have of trying to communicate in an unfamiliar setting or having to engage with an unfamiliar genre? How did you feel? What did you do to help manage the situation? How does this experience inform your approach to developing your students' writing skills?

Looking at the impact of audience

Teachers will often encourage students when writing in English to try and imagine the effect on a person reading the text. This is a way of highlighting the importance of an audience in written communication. The following teaching activity aims to find out if having a real audience (other than the teacher) makes a difference.

If you teach two classes that are at a similar level, you could carry out this activity on your own. However, it would be more interesting to try it out with a colleague who is teaching a class at same or similar level. (It's unlikely to be successful with two classes that are at very different levels because the higher level students will inevitably produce more communicative pieces of writing.) This activity could also be done as a whole-school teacher development project with pairs of teachers who are teaching at the same level comparing writing from their students along the lines indicated below.

How to do it

1 Decide on two or three different genres you will get students in both classes to write. The writing activities don't need to be done back-to-back – it may help to space them across a longer period of time.
2 With one of the classes, put the students in writing pairs. They can be in the same pair for all the tasks or they can change pairs with each writing task. Don't put students in pairs in the other class.
3 If working with a colleague, agree on an approach for teaching each genre that you focus on. It doesn't need to be the same each time, and you can vary the methodology depending on the genre. However, the one key difference will be that the class with paired students will write their texts to their partner (as well as handing it in to you, the teacher). The other class merely writes their text and hands it in to the teacher.
4 When each writing assignment is handed in, make a copy to keep for later evaluation. As the intended audience for the writing, students in the paired class also receive a copy. (For the paired class you could choose to set some peer feedback exercise or not. The important thing is that students have written for an audience.)
5 When students have finished all the writing tasks, evaluate the two class sets of writing, but focus only on one criterion: which class communicates more effectively in their writing? Try to avoid too much consideration of written accuracy and keep the focus on written communicative ability.
6 If you have been working with a colleague, discuss your impressions with each other and see if you agree. Then try to determine what makes one group's writing more communicative and whether having a specific audience has made a difference or not.
7 If you notice any interesting differences between the audience and non-audience group of students, and the writing they produced, you could share this with other colleagues.

Reflection on teaching writing skills

- Writing has been called the 'Cinderella skill' in English language teaching and learning as it can be overlooked in favour of the other three skills (in some course books, for example, a focus on writing occurs only in every second unit). Do you think this is changing at all? Why / Why not?
- One criticism of spending time on process writing skills in the classroom is that it can take quite a lot of class time. Do you believe this is time well spent? What other language skill can be practised a lot when students are engaged in process writing activities?
- Students often have a negative perception of writing. However, if you point out to them that they write most days in order to update their social media profile, they might say, 'that's doing Facebook, it's not writing'. How can you use IT as an aid that helps students develop a more positive attitude towards writing? How can this help them in life?

5 Grammar

An insight into teaching grammar

Before reading

1 The text below begins by referring to a 'built in' grammar syllabus that each student might have. Do you think students learn grammar structures according to a specific order that is 'built in' to their brain? Why / Why not?

2 The text discusses 'doubts about the value of formal instruction' of grammar. What doubts do you think they are?

While reading

3 What key points does the excerpt make about the difference between students acquiring grammar and consciously learning it?

THE EFFECTS OF INSTRUCTION

Since it is generally agreed that learners have a 'built-in' syllabus, even if there is considerable individual variation in both the route and the final destination, the question remains: to what extent – and how – does formal instruction affect the process? Can it be accelerated by the learning of explicit rules, for example, or by form-focussed corrective feedback, or by following a grammatical syllabus?

Doubts about the value of formal instruction – such as the learning and controlled practice of grammar rules – as opposed to naturalistic learning, have a very long history. They resurfaced in the 1970s in the wake of the morpheme studies, and were propelled in particular by Krashen's 'Monitor Theory' (1977). Essentially, Krashen claimed that knowledge learned from formal instruction (e.g., of grammar rules) serves only to monitor or edit output, and, even then, only under certain form-focused conditions. Otherwise, second languages are, like the L1, 'acquired', using subconscious learning mechanisms if, and only if, the learner is exposed to 'comprehensible input'. Moreover, Krashen insisted that there is no 'leakage' from the explicit 'learned system' into the implicit 'acquired' one.

This 'non-interface' position was lent support by studies that compared the order of acquisition in instructed and non-instructed learners (e.g., Pica, 1983), and found little significant difference, leading many scholars to conclude that, in the words of Skehan (1996: 19), "Second language acquisition (SLA) research … has established that teaching does not and cannot determine the way the learner's language will develop."

However, the instructed learners in these comparative studies did seem to achieve higher levels of grammatical competence, suggesting that instruction improves the *rate*, but not the *route*, of SLA (R. Ellis, 1990). A subsequent meta-analysis of nearly 50 studies (Norris and Ortega, 2000) provided confirmation that instructed learners progress at a faster rate, and achieve levels of accuracy and complexity that exceed those of uninstructed learners. These findings would seem to vindicate the need for explicit grammar instruction, and certainly for a 'focus on form' (Long, 1991), including corrective feedback. However, most of these and subsequent studies measured grammar learning by means of artificially-controlled exercises, such as gap-fills and sentence transformations, and not in real communication, and therefore did not necessarily disprove Krashen's argument that explicit knowledge is of use only in monitoring output. As Truscott (2015: 136), reviewing the evidence, concludes, "form-based instruction gave learners conscious knowledge that was very useful for tasks that could be done primarily with conscious knowledge but had only limited (and possibly no) value for tasks that required spontaneous communicative use of the forms."

Hence, the value of learning grammar explicitly (as opposed to simply picking it up incidentally while engaged in communicative tasks, for example), would seem to depend on whether – and the extent to which – explicit knowledge can become implicit. Truscott, above, takes the extreme 'non-interface' position, while others, like Ellis and Shintani (2014: 95) are more circumspect, arguing that explicit instruction can assist the learner "to achieve greater control over a feature that is *already partially acquired* [emphasis added]". Instruction may also have a 'priming' effect, that is, explicit teaching of a grammatical structure may make it more likely that learners will consciously attend to (or 'notice') the structure when they encounter it in naturalistic input, increasing the chance of the item being retained in long-term memory – a phenomenon reported by Schmidt and Frota (1986). Meanwhile, proponents of skill-learning theory take a 'strong interface' position, arguing that "slow, deliberate practice" (DeKeyser 2007: 107) can help 'proceduralize' explicit knowledge, lending support to the traditional 'present-practice-produce' (PPP) instructional sequence. Nevertheless, brain imaging studies have cast doubt on the inter-permeability of the explicit and implicit memory stores, leading at least one neuroscientist to argue that "acquisition is not a process of automatizing rules" (Paradis, 2004, quoted in Ellis, 2008: 754).

Thornbury, S. (2018) 'Learning Grammar' in J. C. Richards & A. Burns (eds.), *The Cambridge Guide to Learning English as a Second Language*, pp. 187–188, Cambridge: Cambridge University Press

After reading

4 What is your opinion on the value of grammar instruction?
5 What do you understand as the difference between explicit and implicit grammar knowledge?
6 What distinction would you make between second language acquisition and second language learning?
7 If you followed the suggestion for a 'focus on form followed by corrective feedback', how might you change your approach to teaching grammar?

Debate the issues

Work together with a group of colleagues and hold a debate on the teaching of grammar.
The motion: *Formal grammar instruction is largely a waste of time.*

How to do it

1. Divide into two teams of about two or three – one for the motion (affirmative) and one against (opposing). You don't have to personally agree with the point of view of your team. Choose someone to be the adjudicator who will run the debate.
2. Decide on a time limit for each speaker – perhaps two to four minutes.
3. Research the topic, but you can also draw on your experience as a language teacher and as a language learner. Try to think of specific examples to back up your claims and try to think of points the other team will make.
4. Invite other colleagues and perhaps students to watch the debate. They can judge which is the winning team.
5. The adjudicator then invites speakers from the teams in the following order:
   - The affirmative team is invited to put forward their arguments.
   - The opposing team then put forward their arguments.
   - There is a short break before the opposing team begins their rebuttal – arguing against points made by the affirmative team.
   - The affirmative team then gives their rebuttal of the opposing team's arguments.
6. The adjudicator then asks the audience to decide which team they think has won the debate – this can be with a show of hands or the audience can write their opinion on a piece of paper.
7. Once the winning team is announced, there can be a more general discussion that includes the audience.
8. If you think it will be difficult to organise a formal debate in this way, you can just discuss the motion in a more general way with colleagues.

Reflection on learning grammar

- What do the activities in Chapter 5 Grammar tell you about different kinds of grammar knowledge?
- Why do you think that some students are good at learning grammar rules, but others are not? Are students who know more rules always the most competent speakers?
- In what ways can you help these different kinds of students?
- How much is it your responsibility to develop a student's grammar knowledge? How much is it the individual student's responsibility?

6 Vocabulary

An insight into teaching vocabulary

Before reading

1 Read the statements below about vocabulary learning and decide if you agree or disagree with them. Think of reasons for your answers.
- It's better to avoid using the student's first language when teaching new words.
- Students need to meet a word more than once in order to understand it and know how to use it.
- Students' ability to have a good understanding of a word is largely reliant on the quality of a teacher's explanation of the word.
- It's a good idea to teach words with similar meanings and form together.

While reading

2 Read the text and compare the ideas in the text with your own from question 1.

How should teachers (or writers) explain words?

Some of the guidelines presented here go beyond the research reviewed in this chapter to draw on points made in other chapters of this book.

1. *Provide clear, simple and brief explanations of meaning.* The research evidence clearly shows that particularly in the first meetings with a word, any explanation should not be complicated or elaborate. Learning a word is a cumulative process, so teachers need not be concerned about providing lots of information about a word when it is first met. What is important is to start the process of learning in a clear way without confusion. There are strong arguments for using learners' first language if this will provide a clear, simple and brief explanation (Lado et al., 1967; Laufer and Shmueli, 1997; Mishima, 1967). The various aspects involved in knowing a word can be built up over a series of meetings with the word. There is no need and clearly no advantage in trying to present these all at once. Elley's (1989) study of vocabulary learning from listening to stories showed that brief definitions had a strong effect on learning.
2. *Draw attention to the generalisable underlying meaning of a word.* If knowledge of a word accumulates over repeated meetings with the word, then learners must be able to see how one meeting relates to the previous meetings. In providing an explanation of a word, the teacher should try to show what is common in the different uses of the word.

3. *Give repeated attention to words.* Knowledge of a word can only accumulate if learners meet the word many times. Repeated meetings can have the effects of strengthening and enriching previous knowledge. There is no need for a teacher to draw attention to a word every time it occurs, but particularly in the early stages of learning, drawing attention increases the chances that learners will notice it on later occasions. Teachers need to see the learning of particular words as a cumulative process. This means that they need to expect not to teach a word all in one meeting. They need to keep coming back to the word to help strengthen and enrich knowledge of the word.
4. *Help learners recognise definitions.* Definitions have certain forms (Bramki and Williams, 1984; Flowerdew, 1992) and may be signalled in various ways. Teachers can help learners by clearly signalling the definitions they provide, by testing learners to diagnose how well they can recognise and interpret definitions, and by providing training in recognising and interpreting definitions. A useful starting point for this is recognising definitions in written text. Bramki and Williams (1984) suggest that learners can be helped to develop skill in making use of lexical familiarisation firstly, by seeing marked-up text which indicates the word, the signal of lexical familiarisation and the definition – plenty of examples are needed at this stage; and secondly, by getting the student to then mark up some examples with the teacher gradually reducing the guidance given. Flowerdew (1992: 216) suggests that teachers and learners should discuss the various forms of definitions as they occur in context.
5. *Prioritise what should be explained about particular words.* There are many things to know about a word, and the different aspects of word knowledge enable different word use skills (Nist and Olejnik, 1995). Some of these aspects of knowledge can be usefully taught, some are best left to be learned through experience, and some may already be known through transfer from the first language or through patterns learned from other English words. When deliberately drawing attention to a word, it is worth considering the learning burden of that word and then deciding what aspect of the word most deserves attention. Most often it will be the meaning of the word, but other useful aspects may be its spelling or pronunciation, its collocates, the grammatical patterning or restrictions on its use through considerations of politeness, formality, dialect or medium.

6. *Help learners remember what is explained.* Understanding and remembering are related but different processes. The way in which a teacher explains a word can affect understanding or it can affect understanding and remembering. In order to help remembering, information needs to be processed thoughtfully and deeply. The quality of mental processing affects the quantity of learning. Teachers can help remembering by showing how the word parts (affixes and stem) relate to the meaning of the word, by helping learners think of a mnemonic keyword that is like the form of the new word, by putting the word in a striking visualisable context, by encouraging learners to retrieve the word form or meaning from their memory while not looking at the text, and by relating the word to previous knowledge such as previous experience or spelling, grammatical, or collocational patterns met before.
7. *Avoid interference from related words.* Words which are similar in form (Laufer, 1989) or meaning (Higa, 1963; Nation, 2000; Tinkham, 1993; Tinkham, 1997; Waring, 1997) are more difficult to learn together than they are to learn separately. When explaining and defining words, it is not helpful to draw attention to other unfamiliar or poorly established words of similar form or which are opposites, synonyms, free associates or members of the same lexical set such as parts of the body, fruit or articles of clothing. The similarity between related items makes it difficult for the learner to remember which was which. Confusion rather than useful learning is often the result. In the early stages of learning it is not helpful to use the opportunity to teach a word as the opportunity to teach other related words. Bolger and Zapata (2011) tested the learning of semantically related and unrelated words in story contexts, finding a slight learning advantage for semantically unrelated items. They suggested that the story context might have overcome much of the disadvantage caused by semantic relatedness. The small difference between the groups may also be at least partly attributed to the fact that the words in the unrelated passage consisted of four sets of related pairs.

Nation, I. S. P. (2013) *Learning Vocabulary in Another Language* (2nd ed.), pp. 126–128.

After reading

3 The text highlights the fact that vocabulary learning is a 'cumulative process', and teachers need to recycle new words and point out different aspects of meaning and use. Think of a word or a lexical set you have taught recently. How can you give students opportunities to meet this word or lexical set again? What different aspects of the meaning, form or use can you point out when you highlight the word(s) another time?

4 The text suggests that teachers can explain certain aspects of new vocabulary, but that students should also experience other aspects for themselves. Which aspects of vocabulary knowledge do you think are best dealt with by teachers and which aspects can students experience for themselves?
5 The text makes reference to the value in training students to recognise and interpret definitions. While it is not explicitly stated, this appears to refer to definitions of new words given in English. Look at an online English–English dictionary (for example, dictionary.cambridge.org) and study some definitions of words you have taught recently. What kind of information do students need training in recognising in the definition (for example, different meanings, different parts of speech etc.)?
6 Point 7 in the text suggests that learning words in lexical sets doesn't help with learning. However, presenting words in lexical sets is a common approach in many course books. What's your experience of students' uptake of new words learned in this way?

Determining the lexical load

Grabe (2009) reports on research that indicates to read successfully students need to be able to understand 95% of the words in a text. A useful resource that gives information about what lexis is understood by learners at different levels is the English Vocabulary Profile (EVP): www.englishprofile.org/wordlists. This tool tags words according to their Common European Framework of Reference (CEFR) level. For this activity, we are going to use English Vocabulary Profile (an alternative tool is the 'Vocabprofile' option on the Compleat Lexical Tutor: www.lextutor.ca) to determine the lexical manageability of a text in relation to the level you would like to use it with. You can do this activity alone, but it is more interesting if you do it with another colleague or as part of a teacher development group.

How to do it

1 Subscribe to English Vocabulary Profile (subscriptions are free). Watch the video showing how to use the tool.
2 Find an authentic text that you think a group of students you are teaching now would enjoy reading and do a word count.
3 Go through the text and underline any words you think may be a little difficult or very difficult for the level of the student group you have in mind.
4 Make a list of these words and then search for their CEFR level on EVP. If the word doesn't appear on EVP, it usually means it is beyond C2 level.
5 Count up the number of words in the text that are above the CEFR level of your students. What is the percentage of these words in the text?
6 If only 5% of the words are likely to be unknown to your students, the level is probably about right. If it is higher, decide whether to simplify the text or find another one more on level.
7 When you use the text in class, get feedback from your students on the words they did and didn't know and whether they found the level of text too easy / manageable / too difficult.
8 If you are doing this activity with colleagues, share your findings with them.

Reflection on teaching vocabulary

- As noted in the introduction to Chapter 6 Vocabulary, meaning of vocabulary is usually dealt with in course books, but sometimes form and use are given less attention. Thinking of your own vocabulary lessons, which of these two aspects of vocabulary learning do you think you could focus on more with your learners? How can you do this?
- What is your preference: dealing with new vocabulary before students read or listen to a text or dealing with it after in context? Does it depend on students' level? Why / Why not?
- Bilingual dictionaries are clearly more efficient at conveying meaning, particularly at lower levels. At higher levels, what aspects of vocabulary knowledge might be missing from bilingual dictionaries? How can you compensate for this if students insist on using bilingual dictionaries?
- What is a good balance between in-class vocabulary learning and vocabulary learning that students do in their own time? How can you encourage them to be systematic about their own learning?

Reference

Grabe, W. (2009) *Reading in a Second Language: Moving from Theory to Practice*. New York: Cambridge University Press.

7 Pronunciation

Insight into teaching pronunciation

Before reading

1 Which of these features of pronunciation do you think are more or less important in determining whether a student is intelligible or not?
- sounds
- word stress
- phrase stress and rhythm
- features of connected speech
- intonation

2 Do you think the priorities change according to students' level?

3 Is phonological intelligibility (understanding different sounds) only an issue with non-native speakers or can there be problems between two native speakers? Can you think of examples?

While reading

4 Read the excerpt and compare the ideas you had in response to questions 1 to 3 with the information in the text.

Pronunciation as a component of intelligibility

There are several features of intelligibility. A person's English is intelligible if the listener can recognize the words and utterances he or she uses and can readily understand the meaning the speaker intends to communicate. Both pronunciation and word choice contribute to intelligibility. Research suggests that for more advanced learners, accurate use of stress, rhythm and intonation in English have a greater impact on intelligibility than accurate pronunciation of vowels and consonants, although this has not been confirmed for basic-level learners (Lane, 2010). Zelinksi (2008) reports that accurate word stress and accurate production of sounds in the stressed syllables are the two features that contribute most to intelligibility. Celce-Murcia et al. (2010: 283) paraphrase Zelinski (2008) who observes:

> ... because native listeners rely on both the word-stress patterns in the speech signal, the interaction between the two is important, so it makes little sense for the learner to focus just on the production of sounds or just the production of word-stress patterns. Special attention needs to be given to the accuracy of segments within strong syllables, as they provide a source of information upon which native listeners depend.

However, intelligibility also depends upon how familiar the listener is with the speaker's accent. An American visiting New Zealand or Singapore for the first time, for example, may have initial difficulty in understanding some aspects of the local varieties of English; however, it quickly becomes intelligible with familiarization. Pronunciation is hence just one factor influencing intelligibility. Intelligibility is also influenced by word choice, rate of speaking and use of grammar, as well as the general coherence of the speaker's discourse.

As noted above, Jenkins (2000) has suggested that some features of standard English are very difficult to master and do not play a crucial role in intelligibility. These include vowel quality, weak forms, connected speech, word stress, rhythm and pitch movement. These features are often included in traditional pronunciation courses and materials, but Jenkins, based on her research on interactions between non-native speakers, has described them as non-core. She suggests that, in teaching pronunciation, the focus should be on an 'international core for phonological intelligibility: a set of unifying features which, at the very least, has the potential to guarantee that pronunciation will not impede successful communication in EIL settings' (2000: 95). The core would consist of those features of pronunciation that are central to mutual intelligibility in contexts of cross-cultural communication. These would be a more realistic target for teaching and learning than the full inventory of features of standard native-speaker pronunciation.

The *core* features identified by Jenkins are:

- Aspiration after word-initial /p/, /t/ and /k/, e.g. *pen* /pen/, not /ben/.
- Vowel-length distinctions, e.g. *beans* /bi:nz/, not /bɪnz/.
- RP (not general American, or GA) pronunciation of the intervocalic *-nt* when it occurs before an unstressed syllable, e.g. *winter* /wɪntə(r)/, not /wɪnə(r)/.
- Full articulation of consonants in word initial clusters, e.g. *strong* /strɒŋ/, not /srɒŋ/.
- Epenthesis (i.e. insertion of a sound into a word in consonant clusters) is preferable to consonant deletion, e.g. *street* /sətə'ri:t/, not /sri:t/.
- Nuclear (tonic) stress production and placement within tone units.
- Adoption of the rhotic variant /r/, e.g. *here* pronounced /hi:r/, not /hɪə/.

Jenkins identifies the following as *non-core* features:

- Substitutions of /θ/, as in *think* /θɪŋk/, resulting in *'tink, 'sink'* or *'fink'*, and of /ð/, as in *this* /ðɪs/, resulting in *'dis', 'zis'* or *'vis'*.
- Pitch movement on the nuclear syllable.
- Weak forms, e.g. *to* pronounced /tu:/, not /tə/.
- Vowel quality, e.g. *cake* /keɪk/ pronounced /kaɪk/.
- Word stress, e.g. *perfectionist, 'per FEC tionist'*, pronounced *'PER fectionist'*.
- Features of connected speech, such as absence of elision, e.g. *facts* /fæks/ pronounced /fækts/, and assimilation, e.g. *good girl* /gʊg gɜ:l/ pronounced /gʊd gɜ:l/.

Richards, J. C. (2015) *Key Issues in Language Teaching*, Cambridge: Cambridge University Press, pp. 344–346.

After reading

5 The text mentions the fact that when native speaker accents become familiar, they are easier to understand. Is this also true of non-native speaker accents? What are the implications of this for you as a teacher?

6 Think of students who you have experience of teaching and who all share the same first language. Which core features on Jenkins' list in the text do you think are most applicable to the needs of these students? How can you help these students deal with these features?

7 Are you surprised by any of the non-core features? Are there any things on this list that you have focused on a lot in class? In light of this list, do you think you might change your approach in teaching pronunciation? Why / Why not?

Learning a difficult sound

Trying to put yourself in the role of student can offer insights on language and learning, and it can help develop your ideas about teaching. This activity is a simple way of recognising challenges your students might face with learning English pronunciation by putting yourself in the position of learner.

How to do it

1 Choose a language you have very little or no knowledge of. Whatever language you choose should include a sound that is difficult for non-native speakers of that language to say.

2 If possible, find a native or very fluent speaker of that language and ask them to demonstrate the sound and give you some example words to practise. You could ask them to record the words. Alternatively, research how this sound is pronounced online.

3 Practise saying the sound as much as possible for a few days.

4 Go back to the native speaker and say the words you have been practising. Ask them for feedback on how close your pronunciation is to that of a native speaker. If you're unable to do this, record yourself saying the words and compare your recording with online examples.

5 You could complete a form like the one below to help structure the activity.

> Language: Swedish
>
> Sound: 'sj'
>
> How to say it: It's a *voiceless vela fricative,* so the place of articulation is at the back of the mouth – the same position as /k/ in English, but the flow of air is released and not blocked.
>
> Sound and spelling: Words that begin with the following letters and followed by a soft vowel sound: sj-, stj-, skj-, stj-, ch-, sch-
>
> Words to practise:
>
> sju (seven) sjuk (sick) skjorta (shirt)
>
> schema (schedule) choklad (chocolate)

6 Once you have completed the activity, answer the following questions:

- How difficult was it to perceive this sound in relation to sounds in English/your first language?
- Once you had understood the place of articulation, were you able to produce the sound?

- If you got feedback from a native speaker, could you sense how far or close you were to being able to say the sound well?
- How much did you practise? Did trying to say the sound correctly become boring or did you want to keep trying to get it right?
- What does this activity tell you about how you deal with students' pronunciation?

Reflection on teaching pronunciation

- In the introduction to Chapter 7 Pronunciation, the distinction between a receptive and productive focus is outlined. What are your thoughts on this distinction, and if you have done some of the activities with your students, has your perception about the distinction changed?
- Much of the literature on phonology suggests that it is valuable for learners to have exposure to a range of accents. How can we help with this in the classroom?
- How motivating do your students find pronunciation activities in general? If you have done any activities in Chapter 7, what was the reaction of your students?
- Who do you think we should accommodate more as far as pronunciation is concerned? Should native speakers make more effort to understand a wider range of accents? Or should non-native speakers try harder to make their accent more intelligible?

8 Discourse

An insight into functional/situational language

Before reading

1 Think of your higher-level learners, perhaps B2 level and above, who are reasonably accurate and can mostly communicate what they want to say. What do you consider their language needs to be in the following three areas?
- naturalness
- appropriateness
- complexity

2 Which of these areas do you think the learners need most work on and how can you help them?

While reading

3 Read the text and compare your thoughts about the needs of high-level learners and the information in the text.
Note: the text refers to Bachman's model of communicative competence. This involves the following components:
- organisational knowledge (grammatical and discourse competence);
- pragmatic competence (functional and sociolinguistic knowledge);
- strategic competence (learners' metacognitive strategies such as planning and monitoring of language production).

The text also refers to a learner called Wes, an adult Japanese immigrant to Hawaii. He was the subject of a three-year study to track the development of his language competence.

7.4 Pragmatic competence

In referring to Bachman's (1990) model of communicative competence in the previous chapter, we noted that *pragmatic competence* (*pragmatic knowledge*) is that aspect of linguistic competence that constitutes the ability to relate language to its contexts of use. This ability varies considerably across learners. Some achieve a high degree of competence both in understanding their interlocutors' communicative purposes, and in producing socially and culturally acceptable responses. Others are less successful. In fact, even advanced non-native speakers seldom achieve the same degree of success as native speakers do on tasks 'where contextualized reaction data are available (as in the case of authentic conversations and institutional talk)' (Bardovi-Harlig, 2001: 14). The absence of certain high-frequency, often idiomatic routines, or 'typical expressions', is frequently cited as characteristic of non-native pragmatics. Bardovi-Harlig observes that 'routines such as *Could you give me a ride/a lift*, as part of a request, or *How clumsy of me*, as part of an apology, make the speech act . . . immediately recognizable to the hearer, and are used more often by NSs [native speakers] than NNSs [non-native speakers]' (2001: 19).

The relation between pragmatic competence and overall language proficiency, particularly in the area of grammar, is unclear. In the case of Wes (Schmidt, 1983), his pragmatic competence, as evidenced by his ability to make requests, relied initially on a limited number of memorized formulae (e.g. '*Shall we go?*'). Over time, and despite the lack of real development in his interlanguage grammar, these became more elaborated, e.g. '*Shall we maybe go out for coffee now, or you want later?*' Matsumuru (2003) has shown that improvement in a group of Japanese learners' command of appropriacy in advice-giving situations was due more to the amount of exposure they had had, rather than to their proficiency in English.

In summarizing the research evidence, Ellis notes that 'pragmalinguistic failure by learners is widely reported in the literature' (1994: 166) and lists such problems as learners using a very limited range of forms for realizing specific speech acts; choosing inappropriate forms; translating directly from their L1; overusing certain politeness markers (such as '*please*'); and erring on the side of verbosity (when making requests, for example).

Following, and building on, Blum-Kulka (1991), Ellis (1997) charts three broad phases in the development of pragmatic competence:

1. a message-orientated stage, in which learners rely on context clues to interpret speaker intentions, and use any means, including gesture and an over-reliance on a few simple formulae, to convey their own meanings;
2. an interlanguage-orientated stage, where a range of strategies are used with varying degrees of success, but still showing evidence of transfer from L1, and also a tendency to verboseness; and
3. an interculturally orientated stage, in which learners approximate closely to native speakers with regard to the use of politeness strategies, although they may still retain certain 'deep' cultural habits, such as the importance attached to status.

Ellis adds that the evidence suggests that very few learners achieve stage 3, even after years of exposure. There is also some doubt as to whether classrooms provide a sufficiently varied social context in which to acquire certain speech acts, a point which we will address shortly.

Apart from the amount and type of instruction available, factors that seem to influence the development of pragmatic competence include the amount of exposure (the more the better, on the whole), and the influence of the learner's first language and culture, an issue which we will now address.

Thornbury, S. and D. Slade (2006) *Conversation: From Description to Pedagogy*, Cambridge: Cambridge University Press, pp. 223–224.

After reading

4 The text indicates two key issues associated with pragmatic competence: the students' ability to understand the communicative purposes of people they speak to in different contexts, and the ability to produce language that is appropriate for the context in which they find themselves. Thinking of your higher-level learners, which of these two issues do you think is more of a challenge for them? Why do you think this is the case – is it a lack of knowledge or is it the influence of the students' first language, or something else?

5 Think of a learner who usually gets good results in grammar and vocabulary tests. Which of Ellis' phases of pragmatic competence could you place this student in? Does this alter your perception of the student's overall level of competence?

6 The text notes Ellis' view that classrooms are limited in their ability to provide students with varied social contexts. How could you provide a variety of social contexts for your learners to help their language learning? What kinds of material and activities could perhaps broaden students' ability to cope with a range of social situations?

Trialling a practice activity

When students do a freer oral practice activity such as a role play, they may not use the target language. This is often an indication that they haven't learned the target language to the point where they can use it spontaneously in a real or very communicative context. However, occasionally, the problem could be with the design of the activity or the way it is set up in class.

Trialling these activities with fluent speakers of English can offer insights into the design of the task and the kind of language that is used.

How to do it

1 Find a course book exercise that aims to provide freer spoken practice of functional/situational language. It will probably be a role play or some kind of simulation.

2 Find fluent speakers of English to participate in the activity. It's important that the participants are not English language teachers who know that they should use any target language.

3 Give the participants the course book exercise. (Make sure there is no reference in the instructions to the target language that should be used in the activity.)

4 Ask the participants to do the exercise following the rubric – don't give them any oral instructions or suggestions.

5 Record their conversation. Then listen to the recording and check if the speakers use the course book target language or not.

6 Choose a key section of the recording and make a transcript of it (this helps you to analyse in detail).

7 Think about the following questions as you study the transcribed excerpt:
- Are there any functional/situational expressions that speakers use that aren't in the course book but are appropriate for the situation?
- What examples of ellipsis (leaving out words – see introduction to Chapter 8) are there in the conversation?

- What do you think determined the language choices the speakers made?
- Could you use the recording and/or transcript with learners? Why / Why not?

8 If you have willing colleagues, this activity could be done as a pair or group teacher development activity, with each teacher making their own recording and feeding back.

Reflection on teaching discourse

- What benefits and drawbacks can you see in having functional/situational language as the main organising principle (or main strand) in a syllabus?
- A core principle of teaching discourse is the idea of language in context. This includes such ideas as: what is being spoken or written about (the topic); who is speaking or writing and who that person's audience is; the relationship between the speaker/listener or writer/reader; how they communicate – face-to-face, online, by phone, etc.; and any conventions associated with the mode of communication. To what extent do listening and reading texts in the course book you use signal this? If they don't, how can you compensate?
- Many aspects of spoken and written discourse can be connected to culture. For example, in Italy a majority of university exams (all subjects) are oral and not written. This means that Italian graduates acquire skills to argue a point of view orally. Think of a language culture that you are familiar with (without necessarily speaking the language to a high level of competence). What bearing do cultural factors have on spoken and written discourse?

Index

Note: Activity names are shown in **bold**. Locators in *italics* refer to figures, though where concurrent with related text these are not distinguished from principal locators.